CHURCH AND STATE
IN SOVIET RUSSIA

The New Russian History

Series Editor: Donald J. Raleigh,
University of North Carolina, Chapel Hill

This series makes examples of the finest work of the most eminent historians in Russia today available to English-language readers. Each volume has been specially prepared with an international audience in mind, and each is introduced by an outstanding Western scholar in the same field.

**THE REFORMS OF
PETER THE GREAT**
Progress Through Coercion in Russia
Evgenii V. Anisimov
*Translated with an introduction by
John T. Alexander*

IN STALIN'S SHADOW
The Career of "Sergo" Ordzhonikidze
Oleg V. Khlevniuk
Translated by David Nordlander
*Edited with an introduction by
Donald J. Raleigh,
with the assistance of Kathy S. Transchel*

**THE EMPERORS AND EMPRESSES
OF RUSSIA**
Rediscovering the Romanovs
Edited by Donald J. Raleigh
Compiled by Akhmed A. Iskenderov

WOMAN IN RUSSIAN HISTORY
From the Tenth to the Twentieth
Century
Natalia Pushkareva
Translated and edited by Eve Levin

MASS UPRISINGS IN THE USSR
Protest and Rebellion in the
Post-Stalin Years
*Translated and edited by
Elaine McClarnand MacKinnon*

**THE RUSSIAN EMPIRE IN THE
EIGHTEENTH CENTURY**
Searching for a Place in the World
Aleksandr B. Kamenskii
Translated and edited by David Griffiths

RUSSIA AFTER THE WAR
Hopes, Illusions, and Disappointments,
1945–1957
Elena Zubkova
Translated and edited by Hugh Ragsdale

LABOR CAMP SOCIALISM
The Gulag in the Soviet
Totalitarian System
Galina Mikhailovna Ivanova
Edited by Donald J. Raleigh
Translated by Carol Flath

OUR DAILY BREAD
Socialist Distribution and the
Art of Survival in Stalin's Russia
Elena Osokina
*Translated and edited by
Kate Transchel
and Greta Bucher*

**CHURCH AND STATE IN
SOVIET RUSSIA**
Russian Orthodoxy from World War II to
the Khruschchev Years
Tatiana A. Chumachenko
Edited and Translated by Edward E. Roslof

CHURCH AND STATE IN SOVIET RUSSIA

RUSSIAN ORTHODOXY FROM WORLD WAR II TO THE KHRUSHCHEV YEARS

Tatiana A. Chumachenko

Edited and Translated by
Edward E. Roslof

M.E. Sharpe
Armonk, New York
London, England

English translation, editorial matter, introduction © 2002 by M. E. Sharpe, Inc. An
earlier version of this work was published in Moscow in 1999 by AIRO-XX under the title
"Gosudarstvo, pravoslavnaia tserkov', veruiushchie, 1941–1961 gg." Copyright © 1999 by
Seriia "Pervaia monografiia" pod red. G.A. Bordiugova, T.A. Chumachenko, and AIRO-XX.

Photos 4, 8, and 10 through 18 courtesy of the Central State Archive of Cinematic and
Photographic Documents.

Library of Congress Cataloging-in-Publication Data

Chumachenko, T.A. (Tat'iana Aleksandrovna)
    [Gosudarstvo, pravoslavnaia tserkov , veruiushchie, 1941–1961 gg. English]
Church and state in Soviet Russia : Russian orthodoxy from World War II to the
Khrushchev years / by Tatiana A. Chumachenko and Edward E. Roslof, editor and
translator.
    p. cm. — (The new Russian history)
Includes bibliographical references and index.
ISBN 0-7656-0748-4 (alk. paper) — ISBN 0-7656-0749-2 (cloth : alk. paper)
 1. Russkaia pravoslavnaia tserkov' -History—20th century. 2. Orthodox Eastern
Church—Soviet Union—History. 3. Church and state—Soviet Union—History.
4. Soviet Union—Church history. I. Roslof, Edward E., 1956– II. Title. III. Series.

BX492.C4813 2002
322'.1094709044—dc21   2002066946

Contents

List of Abbreviations and Acronyms

Agitprop	Agitation and Propaganda Department of the Central Committee of the Communist Party of the Soviet Union
ASSR	Autonomous Soviet Socialist Republic
CPSU	Communist Party of the Soviet Union
Fr.	Father, used as a title for a priest
FSB RF	Federal Security Service of the Russian Federation (1993–present)
GAChO	State Archive of the Chelyabinsk Region
GARF	State Archive of the Russian Federation (formerly TsGAOR USSR)
KGB	Committee for State Security (Soviet secret police, 1954–91)
Komsomol	Young Communist League
MGB	Ministry of State Security (1946–53)
MVD	Ministry of Internal Affairs (1946–60)
NKGB	People's Commissariat for State Security (Soviet secret police, 1941; 1943–46)
NKVD	People's Commissariat for Internal Affairs (Soviet secret police 1934–46)
OGIZ	Association of State Book and Magazine Publishing Houses
OSVOD	Lifeguard Patrol
RGANI	Russian State Archive of Contemporary History (formerly TsKhSD)
RGASPI	Russian State Archive for Social and Political History (formerly the Central Party Archive, and later RTsKhIDNI, the Russian Center for the Preservation and Study of Documents of Modern History)

RSFSR   Russian Soviet Federated Socialist Republic
Sovnarkom   Council of People's Commissars (later the Council of Ministers)
SSR   Soviet Socialist Republic
TASS   Telegraph Agency of the Soviet Union
USSR   Union of Soviet Socialist Republics (1917–91)
ZhMP   *Zhurnal Moskovskoi Patriarkhii* (*Journal of the Moscow Patri-
             archate*)

Editor's Preface

Victims or collaborators? Anyone who studies the history of Soviet Russia is confronted with this stark choice for labeling leaders of the Russian Orthodox Church. Were prominent Orthodox clergymen persecuted by Soviet authorities intent on the complete eradication of religious belief? Or were Orthodox bishops and priests willing accomplices of the regime—perhaps even covert agents for the secret police—who secretly plotted the church's destruction from within?

Tatiana Aleksandrovna Chumachenko's book offers a new perspective on the nature of church-state relations in the crucial period of Soviet history from 1943 to 1961. Using voluminous archival records that are carefully read and analyzed, she redraws the map of personal and institutional relationships between the Orthodox Church and the Soviet government. This history becomes a story filled with personal sacrifices and petty grievances, genuine patriotism and political betrayal. Communists and church leaders collaborated with one another to advance their own agendas. Secret policemen persistently argued for more churches to be opened, while Orthodox bishops exchanged greetings and gifts with high-ranking government officials. Members of both groups advanced their causes and became victims when the political winds shifted.

This book takes a new path in researching Russian Orthodox history in the twentieth century. Chumachenko shows that the Soviet regime collected a wealth of varied material on religion. The reports and correspondence that circulated among high-ranking Soviet bureaucrats were surprisingly free of ideological rhetoric. Instead, they emphasized the practical consequences of policies toward the church. This is not to imply that these bureaucrats as members of the Communist Party did not share a deeply held atheistic worldview. Whenever the debate turned to ideology, their commitment to

Marxist-Leninist materialism was clear. It is remarkable, however, to note how seldom such debates occurred—at least within the highest party and government circles from the early 1940s until the late 1950s. The nation as a whole faced other, more pressing issues stemming from foreign invasion, postwar reconstruction, and Cold War competition. The Russian Orthodox Church willingly accepted and supported national priorities in each of these areas, just as the Soviet government accepted and relied upon support from a social organization that attracted millions of its citizens and spoke with authority to the international community.

Chumachenko enables her readers to understand the human, social, and political factors that allowed the church to become more fully integrated into Soviet society. As a member of a new generation of Russian historians, the author is not bound by the old ideological constraints and so interprets archival documents with critical insight. She chronicles the twenty-year span that saw a dramatic shift in relations between state, church, and believers. The German invasion of Soviet Russia in 1941 brought an abrupt halt to the Stalinist terror against religious organizations. Stalin's meeting with three senior Orthodox bishops in September 1943 marked official recognition of the church in Soviet society. Over the following two decades, except for two brief interludes in 1948–49 and 1954, the Soviet government demonstrated little overt hostility toward or persecution of organized Orthodox activity. This changed in 1961, when the Twenty-first Congress of the Communist Party of the Soviet Union officially adopted a new, radical program of antireligious propaganda that was to guide Soviet policy for the next quarter century.

Chumachenko concentrates primarily on church-state interaction at the highest level. She devotes most of her research to leaders in the Council for Russian Orthodox Church Affairs, the Moscow Patriarchate, the Soviet government, and the Communist Party. Her concern is the process by which national policy on the church was formulated, implemented, and changed. Hers is a history "from above." Yet, she also provides tantalizing evidence of the impact national policy made at the local level. We get glimpses of believers submitting petitions signed by hundreds or thousands of people asking that churches in their towns and villages be reopened. We see local authorities stubbornly rejecting orders signed by Stalin himself when such orders did not fit with their own ideas of dealing with the church. Chumachenko provides a starting point for local studies on the church in the late Soviet era, both by clearly explaining national policy and by pointing historians to archives where additional information can be found. Chumachenko's book is an invaluable resource for historians and students who are interested in Russian studies, the Russian Orthodox Church, and the inner workings of the postwar Soviet government. In addition, it covers topics of interest for those in the general fields of religious history and religious studies. Chumachenko has produced a case study on religious belief in the modern world. Her readers gain an appreciation for the complexities inherent in the struggle between traditional religion and modern secular ideologies—a struggle that will continue to demand our attention for the foreseeable future.

* * *

In an attempt to produce a flowing English translation of Chumachenko's work, I use some license to avoid literal rendering of Russian words and phases. I translate *oblast'* and *krai* as "region" and *raion* as "district." Monastic names are usually transliterated, except for a few that have common English forms. For example, Luke, Alexander, and Peter are used instead of Luka, Aleksandr, and Petr. Soft signs are omitted from personal and place names. I translate references to Council commissioners (*upolnomochennye*) and party or government officials using gender-specific language ("men" and "chairman") to highlight the fact that women did not hold these posts. Also, "clergyman" is used because the Russian Orthodox Church only ordains men. In the text, my editorial notes appear at the bottom of the page and are marked "Ed." to distinguish them from the author's occasional explanatory notes.

I would like to express my gratitude to the author for her enthusiasm and assistance in producing this English-language version of her book. Special thanks also goes to Dilyara Izbragimova for facilitating communication and transmitting material between Ohio and Chelyabinsk. I am grateful to Donald J. Raleigh, the editor of this series and my longtime friend and mentor, for his encouragement and support. Finally, I thank the fine staff at M.E. Sharpe for their assistance in producing this volume.

Edward E. Roslof

Foreword to the Russian Edition

Over the last ten years, Russia has witnessed a significant growth of interest in its national history as a topic for scholarship and cultural life. Russians recall and are eager to follow the advice of the famous Russian historian V.O. Kliuchevskii who wrote: "Without a knowledge of history, we would recognize ourselves only by chance. We would not know how and why we came into the world, how and for what purpose we exist in the world, how and to what ends we should dedicate ourselves." We note that, as a result of social and political clashes in the late 1980s and early 1990s, national interest focused primarily on the twentieth century and particularly on the Soviet era—one of the most complex, dramatic, and tragic periods in our history.

Historical works of various kinds have appeared in recent years thanks to one of the less obvious achievements of the post-Soviet era. I am referring to the easing of restrictions on access to the richest materials in the Russian archives that for decades were guarded with stamps of "secret" and "top secret." Placing new documents in the hands of scholars, of course, forces us to look at many things in our history from a new perspective. We now have more complete and less biased ideas about many things. As a result, our historical works are gradually filling in the "blank spots" of Russian history in the Soviet period.

Many religious topics are included among those now open for research. These include: the history of Russian religious confessions and their relationships with the state; the role of religions such as Christianity, Islam, and Buddhism in the culture, traditions, and everyday life of the peoples of Russia; and the policies of the Communist Party and the Soviet government in the areas of freedom of conscience and profession of faith. Today these issues are reported, discussed, and analyzed on the pages of periodicals—both secular and religious—as well as in scholarly collections and monographs.

Of particular interest is the history of the Russian Orthodox Church and its relationship with the government during the decades of socialism. The study of this issue is no mere mental exercise; it has significant and practical implications for the government and for the slow and painful development of civil society in our country. The Russian Constitution proclaims that we are a secular, democratic, and law-abiding state. Therefore, the current Russian government is obliged to implement policies that conform to international legal standards in the area of freedom of conscience. Such policies relate to religions, churches, and citizens who profess various beliefs and philosophical orientations. As the 1990s showed, these policies must also correspond to Russian traditions and must not appear to be foreign elements thrust on Russia from outside. Such policies should creatively combine the experience of Western democracy and Russian (including even Soviet) experience in solving "the religious question."

This book by Tatiana Aleksandrovna Chumachenko, in my opinion, is part of the most significant stream of new research and writing on Soviet history. The author addresses the extraordinarily interesting and complex subject of relations between the Soviet government and the Russian Orthodox Church between 1943 and 1961. Soviet historians and foreign authors have written about this, and many works have recently appeared. But Chumachenko has successfully found an original approach to the topic.

First, she focuses her attention directly on state activity, various governmental institutions and special organs, and, most of all, on the Council for Russian Orthodox Church Affairs. Even after many decades, society as a whole knows nothing about this particular bureaucracy in the Soviet regime. Even now, in the era of declassified archives, little accurate or objective information has been written about it. In the past, the "ecclesiastical policy" of the government took concrete form in this Council through its decisions, proposals, decrees, and plans—all the things that directly determined the status and activity of the Russian Orthodox Church. Many pages in this book are dedicated to the activity of the Council, and we can now say that we know about the Council not through hearsay but on the basis of high-quality scholarly research.

In this book, activities of the Council for Russian Orthodox Church Affairs are consistently correlated to the Communist Party's position on the "ecclesiastical question." Thus, we can see that over the course of decades the party experimented with diverse approaches to religion and the church because the party's general policy on these issues was diverse. The Council itself experienced various phases. First, Soviet leaders drew it in close to the epicenter of political power in the USSR, then they drove it out to the periphery of state and party interests. The author proves convincingly that the devotion of the Council's leadership to the idea of church-state cooperation was not subject to changes in the political winds. The idea of cooperation was genuine, true, and motivated by a desire to guide the Council's activity for the good of the nation. Thanks to Chumachenko's compelling and impartial descriptions, we can fully experience the drama and tragedy of circumstances that "broke" people. They were forced to abandon legally legitimate positions on church-state relations for a track where administrative pressure was used against believers, clergy, and the religious organizations they created.

The second attractive element of this book is its detailed recreation of the circumstances and conditions of Russian Orthodox Church life in the decades covered. The church of the bleak, evil years of World War II stands before us. Experiencing people's common grief and suffering, the church also stood with them in the triumphant Victory Days. The church awaited the rebirth of the country, the spiritual liberation of the people, and the restoration of ecclesiastical life desecrated in the 1930s. Chumachenko provides a wealth of specific evidence to show that until 1958 the church steadily regained the position it had lost earlier, although it faced difficulties in this process. We also see how the organized church once again felt the heavy hand of power come down upon it, thanks to party and Soviet officials who drifted back to the ideas of the "antireligious struggle" that held sway in the years before World War II. "The Thaw" that occurred in Soviet society after 1956 under Nikita Khrushchev remained an unrealized dream of freedom of conscience for the Orthodox Church. Why? The author offers her own thoughts based on her knowledge of the actual circumstances of those years, but she also allows us to draw our own conclusions.

An outstanding feature of this book is its rich source base. The first serious book on this topic has now appeared. The author draws upon and carefully reads the richest available archival material. There is no place in research for conjecture, hearsay, or unsubstantiated assumptions. Chumachenko uses facts, evidence, and figures to present a living and accurate picture of relations between the Soviet government and the Russian Orthodox Church.

I am convinced that anyone who is interested in Russian history during and after World War II will find this book useful reading.

Mikhail Ivanovich Odintsov,
Professor and Doctor of History

CHURCH AND STATE
IN SOVIET RUSSIA

Introduction

At first glance it seems paradoxical that World War II, the most tragic event in the history of our country, became the salvation of the Russian Orthodox Church.

By the end of the 1930s, relations between the Soviet government and the Russian Orthodox Church had reached a critical point, a point where the word "relations" lost all meaning. As a social institution, the Orthodox Church in the USSR stood on the brink of total destruction.

The financial basis of the church had been destroyed. All its property and capital investments had been nationalized by the 1918 decree of the Council of People's Commissars (Sovnarkom) entitled "On the Separation of the Church from the State and Schools from the Church."

Internal crises within the church, as well as the government's active policy directed toward deepening those crises, led to the disintegration of the church's organizational structure. After the death of Patriarch Tikhon Bellavin in April 1925, the church was unable to elect a new patriarch. In 1935, the church's Holy Synod ceased functioning due to an inability to replenish its ranks with episcopal representatives. In 1939, the episcopacy of the Russian Orthodox Church comprised two metropolitans and two archbishops.* The Moscow Patriarchate was deprived of its publishing activity. While the government permitted publication of the *Journal of the Moscow Patriarchate* in 1931, the magazine appeared only sporadically for four years.

After its advanced theological studies program in Leningrad "voluntarily

---

*In Russian Orthodoxy, the four ranks of bishops (bishop, archbishop, metropolitan, patriarch) denote increasing episcopal seniority, prestige, and authority. A metropolitan oversees a large area centered around a major city, such as St. Petersburg. The patriarch heads the national church and presides over the capital city of Moscow.—Ed.

disbanded" in 1928, the patriarchal church lost the ability to train new clergy.[1] By 1939, only slightly more than one hundred active Orthodox churches could be found throughout the country. In most regions of the USSR, only one church was functioning. Twenty-five regions were designated as "church-less." Not a single monastery was active on our nation's territory.[2]

Success on the "church front" fed the illusions held by most leaders in the government and party bureaucracies that the first socialist state would soon become a truly atheistic society. This idea led to the logical conclusion that both laws on religious groups and governmental organs for implementing those laws were unnecessary. Indeed, in April 1938 the All-Union Central Executive Committee of the USSR abolished both its Commission for Religious Questions and the commission's network of inspectors who worked in regional executive committees. Only regional and local government organs decided religious matters. Complete control over the religious sphere was transferred to the Church Department of the People's Commissariat for Internal Affairs (NKVD).

The situation changed with the advent of World War II. On June 22, 1941, the very first day of the war in Russia, Metropolitan Sergii Stragorodskii (the *locum tenens*, or guardian of the vacant patriarchal throne) stated the patriotic position of the Russian Orthodox Church in his letter "To Pastors and Parishioners of the Orthodox Church of Christ":

> This is not the first time that the Russian people have endured suffering. And on this occasion, with God's help, they will grind the hostile forces of fascism into dust. . . . Our native land is being defended by the force of arms, by the common heroism of its people, and by a general willingness to serve our country in this difficult trial. The Church of Christ confers its blessing on all Orthodox believers in their defense of the holy borders of our Motherland.[3]

Metropolitan Sergii, who became patriarch of Moscow in September 1943, and other Russian Orthodox bishops issued letters and appeals to believers in areas unconquered by the invaders as well as to those in occupied territory. This latter group was called upon to support the partisan movement and to directly participate in it. As military operations approached the borders of the USSR, the church was included in the international antifascist movement. Appeals by Orthodox clergy to their fellow believers stressed patriotic activity by the Russian Orthodox Church and called upon them "to join this holy struggle."

The Soviet government not only encouraged, but also directly supported, initiatives by the Moscow Patriarchate. Government presses printed church leaflets, and state agencies organized the distribution of the leaflets in occupied territory. The Agitation and Propaganda Department (Agitprop) of the Communist Party's Central Committee exercised control over the content of church publications. Clergymen even gave lively sermons to gatherings of

Red Army soldiers—something that was unthinkable only a few years earlier.[4]

National and diocesan Orthodox activity revived after the start of World War II. Orthodox churches and chapels were opened and functioned without any legal registration.

The publication of two books (*The Truth About Religion in Russia* in 1942 and *The Russian Orthodox Church and World War II*, a collection of church documents that appeared in 1943) attested to the initial process for normalizing relations between the government and the Russian Orthodox Church. The government assisted the Moscow Patriarchate during its evacuation from Moscow to the town of Ulyanovsk. With the help of state agencies, a Council of Bishops quickly convened in Ulyanovsk in March 1942 in order to condemn a declaration by the Ukrainian Autocephalous Church.[5] In November 1941, a decree by the Supreme Soviet of the USSR appointed Metropolitan Nikolai Iarushevich as a member of the Extraordinary State Commission to Establish and Investigate War Crimes Committed by the German Fascist Invaders.[6] The Soviet government also permitted general church collections for the national Defense Fund.

The Russian Orthodox Church's energetic collections for the war effort were the most visible forms of its patriotic service. It was more than a public display, however; in financial terms, it was highly significant. During the war years, money and valuables collected by believers and clergy were used to fund a tank column in honor of Dmitrii Donskoi and a fighter squadron in honor of Alexander Nevsky.* Church offerings became resources for hospitals, children's homes, and the children and families of Red Army soldiers. Church contributions to the war effort totaled 300 million rubles.[7]

The first contacts between Metropolitan Sergii and Joseph Stalin, the head of the Soviet government, were directly connected to the project by the Moscow Patriarchate to organize a collection for the tank column. These contacts took the form of an exchange of salutatory telegrams. Metropolitan Sergii telegraphed Stalin on January 5, 1943, and asked about starting collection efforts and about opening a special account in the State Bank. In response, the Moscow Patriarchate in Ulyanovsk received a long-awaited telegram:

> To Sergii, Metropolitan of Moscow and patriarchal *locum tenens.*
>
> Please convey my greetings and the appreciation of the Red Army to Russian Orthodox clergy and believers for their concern about the armored forces of the Red Army. An order for opening a special account in the State Bank has been issued.[8]

---

*Alexander Nevsky and Dmitrii Donskoi were princes of the thirteenth and fourteenth centuries revered in Russian history for leading Russian forces to victory over foreign invaders.—Ed.

From this time forward, the church operated with an expectation of change. The event that became the point of reference for a new era in church–state relations, however, occurred on September 4, 1943. On that day, Stalin met in the Kremlin with bishops of the Orthodox Church—Metropolitans Sergii, Aleksii Simanskii of Leningrad and Novgorod, and Nikolai Iarushevich of Kiev and Galicia (exarch of Ukraine).[9] Later, Georgii Karpov, the chairman of the Council for Russian Orthodox Church Affairs, composed a detailed report on the meeting. This report became the very first document in the Council's archives, preserved in the State Archive of the Russian Federation (GARF).

There is no need to include the document here; its contents became public in 1989 when historians V.A. Alekseev and M.I. Odintsov both published it.[10] An important fact worth highlighting is that Soviet and Russian Orthodox leaders reached a significant concordat at this meeting, which led to major changes in church-state relations.

The government's new policy resulted in normalization of relations with the church and assisted the church in strengthening its financial position, while increasing its authority both domestically and internationally. In October 1943 this new state policy led to the formation of the Council for Russian Orthodox Church Affairs and its network of regional commissioners. The position of the Council's leaders promoted a process that saw church-state relations between 1943 and 1957 develop primarily within a civilized framework, despite attempts to revise church policy in 1948–49 and 1954.

The fifteen years that followed the historic meeting of September 1943 proved to be an exceptional period in the whole history of relations between the Russian Orthodox Church and the Soviet government.

Leaders in Nikita Khrushchev's administration began attacking the church in 1958. At the beginning of the 1960s, this led to a definitive revision of policies that had been laid down during the war years—despite opposition from the Moscow Patriarchate and some staff members on the Council for Russian Orthodox Church Affairs.

Stalin's meeting with the three metropolitans, in the words of D.V. Pospielovsky, "led to many stories, often semilegendary." Publication of Karpov's notes on that meeting opened a new page in our country's historiography, and the issue of church-state relations in the 1940s and 1950s became the subject of special historical investigation. Over the last seven to eight years, many articles and monographs devoted to the topic have appeared. One can identify a specific set of questions that attract the attention of researchers and that are answered from various points of view.

The first question historians asked after they learned about the contents of the discussion between Stalin and the bishops was, "Why?" What caused

Stalin to make such a sharp turn in policy toward the church? Why did this take place in the second half of 1943? Gleb Yakunin proposed several answers to those questions in 1989:

- Patriotic activity by the church caused Stalin to attempt to "channel" the patriotic enthusiasm of believers toward his own interests for the sake of victory over Germany.
- Policies of occupation forces on conquered territory (the opening of churches and the unrestricted performance of church services by the clergy) stimulated the need for liberalized policies on Soviet territory as well.
- Stalin's personal characteristics played a role—the "holy incense of the Orthodox Church" dedicated to "an uncrowned emperor" was not enough, as he sought full glorification.[11]

Alekseev shares Yakunin's views but adds yet another factor, namely, foreign policy. Alekseev thinks that Stalin found it advantageous "to make peace" with the Russian Orthodox Church on the eve of the Teheran Conference. Religious public opinion in the Allied nations would interpret this as a positive change in church-state relations. This would, in turn, sway many issues at the conference in favor of the Soviet leadership.[12]

Such explanations for the reasons behind the turn in Stalinist policy raised another series of questions. First, the patriotic activity of the Russian Orthodox Church began expanding from the very beginning of the war, but, in the words of Pospielovsky, Stalin "was never known to have a special inclination toward gratitude or even consciousness of the services shown him." So, what would have caused him to show gratitude to the Russian Orthodox Church for its actions over the previous thirty months? Second, the year 1943 was a fundamental turning point in the war. The war's outcome was already clear. Did the necessity to demonstrate unity between atheists and believers in the fight against a common enemy still exist? Third, if this was connected with a concrete event (the Teheran Conference), why was this policy not "curtailed" when the war ended, as Pospielovsky rightly asks?

Pospielovsky himself explains the reasons for the change in church policy by Stalin's need to "tame" the Catholic, Protestant, and Orthodox peoples of Western Europe. To do this, he dared not frighten off Russian churches or incite them against him. He had to practice this same religious toleration "at home."[13] M.V. Shkarovskii convincingly argues this point in an article published in the journal *Voprosy istorii* [Questions of History].[14] Information from the archives of the Council for Russian Orthodox Church Affairs also confirms (through calculation of various factors) that the change in church-

[margin handwriting: pregmatism]

state relations was caused by Stalin's pragmatic interests. He wanted to use the Russian Orthodox Church as an instrument for accomplishing his own postwar geopolitical plans.

The second question that is hotly debated in our country's historiography is the nature of Soviet government policies on the church. This question relates to the reasons for changes in policy and, in turn, to the problem of periodization of church-state relations in the 1940s and 1950s.

[margin handwriting: 4 periods]

Without question, M.I. Odintsov has played the leading role in working out this problem.[15] In his monographs and many publications, he has described fundamental principles of the policies toward the church and established four basic periods: (1) 1943 to 1948–49; (2) 1949–54; (3) 1955–57; and (4) 1958–61. While historians S. Gordun and Pospielovsky see the period from 1958 to 1961 as a time of a new direction in policy and a marked change of course, Odintsov believes that an earlier trend was revealed in these years and that the final break with that trend took place at the beginning of the 1960s.[16]

In our view, the task at hand requires fleshing out this chronological framework with specific content. Also, we use archival documents to bolster the argument and to draw general conclusions.

Closely connected with the preceding problem is the question of the activity of the Council for Russian Orthodox Church Affairs. Researchers present diametrically opposed assessments of its activity. Church historians such as Gordun and Pospielovsky (who relies heavily on Gordun's work in his analysis of events in the 1940s) see the members of the Council and its commissioners not simply as "over-procurators" but as "over-procurators* who represented the ideology of militant atheism."[17] One might say that these authors represent the position of the side that suffered—the church. That position compels them to see the Council only as an organ for control over the activity of the Russian Orthodox Church. But, in order to control the church, the Council had to help revive it and guarantee that religious organizations could conduct normal activities. The church could not possibly achieve those ends by its own efforts.

The Council and its chairman, Karpov, saw their main task as implementing and realizing the government's church policies. To fulfill its mission, the Council controlled the whole arena of church-state relations in the country through its commissioners. In the process, Karpov defended the interests of believers and often came into conflict with local government authorities. If this aspect of the work by the Council and its commissioners is not taken

---

*In Imperial Russia, the Russian Orthodox Church fell under the supervision of an over-procurator, a layman who reported directly to the tsar.

into account, one cannot reconstruct a full and objective picture of the relations between the government and the church in the 1940s and 1950s.

Analysis of archival documents, primarily those collected by the Council itself, provides the basis for concluding that Odintsov's viewpoint is the most well-grounded. He writes that the Council's leadership followed legal and constitutional rules in relating to the Russian Orthodox Church, even during crisis situations. The conceptual nature of Odintsov's conclusions requires confirmation by further studying the problem and widening its scope by looking, for example, at the Council's work with its commissioners and its control over implementation of religious policy at the local level.

The work of Church historians most fully represents the position of the Russian Orthodox Church in the 1940s and 1950s.[18] However, this fact must be noted: On the history of the church, Russian researchers avoid any analysis of the position of leaders in the Moscow Patriarchate concerning their relations with state authorities. Confronted with works by Gleb Yakunin and Vladimir Stepanov (who previously used the pseudonym Rusak) that contain indiscriminate and totally unfounded criticism of the patriarchate's activity in the 1940–50s, we must lift the unspoken taboo on this topic. Then, we will be able to present an objective and unbiased analysis of the activity of Russian Orthodox Church leaders with all its positives and negatives from today's standpoint. We will also be able to demonstrate that Orthodox bishops held a spectrum of opinions and views on matters related to policies of the patriarchate.

To a certain extent, these issues are presented in an article by Iu. Degtiarev ("Why Stalin Recognized the Church"),[19] in a 1992 book by Alekseev (*Has "Storming the Heavens" Been Revoked?*),[20] and in articles dedicated to the problem of the elimination of the Uniate Church—Olga Vasileva's "The Vatican in the Crucible of War"[21] and Odintsov's "The Uniates and the Soviet Regime"—that anticipated the publication of archival documents on this topic.[22]

The question of the Russian Orthodox Church's activities during the war years has recently attracted the attention of scholars. However, since analysis of this topic remains focused on the church's patriotic activity during the war, studies on Russian Orthodox relations with the Soviet state in this period are still limited.[23]

M.V. Shkarovskii examines a new historiographical question—the foreign policy of the Russian Orthodox Church in the 1940s and 1950s—in an article ("The Russian Orthodox Church from 1943 to 1957") and a monograph (*The Russian Orthodox Church Under Stalin and Khrushchev*).[24] His monograph draws on a broad historiographical base and presents a full and detailed picture of contemporary scholarship on Russian Orthodox Church history in the 1940s and 1950s by Russian and foreign researchers. Unfortunately, an insufficient base of primary sources (documents from the formerly classified section of the archive for the Council for Russian Orthodox Church Affairs are not included in his analysis) does not permit Shkarovskii to consider questions related to Soviet government policies toward the church. He also does not discuss methods used by the Council and its regional commissioners as their primary means for realizing these policies or the reasons for policy changes during the period under investigation. In my opinion, the use of undocumented historical facts not supported by evidence reduces the value of his work. For example, Shkarovskii writes in his biographical notes that Karpov graduated from theological seminary but does not cite any sources for this information.[25] Karpov himself recorded several times in personnel documents that he was from a family of factory workers and was apprenticed as a metalworker before becoming a sailor in the Soviet navy. Karpov is a key figure in the history of church-state relations for this period, and thus it is not advisable to use evidence from dubious sources when describing him.

Pospielovsky's basic research is unique among publications on the problem of church-state relations.[26] I can only lament that historical works, including those based on Russian archival material, come to us from abroad. Using a wide and varied array of sources, Pospielovsky presents a complex analysis not only of the church's history in the USSR but also its relationship with the government, including the period covered in this book. Nonetheless, I cannot agree with some of his conclusions, most importantly with his above-mentioned stand on the position of leaders in the Council for Russian Orthodox Church Affairs. In particular, Pospielovky repeats Gordun's mistake by labeling the Council as the main obstacle to opening Orthodox churches. In one of his more recent works published in Russia, however, Pospielovsky uses data from the Council's archives and from the former Communist Party archives in Belorussia [now Belarus] to draw different conclusions about the work of the Council and its chairman:

> Karpov and his colleague Polianskii from the Council for Affairs of Religious Cults emphasized that one task for both councils was "to preserve normal church-state relations and to improve them for the good of the Motherland." We must give Karpov and Polianskii their due. They tried to use the "interregnum" of 1954–56 and official slogans about the restoration of "Leninist legality" in defense of the church's legal position.[27]

Thus, a series of problems remain important for historians. The first of these is identifying the factors that influenced changes in religious policy in 1948–49, 1954, and 1958. Another is defining the role of the Communist

Party's ideological structures on the religious question and the degree of its influence on the character and content of government policy toward the church. Examining the work of the Council for Russian Orthodox Church affairs in directing its own personnel in local offices is yet another problem. Historians also want to understand the direction taken by the Council and its commissioners in carrying out the government's religious policy, including specific forms and methods used around the country as well as their correlation with the government's officially declared policy. In a similar vein, researchers need to find the correlation between the Council's leadership and "opinions" about religious policy held by the government and the Central Committee on the one hand and by local government bureaucrats on the other. Finally, historians want to understand both the position of Orthodox Church leaders on state ecclesiastical policy and activities of the Moscow Patriarchate as that policy was transformed.

One must point out that, generally speaking, the question of relations between the Soviet government and the Russian Orthodox Church is still a new topic in our national historiography. The lack of research during the Soviet period on church-state relations eliminates the need to rewrite history or to search for so-called "blank spots" in history books from the period. This topic is also rewarding for historians because the only authorities for contemporary researchers are documented sources.

Documents from the collection of the Council for Russian Orthodox Church Affairs were the main sources for this book. Many of these materials, including the most valuable, are found in the classified collection of the State Archive of the Russian Federation. A unique feature of this collection is that documents were never removed or purged; they have been fully preserved and reflect all aspects of the Council's work. These documents can be divided into two groups. The first are high-level documents from the Council; the second relate to the Council's work with its regional commissioners. Material of special interest in the first group of documents is in files labeled "Memoranda of Instructions by Members of the Government on Matters Relating to the Activity of the Russian Orthodox Church" and "Memoranda of Instructions Received at Meetings with Directive Organs." These are the same documents all marked "top secret," that allow us to form an opinion about the true intentions and motives of Soviet leaders when they chose one course of action over another in deciding "the religious question." These documents also allow us to reconstruct the "kitchen," figuratively speaking, where the government cooked up its religious policy.

The contents of notes from working sessions of Council personnel provide evidence about positions of the entire Council and individual members relating to methods for solving problems of religious policy as it passed through various stages of evolution. "Memoranda of conversations" between representatives from the Council and Orthodox leaders (the patriarch, members of his Holy Synod, and bishops) give us an idea of relationships between those groups.

Studying the second group of archival documents makes it possible to see the complicated process of implementing the Soviet government's policy on the church. Analysis reveals trends in activity by regional commissioners and the nature of the relationships they formed with representatives of local party and state organs as well as with religious organizations. These documents also contain statistical material that facilitates an assessment of levels of religiosity among the population, together with the status and position of the Orthodox Church.

Material from documents contained in the open collection of the Council's archives includes reports on institutions for theological education, minutes from the sessions of the Most Holy Synod of the Patriarch of Moscow and All Russia, and letters sent by Patriarch Aleksii I to the Council and to Karpov personally as its chairman. These documents to some degree reflect the position of the church's leadership on government policies and summarize activities by the episcopacy.

Important sources for addressing the historical problems described above include documents collected by the Agitation and Propaganda Department of the Party Central Committee. These are found in the Russian State Archive for Social and Political History (RGASPI, formerly known as the Central Party Archive and later as the Russian Center for the Preservation and Study of Documents of Modern History) and the Center for the Preservation of Contemporary Documents (TsKhSD). These materials allow us to judge the degree of influence exercised by ideological departments of the party on the character and content of state religious policy, not to mention church-state relations in general.

This study has also relied on published documents. These include the previously mentioned published materials from the Council for Russian Orthodox Church Affairs that were prepared by Odintsov for two journals: *Istoricheskii arkhiv* [Historical Archive] and *Otechestvennye arkhivy* [Archives of Our Native Country]. A two-volume work entitled *The Russian Orthodox Church in the Soviet Era, 1917–1991*, published in 1995, also contains primary sources.[28] This collection is the Russian edition of a work that appeared in Germany during the millennium celebration of the conversion of Russia to Christianity in 1988. Again, we can only regret that such a collection was not published in our own country and that we were forced to publish our own history in documents that were translated twice (from Russian into German and then from German back into Russian). In my opinion, the value of this collection is lessened since it includes only excerpts from documents. Moreover, preference is given to those documents that refer to international aspects of the Russian Orthodox Church's work.

This monograph uses material from Soviet periodicals published in the 1940s and 1950s: the newspapers *Pravda* and *Izvestiia* as well as selected publications by provincial and urban party organizations. Issues of the *Journal of the Moscow Patriarchate* are also used, for they allow us to expose the limits of divergence between the government's official policy and its real policy toward the church as well as between the official position of the church and unpublished statements made by its leaders. Various other publications were useful for this work: recollections of Archbishop Vasilii Krivoshein about Metropolitan Nikolai, autobiographical material from Archbishop Luke Voino-Iasenetskii, a book by Metropolitan Ioann Snychev of St. Petersburg on Metropolitan Manuil Lemeshevskii, and the memoirs of Metropolitan Evlogii Georgievskii.[29]

* * *

I am much indebted to the faculty of the Department of Russian History at Moscow State University for assistance in completing this book and for selecting this research topic. In this connection, I must express words of sincerest appreciation to Professor L.I. Semennikova, Professor E.E. Beilina, and Senior Lecturer N.A. Kovalenko.

I express gratitude to members of the research staff at the Russian archives: D.N. Nokhotovich (GARF) and G.V. Gorskaia (RGASPI). The Moscow Social Science Foundation (President A.V. Kortunov) and the Russian Humanities Research Fund (General Director E.V. Semenov) provided financial support, without which it would have been impossible to study materials from archives in Moscow.

Words of special thanks and gratitude go to D. Kh. Ibragimova for her invaluable help in this work as well as to all those dear people whose support and benevolent assistance made this book possible.

Finally, this work is dedicated to my parents.

Chapter 1

9/4/43

Church and State from World War II Until 1948

The Council for Russian Orthodox Church Affairs and Its Commissioners: Establishment of a Bureaucracy

Stalin's intention to change the nature of church-state relations raised the issue of forming an agency that would implement the government's new ecclesiastical policy. Stalin himself determined the status, function, and even the name for the agency before his meeting on September 4, 1943, with Georgii Karpov, a colonel in the secret police.[1] When Karpov expressed his opinion in favor of creating such an agency under the auspices of the Supreme Soviet of the USSR, Stalin disagreed. He said that it should be a special committee or council for Russian Orthodox Church affairs under the direction of Sovnarkom. With these words, the head of the government clearly wanted to emphasize this essential point: the council would be formed as an organ of executive power. Stalin established its purpose with these words: "The council should be the link between the government and the patriarch. The council itself will not make decisions. Instead, it should report everything to the state and pass on government decisions to the church on the state's behalf."

Karpov was appointed chairman of the newly created body. In this capacity, he participated in Stalin's conversation with the leadership of the Russian Orthodox Church (Metropolitans Sergii, Aleksii, and Nikolai) that took place late in the evening that same day. At the end of the meeting, Stalin informed the bishops that he planned to create a special organ—the Council for Russian Orthodox Church Affairs—and to name Karpov as its chairman. The metropolitans responded favorably to this information, thus showing

15

that they knew Comrade Karpov and respected his appointment. Turning to Karpov, Stalin gave his final instructions: "Choose two or three assistants as members of your Council. Create a staff. But always remember, first that you are not the Over-Procurator of the Holy Synod* and second that your work should heavily emphasize the church's independence."[2]

The building selected for the Council for Russian Orthodox Church Affairs was a two-story detached house located at 20 Kropotkin Street in Moscow. On orders from Viacheslav Molotov,** the building's premises were made available within two weeks—the first floor had been used as apartments, and the second floor had held the offices and library of the Communist Party organization for the city's Frunze region. At the end of September 1943, the new Council's personnel began their work. Its staff originally consisted of a vice chairman, an assistant to the chairman, a corresponding secretary, an assessor, a group of four inspectors, and service personnel. Agents from the People's Commissariat for Internal Affairs (NKVD) occupied leadership positions on the Council.

Karpov headed the Fourth Department of the NKVD's Third Secret Political Directorate from December 1941; the first subsection of his Department had responsibility for "the struggle against church and sectarian counterrevolution." Molotov thought it was natural to combine the duties of that position and those of chairman of the Council for Russian Orthodox Church Affairs. In a conversation on October 13, 1943, he told Karpov, "As long as your official position in the NKGB is not published in the newspapers and isn't officially known, I think it is possible to combine the two jobs. But, we will decide this later."[3] His dual responsibilities continued until March 1955 when Karpov retired from the KGB. K.A. Zaitsev, a NKGB major, was appointed vice chairman of the Council. Karpov nominated him for that position, just as he recommended NKGB Major N.I. Blinov for the post of assistant to the chairman.

The Personnel Division of Sovnarkom's Administrative Department filled the remaining staff positions. According to Karpov's statements, however, employees only reluctantly went to work for the Council. Molotov had to intervene by calling Ia. Chaadaev in the Administrative Department. Molotov

---

*Stalin was referring here to the pattern of Orthodox Church governance in Imperial Russia. The Moscow Patriarchate was abolished, and between 1721 and 1917 the Russian Orthodox Church was ruled by a Holy Synod that was supervised by an Over-Procurator, a layman who reported directly to the tsar and often had enormous influence over the church.—Ed.

**Viacheslav Molotov (1890–1986) was Stalin's protégé and a member of his political entourage. Between 1942 and 1957, he served as first vice chairman of Sovnarkom but fell from power during the de-Stalinization campaign of the late 1950s.—Ed.

ordered him to help the Council in all areas and, along these lines, issued instructions that "all personnel must receive special privileges."[4] As a result, salaries were raised (for example, the Council chairman's salary was increased from 2,500 to 3,900 rubles per month), and members of the Council received the right to use both the Kremlin cafeteria and facilities under the Fourth Directorate of the Soviet Union's Ministry of Health. All other Council personnel were given exemptions from being drafted into active military service.[5] The problem of recruiting personnel for the Council was solved. Staff members of the new state administrative agency set to work.

Sovnarkom approved the "Regulations for the Council of Russian Orthodox Church Affairs" on October 7, 1943, in Decree No. 1095. The regulations defined the basic functions and tasks of the Council:

1. The Council for Russian Orthodox Church Affairs serves as the link between the government of the USSR and the Patriarch of Moscow and All Russia on issues related to the Russian Orthodox Church. . . .

2. The Council for Russian Orthodox Church Affairs is responsible for:

    (a) preliminary review of issues raised by the Patriarch of Moscow and All Russia that require action by the government;

    (b) drafting legal acts and decrees for issues concerning the Russian Orthodox Church, as well as instructions and other orders on their implementation, and presenting these to Sovnarkom USSR for its review;

    (c) oversight for the proper and timely implementation of the government's laws and decrees relating to the church throughout the USSR;

    (d) presentation of recommendations to Sovnarkom USSR on issues relating to the Russian Orthodox Church and presentation of timely informational reports to the government of the USSR on the condition, status, and activity of the Russian Orthodox Church throughout the USSR;

    (e) counting the total number of churches and compilation of statistical reports based on data collected by local administrative bodies.

3. The Council for Russian Orthodox Church Affairs has its own commissioners through Councils of Ministers of union and autonomous republics, regional executive committees, and city executive committees. These commissioners function in accordance with Point 3 of the "Regulations" and instructions from the Council.

4. The Council for Russian Orthodox Church Affairs has the right:
   (a) to demand that central and local administrative organs present essential information and material on issues connected with the Russian Orthodox Church;
   (b) to form commissions for resolution of separate issues.
5. All central administrative offices and authorities in the USSR will coordinate with the Council for Russian Orthodox Church Affairs in advance on measures being implemented in connection with issues relating to the Russian Orthodox Church.
6. The Council for Russian Orthodox Church Affairs has its own stamp and seal.[6]

In status, the Council had the same footing as other committees and commissions that operated under the auspices of Sovnarkom. Sovnarkom Vice Chairman Molotov supervised its activity on behalf of the government. All accounts, reports, and other documents should have been addressed to him but some, "especially on matters of principle," were sent directly to Stalin.[7]

The internal structure of the Council took shape. Its leadership team—the members of the Council—consisted of three men: Chairman Karpov, Vice Chairman Zaitsev, and I.I. Ivanov, leader of the group of inspectors. In accordance with "The Staff Manual for Personnel in the Council for Russian Orthodox Church Affairs" adopted on January 15, 1944, the responsibilities of these Council members included: organization of activity by commissioners through the Council's inspectors, control over patriotic work by the Russian Orthodox Church, control over publications by the church's Holy Synod as well as over activities of the church's theological schools, and organizing the registration of Orthodox bishops. Duties of other Council employees also were established. The assistant to the chairman conducted secret record-keeping. The assessor, who reported to the vice chairman, prepared overviews of the church's activities and status while also tracking both theological schools and the personal registration documents of bishops. A legal consultant for the Council prepared draft legislation, decrees, and instructions relating to the activity of religious organizations; he also provided informational reports on matters that arose in the course of the Council's work. The Council's inspectors were responsible for organizing the work of regional commissioners, preparing statistical summaries, and counting the number of churches and chapels.[8]

During the first months of its existence, the Council experienced all the difficulties characteristic of a newly formed organization. It was plagued by the lack of simple things such as glue, paper, envelopes, and file folders. The problem of providing the Council with folders continued until the end of 1945 when, at a conference with the Council's chairman, Senior Inspector

V. Spiridonov noted that approximately *three hundred* files on requests to open churches had not been properly set up due to the lack of file folders. Obeying mandatory requirements for secrecy in clerical work often hindered or delayed staff members in the fulfillment of their assigned tasks. Council inspectors complained about frequent shuffling of regions under their supervision and "spontaneous" official business trips to the provinces that were often unplanned and carried out on Karpov's personal orders. Unexpected "rush jobs" also disrupted staff work. For example, in January and February 1945 the whole office was busy preparing for a national council of the Russian Orthodox Church.[9]

The primary complication in these early years, however, came from another source. Workers in the Council for Russian Orthodox Affairs, the majority of whom formerly served in the state bureaucracy, lacked work experience or even knowledge essential for the specialized task of interacting with religious organizations under the new ecclesiastical policy. The Council's leaders were significantly less educated than church leaders. The only member of the Council who had more than a secondary education was G.T. Utkin, head of the department for central church administration. Other Council staff members with higher education included a translator, the corresponding secretary K.G. Anisimov (with a degree in history), and the legal consultant I.V. Pokrovskii (with a law degree).[10]

Work itself provided the necessary experience. Mistakes and errors forced Council personnel to seek new and more effective methods for organizing their activity. Staff turnover led to the hiring of new people. Thus, K.A. Zaitsev was relieved of his position as vice chairman of the Council in March 1945. He was replaced by S.K. Belyshev, a lieutenant-colonel in the secret police, on Karpov's recommendation.[11] K.G. Anisimov resigned as corresponding secretary in October 1946, and P.I. Barashkov took his place. The Council's structure was also revised many times. In January 1945, its leaders decided to create two divisions: an inspectorate and a department on central administrative affairs for the Russian Orthodox Church.

At the end of 1945, the staff makeup was discussed anew. The Council adopted a motion to form a secret section, whose staff would be responsible for receiving, expediting, registering, and filing classified documents. A new position of statistician was created to more accurately count churches and chapels. The Council also decided to increase the size of its staff.[12] Karpov presented this proposal to the government at the beginning of 1946. In a report to Molotov, Karpov wrote, "The staff of the Council as approved in 1943 is not sufficient for its increased volume of work and at present requires certain structural changes as well as a negligible increase in personnel."[13]

Sovnarkom ratified the new structure and staff of the Council through special Decree No. 1506 on February 2, 1946, entitled "Ratification of the Structure, Staff, and Official Salary Scales for Workers in the Council for Russian Orthodox Church Affairs." In accordance with this decision, the Council's staff in 1946 included thirty-two workers in operations and twenty-one people in administration.[14] The number of individuals employed later changed, but the Council's structure as a whole remained unaltered for the rest of Karpov's tenure.

While resolving organizational problems related to the work of the staff, Karpov and other members of the Council took steps to strengthen their local representatives—the Council's commissioners. The office of commissioner was created to implement certain tasks assigned to the Council, namely; conveying to local authorities decrees and decisions of the government concerning various Russian Orthodox Church organizations and putting into practice the government's new policy on the church.

These new responsibilities were implemented through the Councils of Ministers of union and autonomous republics and through regional executive committees. Appointing commissioners for regions freed from Nazi occupation and for areas having active churches had the highest priority.

The question of forming a cadre of commissioners was decided at the highest level. After meeting with the vice chairman of Sovnarkom on October 12, 1943, Karpov wrote: "Comrade Molotov thinks that it is essential to appoint members of the secret police as commissioners in regions newly freed from Nazi occupation. Regional committees of the Communist Party should be involved in the selection of commissioners."[15] Duties of commissioners were spelled out in the Council's Regulations of October 7, 1943. Salaries and "other forms of compensation" for commissioners were comparable with those in such positions as head of administration in a republic-level Council of Ministers or a department head of a regional executive committee. Funds from the local budget had to finance the commissioner's position. A special decree of Sovnarkom's Military Conscription Commission gave all commissioners deferments from the draft.[16]

Work on filling commissioner slots began immediately after the Council was established. On December 18, 1943, Sovnarkom USSR approved the Council's recommendation to establish eighty-nine positions for its commissioners throughout the country.[17]

The process of creating regional offices for the Council went slowly, however. Corresponding secretary Anisimov reported on this at the Council's session on February 28, 1944. At that time only forty-three out of the eighty-nine individual slots had been filled; no one had been appointed to ten regions in Belorussia or twenty in Ukraine. The Council decided to send telegrams to local officials "categorically demanding that they appoint someone to the position of commissioner in accordance with instructions from the government." The Council also decided at this session "to ask the State Appointment Commission of Sovnarkom about establishing commissioners in regions where they are needed but which were not stipulated in instructions from Sovnarkom on December 18, 1943 (such as the Karelo-Finnish ASSR, Kabardino-Balkar ASSR, and the regions of Yakutia and Astrakhan)."[18]

Appointment of commissioners in eastern regions of the country occurred as these regions were freed from occupation. In western regions, the selection of staff was basically completed by April 1944. The number of commissioners reached its height at the end of 1946 when the Council's local staff stood at 112 men.[19]

The first question of interest to the Council related to working conditions for the newly appointed commissioners. Heightened interest in the organization of workspace for commissioners undoubtedly resulted from the nature of the Council's work, which was conducted under the cloak of strictest secrecy. Therefore, the first reports by the Council's inspectors on the results of their visits to local offices began, as a rule, with a detailed description of the working space of each commissioner. The report explained where working files related to opening churches were kept, where the card file was located, and so forth. In accordance with Council requirements, every commissioner was to be assigned a separate office for receiving believers and clergy and workspace for a secretary-typist (a support staff position allocated to each commissioner) that was completely separate from the commissioner's office.

Fulfilling these conditions was certainly difficult in wartime. When the Council for the Affairs of Religious Cults was formed in May 1944 with its own set of commissioners who demanded identical workspace, regional executive committees faced the problem of immediately setting up four isolated offices. Initial reports from commissioners attest to this and abound with complaints about the lack of private offices, furniture, and so forth. Thus, at the end of 1944 Commissioner Kuzovkov from Kaluga even asked the Council to release him from his duties because he did "not have either a place to work or an apartment in which to live, despite the fact that leaders of the regional executive committee are promising to provide everything." Kuzovkov had to meet with clergy and believers on the street.[20] The commissioner in Estonia began working in February 1945 but by August still did not have an office and received clergy in his own apartment.[21] Karpov informed the government in July 1948 that "commissioners in the Bobruisk and Polotsk regions of Belorussia still have not been assigned office space. They receive visitors, including clergy, in offices that issue hunting licenses."[22]

Although the issue of arranging office space was resolved over time,

Karpov faced pressing and ongoing problems with local authorities who assigned commissioners to tasks unrelated to their official duties. Regional party and executive committees often sent commissioners on lengthy business trips for various purposes, such as organization of the harvest and state grain collection, supervision of tractor repair, and preparation of collective farms for spring planting.

The Council chairman categorically opposed such treatment of commissioners and asked the government for assistance. In response to his request, Molotov sent a telegram to regional executive committees and to republic-level Councils of Ministers on March 29, 1945. This telegram characterized the unsatisfied office needs of the Council's commissioners as "political devaluation of the role of commissioners." In addition, the telegram specifically instructed them:

1. To assign commissioners the space needed to conduct their work (an office and a reception area).
2. To stop assigning commissioners to other tasks without the Council's consent or sending them on extended business trips unrelated to their official responsibilities.
3. To assist commissioners in acquiring manufactured and rationed goods as you would the heads of departments in regional executive committees or administrative heads of republic-level Councils of Ministers.
4. To pay administrative and management expenses for the commissioner's staff from the budget of regional executive committee or the administrative department of the republic-level Council of Ministers.
5. Supervision of the work by commissioners is to be carried out personally by chairmen of regional executive committees or their first vice chairmen.

V. Molotov, Vice Chairman of Sovnarkom USSR[23]

One can assess the reaction of local officials to this telegram from the following example. When Commissioner Romanov from Kirovograd cited Molotov's telegram before a planned business trip, Chairman Ishchenko of the regional executive committee declared, "Telegrams are telegrams, but you will go on the business trip. Churches and priests won't go anywhere while you are away."[24]

Postwar destruction, combined with the necessity and complexity of restoring the domestic economy, forced local government bodies to give priority to problems, demands, and duties that most urgently needed to be addressed. For these reasons, they apparently often ignored telegrams, even those signed by the deputy head of state. Chairman Karpov of the Council for Russian Orthodox Church Affairs and Chairman I.V. Polianskii of the Council for Affairs of Religious Cults several times requested that the government and the Party Central Committee intervene. The situation did not change, however, for the duration of the 1940s. In 1947 alone, 70 of the 104 commissioners working for the Council for Russian Orthodox Church Affairs traveled throughout their regions on long business trips not connected with their official duties on orders from their regional party or executive committees. The commissioner in Lvov spent 201 days that year on such trips; the commissioner in Kaluga—130 days; in Briansk—212 days; in Tambov—129 days; in the Tatar ASSR—101 days.[25] The results of these extended absences by commissioners—canceled office hours and accumulated unresolved matters related to activities of religious organizations or the opening of churches—aroused discontent on the part of clergy and believers. This discontent fed their feelings of mistrust toward the new bureaucracy and their lack of confidence in the possibility of stable, long-term relations between church and state.

Karpov constantly discussed problems related to the issue of financial security for commissioners in his written reports to the government throughout the 1940s. He noted significant "limitations" on commissioners "in the plan for financial support" compared with other workers in regional bureaucracy. The Council chairman observed correctly that this practice "did not promote an increase in the number of those wishing to accept this duty." The Council constantly sent letters and telegrams to local officials demanding that they obey relevant sections of the "Regulations on the Council for Russian Orthodox Church Affairs." Nonetheless, many regions paid supplemental salaries for commissioners only irregularly. Outside Russia—for example in Ukraine and Belorussia—supplemental salaries for so-called "social life" and "other types of support" were generally never paid.

During the period of establishing his staff, Karpov often criticized regional party committees for their formal approach to the selection and appointment of candidates to the post of Council commissioner. Formalism was obvious in Karpov's opinion because of the appointment of sick, illiterate, or elderly men whom regional committees saw as unsuitable for more responsible work. As Karpov noted in his written report to the government in December 1946, "In terms of health, twenty men are either invalids or seriously ill (with tuberculosis, stomach ulcers, fits, etc.). One can hardly expect effective results in the work and liveliness of such commissioners."[26]

Out of 106 commissioners serving on January 1, 1947, over 50 men were age fifty or older, 42 were in their forties, 13 in their thirties, and only one was under thirty.[27]

The Council's leadership was also dissatisfied with the educational level of its commissioners. As of July 15, 1948, eighteen commissioners had completed a program in higher education, eleven had some higher education, twenty-four had a secondary education, twenty-six had some secondary education, and twenty-three had only an elementary education.[28]

But the level of education alone did not concern leaders on the Council. In those years, especially in wartime conditions, education did not determine personnel decisions. Responsibility, initiative, motivation, and an ability to do assigned tasks were highly prized. In addition to these qualities, work with a specific social segment of the population such as believers and clergy demanded something more—a specific understanding of relationships and evidence of tact, tolerance, and respect for people holding a different worldview. The nature of the new relations between government organs and religious organizations demanded signs of these qualities. When the Council for Russian Orthodox Church Affairs and the Moscow Patriarchate started receiving the first applications for opening churches, they also got complaints about crude and tactless treatment of believers and clergy by some commissioners. One such complaint said, "If you appeal to the commissioner about the illegal closure of a chapel, he will close three of them." Others complained about commissioners using administrative pressure. One commissioner reportedly said, "If I agree, you can send a priest to a parish; if I don't, you can't." Conflict between the Orthodox Church's exarch in Ukraine, Metropolitan Ioann of Kiev and Galicia, and the Council's commissioner for Ukraine, I. Khodchenko, required Karpov's intervention. Finding himself in a very complicated situation, Karpov took a simple position. In a letter to the Central Committee of Ukrainian Communist Party on April 24, 1945, addressed to its First Secretary N.S. Khrushchev and to L.R. Korniets of the Ukrainian Council of Ministers, Karpov laid out the facts of Khodchenko's tactless treatment of the metropolitan. Karpov also informed them of the commissioner's diktats on various issues, including the placement of clergy in Ukraine, and his scornful attitude toward problems arising with the metropolitan. The Council chairman evaluated the activities of Commissioner Khodchenko as "utterly impermissible and obviously contrary to the goals set out by the government." Karpov asked that steps be taken and proposed that "Comrade Khodchenko be immediately released from his position as commissioner for the Council for Russian Orthodox Church Affairs and a new candidate be approved by a decision of the Secretariat of the Central Committee of the Communist Party (Bolshevik) of Ukraine." Karpov also advised that "the chairman of the Council of Ministers for the Ukrainian SSR receive the Ukrainian exarch Metropolitan Ioann and that this event be publicized in the republic's press. This will be positively regarded in the current circumstances."[29] Karpov's information apparently was taken only under advisement. Khodchenko held the position of commissioner for an additional five years and, as archival documents attest, found grounds for compromise in his relations with the metropolitan.

Diktats, rudeness, and contempt for issues raised by religious organizations—all these resulted from the worldview that many commissioners had formed in previous decades. As a result, they carried into the 1940s those norms for relations with clergy and believers that had been characteristic of the 1930s. In most cases men appointed as commissioners had proven themselves as active campaigners against "religious obscurantism" in the past. Council Inspector N. Mitin's evaluation of Commissioner Tiunov from Krasnodar typified the evaluations of many other commissioners. Mitin's report to the Council's chairman, entitled "Results of My Inspection Tour of the Krasnodar Area," reads: "In recent years, Comrade Commissioner Tiunov has worked in antireligious propaganda by presenting reports to meetings of party activists, to collectives, etc. . . . Workers know Comrade Tiunov to be an active antireligious propagandist. . . . Tiunov had great difficulty understanding my explanations of procedures for applying prevailing statutes on the church to his practical work."[30]

From the perspective of local and regional party leaders, only personnel with such backgrounds could follow the "true" and "correct line" in relation to the church. That approach also indirectly reveals the real position of the party apparatus toward the new ecclesiastical policy of the government. Party functionaries believed that relations with the church were a temporary, necessary, and tactical concession for the sake of achieving the main goal of that time—victory over Nazi Germany.

Council leaders informed the government in January 1947 that, out of the 106 men in the Council's local offices, "Seventy-five commissioners meet the requirements of the position and the Council has little information on twelve others, but nineteen commissioners must be removed because they are unqualified for their positions (they are rude, tactless, do not want to work, or tolerate illegal contact with clergy)."[31] Then, Karpov wrote a separate report to Kliment Voroshilov* asking permission for the Council to conduct a review of all commissioners during the first quarter of 1947 in conjunction with the Central Committee's Department for Personnel Administration.[32] Permission was never given. Apparently, Karpov's request was seen as inexpedient and untimely.

For leaders of the Council, the first step toward a basic solution of their personnel problem with commissioners was a change in financing the posi-

---

*K.E. Voroshilov (1881–1969) was a member of Stalin's inner circle, a Marshall of the Soviet Union and, in the 1940s, a vice chairman of Sovnarkom.—Ed.

tions. The Council wanted to have commissioners paid from the national budget instead of from local budgets. On the one hand, this step would ensure financial security for commissioners. Higher salaries and privileges arising from higher status would allow officials in Moscow to attract more active and competent people for local positions. On the other hand, financial independence from the local budget would give commissioners more independence and their inherently dualistic status would end. Under the existing system, they had to follow the Council's orders and to report progress on assigned tasks while also constantly trying to take into account the opinion of local authorities that did not always agree with the opinion of the Council for Russian Orthodox Church Affairs.

At the same time, Karpov repeatedly proposed that the government approve those recommended for commissioner positions only after the Council or the Central Committee's Department for Personnel Administration had discussed the candidates. Such a process would allow the Council's leadership to influence the composition of its regional staff.

Neither the government nor the Central Committee, however, supported any of these initiatives. The funding mechanism did not change. The appointment process that just required "agreement" on a candidate was not followed in most cases. The Council could summon to Moscow only those commissioners who had already been confirmed by regional committees in order to "become acquainted" with them.

Failing to receive authorization "from above" to exercise its right to influence the selection and appointment of local staff members, the Council for Russian Orthodox Church Affairs solved the problem of strengthening its cadres of commissioners and effectively organizing their work within the limits imposed by the Regulations of October 7, 1943.

The Council's Division of Inspectors assumed primary responsibility for the task of guiding commissioners. Karpov often noted the importance and responsibility of the inspectors' work. He stressed this point in particular during a conference with inspectors at the end of 1945 by saying, "Inspectors do the Council's most productive work. Shortcomings in the way that inspectors supervise commissioners indicate a failure in fulfilling our primary task."[33] Even today, that statement by the Council's president seems totally correct from the perspective of fulfilling the primary task given to the Council—implementation of the Soviet government's policy on the church. Fulfillment of this task was dependent on the ability and skill of the central bureaucracy to control and direct the activities of its commissioners.

Council leaders developed various ways for the central and local bureaucracies to interrelate. Commissioners were required to submit quarterly informational reports that, according to orders from the Council, covered all aspects of their work. Commissioners were regularly summoned to Moscow to report on their work over longer time periods (six months or a year). Twice every quarter, inspectors for the Council scheduled visits to local offices to verify the activity of the commissioner and provide him with needed assistance. In addition, the Council itself sent out detailed written instructions, instructional letters, clarifications, and recommendations. From 1944 to 1947, the Council sent commissioners over forty instructional letters, some of which took the form of small brochures. Instructional letters not only contained official material but also served as a unique way to broadcast the experience of commissioners in various regions of the country. On the basis of analysis and generalizations from the informational reports, the Council's Division of Inspectors singled out positive points in local work and noted actions by certain commissioners that fell under the category of "improper conduct" or "mistakes." This analysis was included without fail in the next instructional letter. Group conferences for commissioners enabled face-to-face exchanges of experience (the first of these was organized in Moscow as early as May 1944) as did seminars on specific problems for commissioners in regions where such problems existed. For example, seminars discussed controlling activity in institutions for theological education and issues connected with the activity of monasteries.

In its early years, the Council defined the tasks confronting commissioners as follows:

- Inventory and registration of active Orthodox churches, chapels, and monasteries.
- Registration of religious communities.
- Registration of clergy.
- Inventory of inactive buildings formerly used by the Orthodox Church for religious rites.
- Review of petitions from groups of believers for opening churches or chapels.
- Preparation, verification, and formulation of documents connected with registration of religious communities.

Various factors, however, interfered with the completion of these tasks. The main one was that regional executive committees and party committees ordered commissioners on trips for other business. A general summary of visits by inspectors during the first quarter of 1944 to the regions of Gorky, Kursk, Molotov, and Penza, among others, concluded, "The inventory of churches and cultic property is unsatisfactory."[34] The Council also gave an unsatisfactory grade to the work of many commissioners for 1944 in response to their reports. Here are some excerpts from the minutes of the Council's sessions:

> Session of the Council for Russian Orthodox Church Affairs for February 2, 1944. Heard a report of the Council's commissioner for the Yaroslavl region. Resolved to note the following shortcomings: from October 1943 through February 1944, he received 115 applications from believers for opening churches. As of February 15, 18 applications had been reviewed (all petitions were denied), 48 had been sent to the area executive committees for verification, 49 applications had not been reviewed. . . . The plan for doing an inventory of active and inactive churches had not been fulfilled.[35]
>
> Session of the Council for Russian Orthodox Church Affairs for January 18, 1945. Heard from Comrade Nesulenko, Council commissioner from Sumy. Resolved to note the following shortcomings: as of now, the inventory of active churches and chapels has not been completed; the inventory of inactive ones has not begun. . . . Registration of communities and clergy has not been completed: as of December 27, 1944, only 24 out of 244 communities have been registered.[36]
>
> Session of the Council for Russian Orthodox Church Affairs for March 28, 1945. Heard a report from Comrade Amarantov, Council commissioner from Rostov. Resolved to note the following shortcomings: as of March 1945, over 50 percent of active churches have not been registered.[37]

During their trips to commissioner offices, inspectors and members of the Council took it upon themselves to review and act on petitions submitted by believers. While in Tambov in January 1945, Karpov "examined all [of the seventy-four applications not reviewed by the commissioner] and issued orders to open twelve churches."[38] Council member Utkin during a business trip to Saratov in October 1947 "reviewed applications from believers and noted those which should be given positive responses."[39]

Council instructions dated February 5, 1944, required commissioners to submit their quarterly informational reports no later than the first day of the month following the end of the quarter.[40] But the majority submitted their reports late. The first section of an instructional letter for September 1944 was devoted to the issue of work discipline for commissioners. Citing facts related to long delays in submitting local reports and calling these "a gross violation of work discipline," Karpov pointed out that such behavior was intolerable in wartime.[41] The situation did not improve, however. In November 1945, the Council's Senior Inspector Spiridonov reported to Karpov that as of November 1 the Council had received only 66 out of 107 reports from commissioners.[42]

Contents of reports and registration of documents relating to applications from believers also evoked criticism on the part of the Council. Carelessness during registration, mistakes, and incomplete or unproven numerical data— all caused confusion. These problems led to the need to recheck, collate, and demand the presentation of new data. An example of such a mistake is found in a recommendation to the Council from Commissioner Trushin from Moscow to open a church in the village of Vosnesensk in the Stupino district. Verification of the documents revealed that no such district existed in the Moscow region, although there was a town named Stupino.[43] In the end, such problems lengthened the time for making decisions on opening churches or chapels.

Spontaneous action by many commissioners, who in Karpov's words "insufficiently mastered the Council's instructions on the question of procedures for opening churches," also led to extra red tape, to additional troubles for believers, and in some cases even to their bitter disappointment. Some commissioners made final decisions on their own on petitions from believers for opening churches. For example, Commissioner Kushnarev from Leningrad wrote in his report to the Council, "I received eighty-two applications from believers for opening churches. I reviewed all applications, and applicants were informed of the results of my decisions through executive committees of regional and city soviets."[44] Commissioner Gostev from Voronezh even created and reproduced an official form that read: "Certificate given to the community of (name of church) to verify that it has been registered by me as No. _____."[45] Gostev sent a copy of the certification to the Council for Russian Orthodox Church Affairs. Such decisions were revoked, and applications by believers were reviewed anew in accordance with proper procedure.

Many commissioners shared a common desire to compose various types of instructions and circulars addressed to city and regional executive committees, religious organizations, or clergy within their jurisdiction. Commissioners often gave instructions in letters to local authorities regarding issues that related strictly to the commissioner's own activity: analysis of complaints from believers and clergy, collection of information on patriotic work by religious organizations, and the like. The Council's Division of Inspectors, drawing upon the contents of the first reports by commissioners, drafted an instructional letter that assessed such activity as "contradicting Instructions from the Council for Russian Orthodox Church Affairs dated February 2, 1944" and pointed out that sending similar letters in the future would not be tolerated.[46] "Distribution of letters of an instructional nature without prior consent of the Council" remained, however, a widespread phenomenon in the activity of many commissioners.[47] At the end of the 1940s, Agitprop used these events to argue in support of its accusation that the Council for Russian Orthodox Church Affairs had exceeded its authority.

The Council reacted strongly to evidence of correspondence between commissioners and clergy or regional religious groups. The first letters from the Council contained the constant reminder that "it is not necessary to correspond with clergy." This preoccupation of Council leaders was explained by the fact that practically all activity by the Council was cloaked in the strictest secrecy. This was true not only in external matters but also in internal ones among sections of its bureaucracy. All documentation—decisions and orders of the government on issues relating to the Orthodox Church, Council correspondence with various Soviet institutions and departments, and reports to the government and Central Committee—passed through the Secrecy Classification Department (*Sekretnyi otdel*) and were stamped "secret" or "top secret." Correspondence on particular issues assigned to commissioners was considered classified: composite statistical data on active and inactive churches and chapels, information on the status and activity of the Moscow Patriarchate and clergy, the state of religiosity among the population, and correspondence with various organizations and departments on matters related to the Orthodox Church. References in ordinary correspondence to secret governmental decisions and instructions were also forbidden.[48] The Council's chairman demanded great care when working with classified materials. He punished carelessness as being "the loss of political vigilance." Thus, Karpov ordered that Commissioner Zagorodnii from the western region be dismissed from his position for losing secret Council instructions for commissioners dated February 5, 1944.[49]

In matters concerning Orthodox clergy, generally neither bishops nor rank-and-file clergymen had the right even to read documents that directly related to church activity. The Council's chairman ordered, "The Sovnarkom Decree dated November 28, 1943, No. 1325, entitled 'Procedures for Opening Churches,' and 'Instructions from the Council for Russian Orthodox Church Affairs for Commissioners' dated February 5, 1944, are confidential. Therefore, you should use them for work-related purposes, and you are forbidden from making them public to believers or clergy."[50] Clergy discovered ways to get around this requirement and to receive copies of necessary documents, sometimes with the help of commissioners. For example, Commissioner Romanov from Kirovograd "issued" Bishop Sergii of Kirovograd and Odessa a copy of the government's decision of November 28, 1943, and supported his explanations concerning the application of that document by excerpts from the instructions dated February 5, 1944.[51] Such incidents did not, of course, go unnoticed by the Council's leadership. They were labeled "mistakes" and "improper actions of commissioners." Orders followed stating that it was impermissible to "publish" classified documents and forbidden to correspond with clergy. Also, commissioners were limited to oral explanations of decisions.

By demanding that commissioners limit themselves only to oral contacts with representatives of the clergy, the Council possibly was motivated by more than just a desire to preserve secret information. Clergy regarded many aspects of the work by certain commissioners as interference in the internal affairs of religious organizations. Letters, notes, and "orders" of such commissioners became documentation and might become grounds for proving accusations that the Council for Russian Orthodox Church Affairs and its bureaucracy had violated existing statutes on freedom of conscience. Keeping in mind the Moscow Patriarchate's active international contacts, Council leaders tried to head off such accusations.

Instances of interference by commissioners in the internal life of religious organizations were numerous enough, however, especially during the second half of the 1940s. Doubtlessly, the activity of religious organizations in the Soviet period was always and everywhere controlled. It is important to stress that, especially in these years and especially by these leaders of the Council, instances of interference in the internal life of religious groups was identified as such and was both regarded and condemned as a violation of statutes on freedom of conscience.

An inventory of active and inactive churches and chapels for the whole country was mostly finished by the second half of 1946. The Council then directed its commissioners toward a new task—systematically studying the status and activity of the church.[52] Karpov gave a specific explanation of the new task in an instructional letter dated January 9, 1947: "Now, commissioners direct their primary attention to a deeper and more detailed study of processes taking place in church circles, of clergy cadres, of activity by theological schools, of the status of monasteries, and of current implementation of Soviet laws."[53]

Trying to accomplish these newly assigned tasks, many commissioners demanded written reports from clergy and religious communities containing the needed information. Commissioners also arranged for financial audits of parish churches and controlled contents of sermons by churchmen. Commissioner Tikhonov from Novgorod even composed a "Questionnaire" for regional clergy and sent it to all senior parish priests to get answers to eight questions on the conduct of services during Easter week.[54] As a direct result of the analysis of informational reports for the third quarter of 1946, the Council released an instructional letter with strict instructions: "Even the appearance of interference in the internal affairs of religious organizations is forbidden. . . . We forbid control over sermons. . . . You cannot make special demands of clergy for the purpose of receiving information from them about church life. . . . You must clarify all pertinent issues by means of personal visits, reviewing complaints, and tactful casual conversations held with trusted individuals from the ranks of the clergy."[55]

An analysis of reports from some commissioners leads to the conclusion, however, that they by no means considered activity forbidden by the Council as a violation of the law. On the contrary, they saw it as a direct requirement of their job. One might explain this attitude by their lack of competence on issues concerning legal relations with the church at the time, but this does not appear to have been the only reason. Some commissioners interpreted the fundamental change in church-state relations as a change in the church's status in the sociopolitical system. They began to regard religious organizations and associations of believers as a component of that system or as a new link in the developing structure of various communities, associations, and unions of Soviet citizens. Out of this came an attempt by commissioners "to introduce order" into religious communities under their jurisdiction, to control them, to suggest what must be done, and "to join believers to the interests and aspirations of the Soviet people."

Commissioner Smirnov from Sverdlovsk particularly insisted that a diocesan council be held, "contrary to the stubborn unwillingness of the bishop to limit his individual personal power." Moreover, Smirnov obtained, reviewed, and approved a proposed plan of the diocesan council's work that had been submitted to the bishop.[56] Commissioner Gorbachev from Briansk revoked the registration of a priest from a rural parish without the bishop's consent "for the purpose of improving the church's internal health."[57] Commissioner Sergievskii from Vladimir called attention to a decline in the qualifications of clergy and their backwardness in relation to the cultural and political level of the population. In his opinion, church sermons should be "sharpened politically."[58]

During the preparatory period for elections to the Supreme Soviet in February 1946, some commissioners traveled around their areas for the special purpose of recruiting clergy to conduct the election campaign.[59] Curiously, one must note instances where some commissioners read reports on antireligious topics to groups of clergy.[60]

Many commissioners intervened when conflicts arose among members of religious communities or among clergy and their parish councils. Commissioner Efimov from Chelyabinsk reviewed the minutes of a parish meeting for St. Simon's Church in Chelyabinsk and then sent a letter to the parish council in which he explained: "The decision to reinstate Deacon Pikhtovnikov to his position, despite his removal by order of the diocesan bishop, violated article 26 of the 'Regulations for Administration of the Russian Orthodox

Church.' Also, the decision at the general meeting to give the deacon monetary assistance in the sum of 1,500 rubles is illegal."

Efimov sent a letter with the following proposal to Fr. Ashikhmin, the senior priest of that church: "I ask that you explain your aforementioned violation to all members of your parish leadership and repeal your decision. Remove Citizen Popovkin from the parish's leadership for raising the issue of monetary support for Pikhtovnikov at the meeting and give me information about other persons who supported rendering monetary aid to Pikhtovnikov." The commissioner's activity received an unambiguous evaluation from the Council for Russian Orthodox Church Affairs: "This is direct interference in the church's internal affairs."[61]

Council leaders maintained strict control over its commissioners' relations with clergy, especially with diocesan bishops. Those relations fell between two extremes. The first extreme was strikingly manifested in Saratov by the absence of any contact between Commissioner Polubabkin and Bishop Boris Vik. Bishop Boris complained to Karpov about the commissioner's conduct during the Council chairman's visit to Saratov. Karpov later wrote:

> The commissioner advised the bishop to appeal to the city soviet a second time in connection with the bishop's request to open a second church in the town. When Boris objected that it was the commissioner's duty, Polubabkin said, "It's inconvenient for me to do that. They might think that I am helping you. You send a letter first, and then I will send one." Polubabkin refused to go with the bishop to a workers' settlement in order to look at a chapel by saying, "Go with you in the same car? No, that isn't possible." The bishop invited Polubabkin to a celebration on the bishop's name day.* The commissioner replied, "I don't celebrate my own name day, much less anyone else's." Then, Polubabkin purposely left town on a business trip on the bishop's name day.[62]

In such cases, the Council issued the following instructions: "Do not decline invitations to participate in celebratory gatherings" and "Do not decline invitations from clergy for dinner and celebratory prayer services, because this might be interpreted as disdain on the part of the Council's commissioners."[63]

The other extreme was designated in Council documents as "close contact with clergy" and "having criminal connections." Specific breaches of

---

*In Russian tradition, people celebrate the day of the saint for whom they are named. This is called one's name day [*imeniny*]. For the bishop, this would have been St. Boris's Day.—Ed.

conduct fell under these formulations: "frequent meetings with the bishop in his home," "participation of commissioners in drinking bouts," "overly familiar relations with clergy," "acceptance of gifts and refreshments," and so forth. The commissioner for Belorussia was removed from his position and arrested "for systematically getting drunk with the archbishop of Minsk and Belorussia." Commissioners Shcherbakov from Zhitomir and Ibadov from the Uzbek Republic were "caught taking bribes" and arrested.[64] During 1945–46, commissioners from four regions lost their jobs "for receiving bribes, improper conduct, and collusion with lay activists and clergy."[65]

Overall, bribes became a serious problem for leaders of the Council for Russian Orthodox Church Affairs. Believers petitioning for opening churches or clergy and churchmen seeking positive answers to their requests gave commissioners money—"accidentally left" in the office or sent by mail—as "holiday gifts" and "compensation to the office for additional work." Cases of bribery by believers and clergy appeared practically everywhere. Commissioners reacted in various ways. One bought office equipment with the money. Another gave back "gifts" and limited his response to "explanations about the incorrectness of the crime." Commissioner Grishin from Tula contributed the money to the Defense Fund. As early as 1944 in an instructional letter dated September 14, the Council carefully explained how commissioners should act when believers and churchmen offered bribes. The Council reminded them that giving and receiving bribes was punishable by five years in prison. It especially stressed that "under no circumstances can bribes be taken and passed on for any state or societal purposes."[66]

Karpov held a special conference in June 1945 dedicated to reviewing material "on the conduct of some commissioners that has compromised the Council." The conference adopted the following decisions:

   a. Pass on statements* received directly by the Council to Regional Committees and republic-level Central Committees of the Communist Party for verification and action.

   b. Return material received on these matters from local offices of the NKGB and ask them to be sent directly to Regional Committees or republic-level Central Committees of the Communist Party.

   c. Ask a bishop to provide a written statement when he verbally accuses any commissioner of improper conduct in conversations with Council staff.[67]

Thus, leaders of the Council officially abrogated Council responsibility for the conduct of some commissioners. That responsibility should have been

---

*Statements on "improper" conduct of commissioners.

borne by regional or republic-level committees of the party that recommended a member of their own party organization to be a commissioner.

Another interesting incident took place during the conference that was not directly related to the review of this problem. It very clearly captures the personal qualities of some clergy. A resolution was adopted relating to the specific case of Commissioner Teptiarev from Chkalov that read, "Write a letter to the Party's Regional Committee for Chkalov informing them that the priest Arkhangelskii once slandered the commissioner for the Gorky region and, therefore, the facts about improper conduct by Commissioner Teptiarev must be carefully verified."[68]

Mistakes, errors, and shortcomings in the work of commissioners as well as inspectors for the Council were unavoidable, if only because Council employees at both the national and local levels were engaged in a completely new task, at least for them, of building relations with religious organizations, clergy, and believers. To be exact, they were given the task of constructing church-state relations and not destroying them, which was contrary to the usual approach by Soviet bureaucrats over the previous two decades. Doubts about the stability and longevity of the government's new policy toward the church gave rise to a feeling of uncertainty about their own future. They did not know if, under new circumstances, the work of commissioners would be regarded as "collaboration with enemies of the people" or "assistance to counterrevolutionary forces"—after all, in the recent past, clergy, believers, and even the Orthodox Church as a whole fell into those categories. Uncertainty in turn led to inertia on the job, negligence, and an unwillingness to do the job as the Council demanded. Leaders of the Council attempted to get rid of such personnel (in solving problems with cadres, Karpov possibly used channels available through his other position in state security that, in the words of Molotov, "was not advertised in the press"). In 1945, thirty-one new men were appointed to commissioner positions, and nineteen in 1946.[69] Council personnel serving as commissioners and staff stabilized with the departure of people who had taken positions accidentally or had compromised themselves. A distinct core of workers in commissioner positions had emerged by 1947; they possessed experience and the ability to make competent decisions. In 1947, twelve men had served as commissioners since the formation of the Council in 1943, and forty-four had served since 1944.[70] Spontaneous action in the provinces combined with constant control and surveillance—the methods for interrelating and working developed by the Council—enabled the establishment of a new bureaucracy. These also helped, in Karpov's words, "in gaining political experience and tactical orientation" by commissioners and staff members of the Council for Russian Orthodox Church Affairs.

One document attests that such work was very significant from the leadership's point of view. That document, prepared by Council staff, was an Edict of "Awards for Successful Performance" for staff and commissioners for the Council for Russian Orthodox Church Affairs. It recommended the Order of the Red Banner of Labor to five men (Council chairman G. Karpov, Council members N. Utkin and I. Ivanov, and Commissioners Kushnarev from Leningrad and Trushin from Moscow), the Emblem of Honor to eight people, and the Devoted Service medal to seventeen people.[71] The document was dated August 22, 1945. The chairman of the Supreme Soviet of the USSR never signed this proposal, but its preparation alone serves as eloquent testimony of how the Council's leaders recognized and highly valued the work of their staff in this complex period.

Karpov fulfilled the task given to him in September 1943 by the head of state who said, "Choose assistants for yourself. Create a staff." He fulfilled that task brilliantly. In wartime, he created a completely new structure in the Soviet government and assembled a staff that could operationally and competently discharge the functions laid upon it at that time by Soviet leaders.

Organization of a Council for Russian Orthodox Church Affairs and its staff of local commissioners was an exceptionally significant event for the nation's religious believers. Contacts between organs of state power, religious organizations, and church communities took place on official terms. Action by the Council and its regional commissioners regulated those terms and provided a certain amount of stability. Believers and clergy had a new opportunity not only to express their needs but also to be heard. The Council for Russian Orthodox Church Affairs, despite the limitations of its competency, played a significant role in the cause of defending the rights of religious organizations, clergy and believers.

The Moscow Patriarchate Under the Government's New Policy on Religion

The church's episcopal leaders accepted the conditions of the compromise offered by Stalin. This placed the Russian Orthodox Church in the complex and contradictory position of a preferentially protected confession that was simultaneously controlled by the state. The desire to preserve the church as an active institution required its leaders not only "to extol a regime that fought against God" (D.V. Pospielovsky) but also to follow that regime's political course. "Preferences" and "recommendations" from the Council for Russian Orthodox Church Affairs became guidelines for action by the Moscow Patriarchate, not only in political matters but also in the church's internal problems.

Survival

Thanks to the active "assistance" of the government, primarily through the secret police, renovationist activity in the Russian Orthodox Church ended. Renovationism was the largest pro-Soviet schism in the church.*

In a report to Stalin on October 12, 1943, Karpov made the following proposal:

> The renovationist movement earlier played a constructive role but in recent years has lost its significance and base of support. On this basis, and taking into account the patriotic stance of the Sergiite church, the Council for Russian Orthodox Church Affairs has decided not to prevent either the dissolution of the renovationist church or the transfer of renovationist clergy and parishes to the patriarchal, Sergiite church.

Stalin wrote alongside this paragraph, "Comrade Karpov, I agree with you."[72] The Council immediately instructed its local commissioners accordingly. The future of renovationist clergy and believers was decided. Patriarch Sergii Stragorodskii was informed of a "request" related to "a preference that he not set strict requirements for receiving renovationist clergy in the interest of speeding up their transfer." The patriarch agreed but noted that he could not get around basic canonical requirements and, in particular, "did not see any possibility for using Alexander Vvedenskii in the church since he has been married three times."[73] But at a session of the Holy Synod in December 1943, Patriarch Sergii issued the following statement concerning many renovationist bishops who had expressed "hope in reuniting with the patriarchal church": "Apparently one of those moments, when the church goes out to meet the prodigal son and assists in his conversion, is imminent. . . . The Russian Orthodox Church can make individual exceptions for a certain category of persons."[74]

An active process began wherein renovationist clergy and whole parishes returned to the patriarchal church. The government's policies supporting Sergii caused dismay and panic in leading renovationist circles. Renovationist leader Vvedenskii launched a series of attempts to activate his church and thereby enlist the support of the Council for Russian Orthodox Church Affairs. During a meeting with Karpov, Vvedenskii petitioned for opening new churches in Moscow and for appointing and reassigning renovationist bishops through-

---

*The renovationist movement, also known as the Living Church, divided the Russian Orthodox Church from 1922 to 1946. Renovationists attempted (unsuccessfully) to combine the beliefs of Orthodox Christianity with the political and social goals of Bolshevism. Renovationism also allowed the remarriage of parish clergy and the marriage of bishops, both of which were forbidden by traditional Orthodox canons. Metropolitan Alexander Vvedenskii led the schism for five years until 1946.—Ed.

out the country. For example, he wanted to appoint Metropolitan Filaret Iatsenko as exarch of Ukraine. Vvedenskii also raised the question of forming a patriarchate within the renovationist church in order to make it equal in status with the Sergiite church.[75] Karpov hedged in his formal response by saying "transfers of renovationist clergy and parishes are an internal church matter." But, he also noted, "it would be improper for Vvedenskii or his clergy to take any measures or conduct any agitation for reversing the exodus of churches."[76]

Nevertheless, Vvedenskii made several attempts to transfer to the jurisdiction of the patriarchal church on the condition that he keep his rank of metropolitan.[77] Patriarch Sergii and then patriarchal *locum tenens* Metropolitan Aleksii categorically objected to any negotiations with Alexander Vvedenskii. But the Synod thought it was possible to meet Vitalii Vvedenskii* halfway (during his meeting with Karpov, Alexander claimed that Vitalii Vvedenskii would sooner die than transfer to the patriarchal church).[78] By action of the patriarchal Synod on March 3, 1944, Vitalii Vvedenskii was received with the rank of archbishop and placed in retirement. A short time later, he was appointed as temporary administrator of the Orlov diocese.[79]

Karpov reported to the government that Alexander Vvedenskii, understanding the hopelessness of his position, "began to advance a series of unscrupulous proposals, such as union with the Old Believers or with the Catholics or even the formation of a totally new sect. He even began provocative actions aimed at compromising the patriarchal Synod and expressed his dissatisfaction by saying, 'This is an escapade by the government' and 'this whole comedy is being staged for the West.'"[80]

Only 147 renovationist churches remained in the USSR by August 1944, and the majority of these were located in the Krasnodar and Stavropol regions. Out of six renovationist churches in Moscow, only one remained— the Church of St. Pimen where Alexander Vvendenskii himself served along with his sons. Karpov informed the government that parishioners at St. Pimen's constantly complained about Metropolitan Vvendenskii and his sons "conducting church services while obviously drunk, using foul language, and causing a scandal."[81]

The Council concluded in August 1944 that "the issue of liquidating the renovationist church is looming" and that the Council "thinks it is possible to accelerate the process of [renovationism's] disintegration." To this end, Karpov proposed that Metropolitan Vasilii Kozhin of Stavropol and Archbishop Vladimir Ivanov of Krasnodar "can appeal to the remaining

---

*Metropolitan Vitalii Vvedenskii was an unmarried bishop who led renovationism for much of the 1930s. He was not related to Alexander Vvedenskii.—Ed.

renovationist clergy with a statement on severing ties with Metropolitan Alexander Vvedenskii due to his immoral conduct and with a recommendation to follow their example and transfer to the Russian Orthodox Church."[82]

The renovationist movement quickly lost support. It finally departed from the scene with the death of Alexander Vvedenskii in 1946, although renovationist churches continued to be active in some regions until 1948.

After normalization of relations between the government and the Moscow Patriarchate in the fall of 1943, other schismatic groups that had previously broken away from the Russian Orthodox Church came to naught and ceased to exist. Included in this list were the Grigoriites, the True Orthodox Church, and the Josephites.[83]

Starting in 1943, the Moscow Patriarchate actively renewed ties with both foreign Orthodox churches in Eastern Europe and other Eastern Orthodox patriarchates. The level of representation by foreign Orthodox churches at the National Council of the Russian Orthodox Church in 1945 testified to the growing authority of the Russian Orthodox Church and its heightened influence in the Orthodox world. Honored guests at this National Council included the leaders of churches from Alexandria, Antioch, and Georgia, representatives of the patriarchs of Constantinople and Jerusalem, and delegations from the Serbian and Romanian churches—in all, three patriarchs, four metropolitans, an archbishop, and four bishops accompanied by over twenty other members of their delegations.[84]

The agenda for the National Council of the Russian Orthodox Church that met from January 31 to February 2, 1945, consisted of two items: acceptance of the "Regulation for Administration of the Russian Orthodox Church" and selection of a patriarch of Moscow and All Russia. Patriarch Sergii had died on May 15, 1944. In accordance with his written will, Metropolitan Aleksii of Leningrad and Novgorod became patriarchal *locum tenens*. Questions of where and how a new patriarch would be selected were decided within the government. Karpov supported Metropolitan Aleksii's "preference" that "the patriarchal election be conducted by a National Church Council of bishops, clergy and laity, not by an Episcopal Council comprised only of bishops."[85] A Council of Russian Orthodox Bishops nominated Metropolitan Aleksii as the sole candidate for the patriarchal throne in November 1944,[86] and he was unanimously selected as patriarch of Moscow and All Russia through an open ballot taken at the second session of the National Church Council on February 2, 1945.[87]

Both the Holy Synod and the Council for Russian Orthodox Church Affairs worked along parallel tracks on the "Regulation for Administration of the Russian Orthodox Church." Archbishop Grigorii Chukov of Saratov and Stalingrad presented a report on the Regulation to the Synod at its session on

October 28, 1943.[88] Council Vice Chairman Zaitsev was responsible for preparation of the draft Regulation; in Council minutes, the document passed as the "Charter of the Russian Orthodox Church." The Council of Russian Orthodox Bishops held in November 1944 heard a draft of the coordinated Regulation. Sovnarkom ratified the Regulation on January 28, 1945 (Decision No. 162), and the National Church Council unanimously adopted it at its first session on January 31.[89]

The Regulation as adopted established "in the highest degree" a centralized church administration using the church's hierarchical structure[90] and vaguely defined the rights and prerogatives of the patriarch and diocesan bishops. The principles of administration that were established facilitated government influence over the entire Russian Orthodox Church through the patriarch, especially because the Regulation did not specifically describe the host of matters that the patriarch was required to submit to the Council for Russian Orthodox Church Affairs for approval.

From the government's perspective, however, the significance of the National Church Council of 1945 was not limited to resolving the two main agenda items. The National Council was supposed to show representatives of foreign Orthodox churches the growing power of the Russian Orthodox Church in the USSR. They were to see both political and financial power flowing from government support, which in turn was to become a decisive factor when the financially needy Eastern Orthodox patriarchs set their own political priorities. In addition, the National Church Council was to demonstrate the unity of Orthodox churches to the international community as well as the reality of claims by the Moscow patriarchate to "leadership" of the whole Orthodox world. This was especially important for officials already planning a political confrontation between the USSR and the Vatican. It also explains the attention devoted by the Soviet government to preparations for the National Church Council. The Council for Russian Orthodox Church Affairs developed a special plan for arrangements relating to the preparation and conduct of the National Church Council. Molotov, in turn, reviewed and approved that plan. Representatives of the Moscow Patriarchate discussed in advance the persons being invited from abroad. The People's Commissariat of Foreign Affairs gathered information about these persons and members of their retinues.[91] The Council for Russian Orthodox Church Affairs discussed and approved the National Church Council's formal greetings, appeals, and political declarations. The government provided transportation for Soviet participants in the National Church Council. It sent telegrams to regional executive committees requiring them "to provide unimpeded travel to the National Church Council for the bishop and two diocesan representatives." Government orders for staging the National Church Council allotted furniture, delivered food, and reserved rooms in the National Hotel. The People's Commissariat of Trade provided twenty meters of heavy cloth, sixty-five meters of white and colored silk, and thirty-five meters of carpet runner. On orders from Sovnarkom, the Moscow City Executive Committee allotted 5.5 tons of fuel from its own reserves for automobile transportation serving delegates to the National Church Council. Twenty-eight valuable religious objects from the collection of the Historical Museum and ninety-seven from the museum at the Holy Trinity Monastery of St. Sergius were placed, free of charge, at the disposal of the patriarchal *locum tenens* (soon-to-be patriarch) Metropolitan Aleksii. The government assisted the patriarchate in acquiring gifts for the Eastern Orthodox patriarchs. The Moscow Patriarchate hosted a concert by the State Orchestra under the direction of Nikolai Golovanov* for delegates and guests to the National Church Council. A film was made on the work of the National Church Council.[92]

As chairman of the Council for Russian Orthodox Church Affairs, Karpov appeared in person at the National Church Council on the first day of its meetings to give greetings on behalf of the Soviet government. He offered, "Best wishes for successful and productive work in the organization of a national church administration."[93]

The grandeur and splendor of the arrangements, as well as the level of service provided to members and guests attending the National Church Council, were intended to make a positive impression and to be conducive in no small degree for successful resolution of the tasks set by the government. These goals were achieved, as testified indirectly by the fact that Karpov received the state's highest award for excellence, the Order of Lenin, in February 1945.[94]

Another meeting between Stalin and leaders of the Moscow Patriarchate took place and was devoted to the work of the Russian Orthodox Church in foreign policy. It was held on April 10, 1945. Contents of correspondence between Patriarch Aleksii and Karpov attest to the fact that this meeting was dedicated to problems of international policy. In addition, the meeting at the Kremlin was attended by people directly related to foreign relations: Metropolitan Nikolai Iarushevich, who was already representing himself as minister of foreign affairs for the Moscow Patriarchate (since spring 1945 he headed the newly formed Department of External Relations of the Moscow Patriarchate); Protopresbyter Nikolai Kolchitskii, head of Patriarchal Affairs; and Molotov for the Soviet government in his role as head of the People's Commissariat of Foreign Affairs.[95]

---

*N.S. Golovanov (1891–1953) was a highly esteemed orchestral director in the Soviet Union and a professor at the Moscow Conservatory. From 1948 until his death, he was conductor of the Bolshoi Theater Orchestra.—Ed.

foreign policy

Manipulation

RC pers.! Vatican

The Russian Orthodox Church's involvement in foreign policy began in the spring of 1945. Delegations from the Moscow Patriarchate visited Bulgaria, Yugoslavia, and Romania. In May, a historic first took place when Patriarch Aleksii of Moscow and All Russia traveled on a pilgrimage to the Holy Land.[96]

The Moscow Patriarchate was forced in the spring of 1945 to start implementing a plan by the Soviet government to liquidate the Greco-Catholic Church* in western regions of Ukraine and in the Carpathians. Stalin regarded this large-scale action as part of an emerging struggle against the Vatican. In the contemporary mass media,[97] the papacy began to be characterized as "a defender of fascism, striving to strengthen its influence in the postwar world," with the Uniate (Greco-Catholic) Church presented as an "accomplice" to the papacy. From another perspective, the Soviet government feared the possible transfer of Uniate clergy to Catholicism. Polianskii, chairman of the Council for Affairs of Religious Cults, did not exclude such a possible course of events. He wrote a report to the government on March 13, 1945, saying, "We should expect that the Greco-Catholic Church and especially its hierarchy led by Metropolitan Joseph Slipy will attempt a complete transfer to Catholicism and eliminate the last signs of the Eastern Rite."[98] It goes without saying that such a possibility had to be ruled out, and Soviet leaders chose a course for liquidating the Uniate Church in the USSR and uniting it with the Russian Orthodox Church.

The Council for Russian Orthodox Church Affairs received instructions from Molotov on March 2, 1945, telling it to study matters connected with the Greco-Catholic Church. By March 14, the Council worked out measures "for tearing parishes of the Uniate Church in the USSR away from the Vatican and subsequently joining them with the Russian Orthodox Church." The Council planned: to organize an Orthodox diocese in the town of Lvov that would unite parishes of the Lvov, Drogobych, Stanislav, and Ternopol regions; to give the bishop and all churchmen in that diocese the right to conduct missionary work; to organize an Orthodox brotherhood and grant it the right to conduct missionary and charitable activity; to issue a special appeal from the patriarch and Holy Synod to clergy and laity of the Uniate Church and to distribute that appeal widely throughout Uniate parishes; to organize an initiating group within the Uniate Church that would solemnly announce a break with the Vatican and call on Uniate clergy to rejoin Orthodoxy. The Holy Synod organized a missionary council for the purpose of fulfilling this

---

*The Greco-Catholic Church was formed by the Union of Brest in 1596. Also known as Uniates and Catholics of the Eastern Rite, these Christians accept the supremacy of the pope and Roman Catholic doctrine while maintaining Orthodox liturgy and ritual.—Ed.

plan. The Moscow Patriarchate was granted the right to have its own printing house with a single printing press in order to print liturgical books.
Courses in pastoral theology were planned for Kiev, Lvov, Lutsk, and Minsk
to prepare cadres of clergy for parishes in the western Ukraine and the
Carpathians.

Stalin wrote "I agree" on the plan and the measures it outlined. This plan
became the blueprint for subsequent activity by the Council in eliminating
the Greco-Catholic Church on the territory of the Soviet Union.[99]

From that moment on the Moscow Patriarchate was engaged in the battle
for "reunification" of the Uniate and Orthodox Churches. In March 1945,
Karpov asked Molotov to approve a draft of the appeal from the patriarch of
Moscow and All Russia to clergy and laity of the Greco-Catholic Church.
This appeal, in Karpov's opinion, "should play a positive role in conjunction
with other measures."[100] Reproduced in 10,000 copies, the appeal was distributed in regions of western Ukraine and said, "I pray to you, brothers,
observe a unity of spirit with us in a union of peace. Sever and dissolve ties
with the Vatican, which leads you to darkness and spiritual destruction through
its religious errors and wants to force you to turn your back on the whole
world."[101]

Metropolitan Slipy, five bishops, and other clergy of the Uniate Church
were arrested in April 1945 "for energetic, traitorous, and collaborative activity in support of German occupation forces." This announcement was not
published in *L'vov Pravda* until a year later, in March 1946.

Following these arrests in April 1945, Fr. G. Kostelnik, Fr. Mikhail
(M. Melnik), and Fr. Antonii (A. Pelvetskii) formed an initiating group within
the Uniate Church. The group declared its break with the Vatican, called on
Uniate clergy to rejoin Orthodoxy, and conducted a broad agitation campaign among believers.

For its part, the Moscow Patriarchate did everything possible to "facili-
tate and accelerate" the unification process. In connection with the activity
of Kostelnik's group, Patriarch Aleksii decided it was necessary to present
his own "ideas" to the Council for Russian Orthodox Church Affairs. Karpov
in turn forwarded them to First Secretary of the Central Committee Nikita
Khrushchev. Patriarch Aleksii thought, in particular, that convening an all-
Uniate church council was "pointless because the question of reunification
will be decided by each parish at its own diocesan congress." The patriarch
considered it essential to convene diocesan congresses that were, in his opinion, "not only reasonable but also advantageous by indicating that unification is occurring by free choice of Uniate clergy and not under pressure from
Orthodox clerical authorities with the support of the regime." Patriarch Aleksii
added that patriarchate and exarchate can:

a. open wide the gates to the Orthodox Church by accepting applications individually and not limiting reception through "the narrow gate" of the initiating group.

b. Not insist on a rapid, forced change in external forms of the liturgy or even in the external appearance of clergy (shaving of beards and mustaches). The essentials are important: the Orthodox version of the Nicene Creed; praying for the patriarch and his bishops, not the pope; celebrating Easter according to the Orthodox calendar.

c. Consecrate eligible priests as bishops.[102]

As is well known, the Church Council held in Lvov in March 1946 adopted a resolution ending the church formed by the Union of Brest in 1596. The decision was "to leave Rome and return to our mother Holy Orthodox faith and Russian Orthodox Church."[103]

Undoubtedly many supporters of Orthodoxy lived among the Greco-Catholics in the western regions of Ukraine, and they genuinely desired to unite with the Russian Orthodox Church. But the coercive methods used during this campaign, pressure from state organs, and terror by the security services—all these in the final analysis could not help but discredit the idea of reunification and turn many believers and clergy against it.

Events in Ukraine provoked widespread response from abroad. Karpov wrote about this to the government in April 1946, commenting on "negative comments, including slanderous ones (on mass arrests of bishops and clergy, that only forty priests agreed with the decisions of the church council, and that the council's organizers were not members of the clergy)." In response, the Council for Russian Orthodox Church Affairs presented a proposal for "an interview with members of the Presidium of the Church Council by a correspondent from TASS," considering "it expedient to distribute this interview through TASS to international magazines and publish it in the *Journal of the Moscow Patriarchate*."[104] After the proposal was reviewed by Andrei Vyshinskii* and sanctioned by Molotov, the "interview" was indeed published in the *Journal of the Moscow Patriarchate* (1946, no. 4).

After the Lvov Church Council, the Council for Russian Orthodox Church Affairs together with the Council for Affairs of Religious Cults used their commissioners in Ukraine to unite the remaining Greco-Catholic churches and Uniate clergy with the Russian Orthodox Church. Khrushchev controlled

---

*A.Ia. Vyshinskii (1883–1954) at this time held a leading position in the Ministry of Foreign Affairs and later became head of that Ministry. He is best known as the chief prosecutor during the show trials of the 1930s that condemned Stalin's political opponents to death.—Ed.

this work on behalf of the Ukrainian government in his capacity as first secretary of the Central Committee for the Ukrainian Communist Party. Overall, Karpov was dissatisfied with the slow pace of the process for annexation and registration of former Uniate parishes and clergy. By the fall of 1946, the Council had responded to a summary report by Inspector Petrunis on a visit to Lvov region by passing a resolution on "the unsatisfactory situation" in the region. It proposed that Khodchenko require Commissioner Vishnevskii from Lvov to complete the registration of clergy and parish communities no later than February 1, 1947.[105] Karpov repeatedly instructed church leaders that "in western regions of Ukraine the process of reuniting Uniates with Orthodoxy was proceeding very slowly" and asked them to take steps to speed it up. (Karpov was dissatisfied because good relations had not developed between Archbishop Makarii of Lvov and Protopresbyter Kostelnik and because Patriarch Aleksii thought preaching was a priority in the struggle with the Uniates).[106]

Finally, Karpov announced to the government at the beginning of 1948 that "officially the unification of parishes* is basically complete and the goal has been achieved for ending the submission of that Church to the Roman Pope." According to the Council's data for January 1, 1948, some 2,491 out of a total of 2,718 Uniate churches in the western regions of Ukraine had united with the Orthodox Church. Services were being conducted in only 188 parishes of those that did not reunite. Seventy-five Uniate priests stubbornly refused to join. Only eighteen of these conducted services, and the remainder became financially dependent on relatives, worked in agriculture, or found jobs in civil institutions.[107]

Karpov noted in the same report that reunification was "in a very preliminary stage in the Carpathian region and that the process would be different because it still had not been possible to form an initiating group out of Uniate clergy for the purpose of carrying out a return to Orthodoxy."[108] A plan with measures "for weakening the position" of the Uniate Church in the Carpathians was worked out in the fall of 1947 in cooperation with the Council for Affairs of Religious Cults. As Karpov and Polianskii noted, "implementation of these measures in connection with the death of Bishop Romzha** is quite timely and might weaken Catholic influence in Ukraine's Carpathian region."[109] Implementation of the plan was officially completed in August 1949 when, at a meeting in the Mukachev Monastery, Greco-Catholics decided to abrogate the Uzhgorod Union of 1649 and to reunite with the Russian Orthodox Church.

---

*In western regions of Ukraine.
**Bishop Romzha, head of the Carpathian Greco-Catholic Church, was killed in an automobile accident in September 1947.

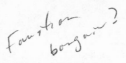

In a letter to Stalin, Molotov, Voroshilov, Suslov,* and Malenkov** dated September 24, 1949, Karpov stated, "The Council reports that orders of the government for elimination of the Uniate Church have been carried out." A total of 3,001 Uniate parish churches with 1,242 priests and 463 deacons had reunited with the Russian Orthodox Church by August 1949. Altogether, 133 priests transferred to other work, but some of these continued to perform religious rites illegally. Karpov also indicated that twelve Greco-Catholic monasteries with 306 monks "stubbornly refuse to reunite." He thought that there was no longer any base of support for the monasteries due to the absence of Greco-Catholic bishops and parish churches in the USSR. These monasteries were also strongholds for illegal church activity by clergy who had refused to reunite with Orthodoxy. For these reasons, Karpov thought it was necessary to take measures to close the monasteries.[110]

The Greco-Catholic (Uniate) Church ceased to exist legally in the USSR thanks to the grandiose political measures implemented between 1946 and 1949. During this period, the Moscow Patriarchate brought more than 3,000 churches into its jurisdiction, a fact that undoubtedly helped strengthen its financial status.

In return for its active, open and pro-Stalinist activity in foreign affairs, the Orthodox Church received relative freedom within the country. But this freedom was only relative. All aspects of Russian Orthodox Church life fell under the strict control and constant surveillance of various government agencies including, of course, the Council for Russian Orthodox Church Affairs.

The Russian Orthodox episcopacy served as the main link through which the Council exercised control over the church and, in many ways, directed the character of church activity within the country. The Council was primarily interested in matters of influencing personnel who entered the higher clergy (those ordained into the ranks of bishop, archbishop, and metropolitan) in addition to matters of appointing and transferring bishops to the nation's dioceses. Karpov defined the procedure for appointing higher clergy in these terms, "a) the patriarch requests the Council's approval only for appointments to his Holy Synod and of bishops and ranking diocesan clergy." The word "only" did not fool anyone, since personnel decisions by regional diocesan bishops also had to be approved by commissioners for the Council.

---

*M.A. Suslov (1902–1982) was a leading communist. After Stalin's death, he became the chief ideologist for the Communist Party of the Soviet Union.—Ed.

**G.M. Malenkov (1902–1988) was a close associate of Stalin and a leading figure in the political repression of the 1930s through the early 1950s. Malenkov lost to Nikita Khrushchev in the political struggle for power that followed Stalin's death in 1953.—Ed.

In fact, bishops could independently appoint "only" associate priests and deacons.[111]

From 1943 to 1947, the Council decided appointments and transfers of bishops generally without restrictions. Karpov only rarely expressed a negative opinion about a given candidate. More often, the Council reacted by saying, "the Council does not have any objection." Sometimes, the required agreement was delayed in cases where, in the government's opinion, a suitable candidate for a vacant diocese had not been identified. This was the case in finding a replacement for the position of exarch to Ukraine after Metropolitan Nikolai Iarushevich was chosen as a permanent member of the Holy Synod in the fall of 1943. The Ukrainian NKVD, Central Committee, and Council of Ministers, together with the Council for Russian Orthodox Church Affairs, and the Soviet government, took six months to work out an "agreement." Archbishops Sergii Grishin of Gorky[112] and Antonii Romanovskii of Stavropol[113] were scrutinized as possible candidates for the post. Finally, Archbishop Ioann Sokolov of Yaroslavl was promoted to the rank of metropolitan and appointed exarch of Ukraine in February 1944.[114]

The Soviet government took a special interest in the appointment to the Lvov diocese as part of the campaign to liquidate the Uniate Church in western Ukraine. A decision by the Holy Synod on March 10, 1945, sent Bishop Nikon of Donets and Voroshilovgrad to the Lvov see.[115] Soviet officialdom, however, saw otherwise. M.F. Oksiiuk, formerly an instructor at the Kiev Theological Academy, was named as candidate for the Lvov diocese. He was tonsured as a monk on April 20, consecrated as bishop on April 21, and installed as Bishop Makarii of Lvov and Ternopol on April 22.[116] In another instance (although this case was hardly unique) the Holy Synod did not obey Karpov's recommendation. During a conversation on August 15, 1944, Karpov and Metropolitan Aleksii discussed a visit by Archbishop Aleksii of Yaroslavl to America. "Karpov expressed his opinion that the archbishop should properly go to America with the title of metropolitan. Aleksii immediately agreed to bring up the archbishop's appointment at the very next session of the Holy Synod—well in advance of his departure for America. Aleksii asked that this be kept secret in the meantime, mainly so that it did not become a topic of discussion by bishops prior to convening the Holy Synod."[117] Karpov's "opinion" did not become reality. Later, plans were drawn up to nominate Archbishop Aleksii as a candidate for the position of metropolitan of America, but they also were not carried out.[118]

On January 1, 1948, the episcopacy of the Russian Orthodox Church consisted of three metropolitans, twenty-four archbishops, and forty-two bishops, with the patriarch at their head. Twenty bishops with advanced theological education also had secular education (ten with higher education, eight with incomplete higher education, and two with secondary education). Twenty-four bishops had academic degrees in theology, and three had secular academic degrees. Fifty-two of the seventy men became bishops between 1941 and 1947. Thirty-two of the total number of bishops in 1948 had formerly been tried and convicted.[119]

Archival documents reveal that the Council for Russian Orthodox Church Affairs possessed more complete information than church leaders on the activity and personal life of bishops. The patriarch first learned of many things during his visits to the Council. In addition, he asked Karpov several times to provide him with a copy of a commissioner's review of some bishop that would serve as supplemental information for the Holy Synod.

The Council had "personal observation files" on all higher clergy.[120] Inspectors regularly checked the condition of these files in local offices, and the Council used summaries of these files in accepting specific recommendations concerning diocesan bishops. For example, after returning from a visit to Chkalov region in August 1945, Council member Utkin proposed to transfer Archpriest Arkhangelskii to another diocese because of his "hostile" relations with Bishop Manuil "and to make Bishop Manuil understand his mistakes and help him eliminate them."[121] Similarly, after a visit to the Saratov region in 1947 in connection with a conflict between the local commissioner and Bishop Boris, Utkin concluded that "there is no pressing need to remove him (Bishop Boris) from that diocese."[122]

Sustained activity by bishops who tried to revive religious life in their assigned dioceses raised anxiety in the Council. Hierarchs like Archbishop Luke Voino-Iasenetskii, Bishop Manuil Lemeshevskii, and Archbishop Grigorii Chukov, among others, had endured prisons, Stalinist camps, and exile but managed to preserve a deep spirituality, an uncompromising attitude, and a genuine desire to serve the church. Archbishop Luke's energetic religious activity, together with his strong and sharp opinions, constantly provoked displeasure and complaints from regional leaders in both Krasnoyarsk and Tambov.[123] Owing to Archbishop Luke's "improper conduct, attacks, and host of improper claims," Karpov denied Patriarch Sergii's request to transfer Luke to the Tula diocese due to his poor health.[124] Luke was awarded the highest level of the Stalin Prize in 1946 for his work in purulent surgery, and this undoubtedly accounted for his transfer the Crimean diocese in May 1946.

A certain segment of the episcopacy showed little interest in church life in Karpov's opinion. He informed the government that some hierarchs lived in luxurious private homes maintained by large numbers of servants. These bishops led "a grand lifestyle" and concentrated their attention mainly on collecting money for the diocesan treasury.[125] Believers and members of parish councils sent many complaints to the patriarchate and Council about diocesan bishops who seized church funds, charged set fees for appointing priests to rich parishes, were rude, or committed "lecherous acts."[126] In May 1947, the Holy Synod heard a report from the Archbishop of Minsk and Belorussia that presented serious accusations against former Archbishop Vasilii Ratmirov of Minsk. He was accused of: purposely understating his diocese's income; appropriating money assessed to parishes for construction of his house (in fact, the government provided the house); misappropriating money given by parishes to support the seminary in Zhirovits (Vasilii placed fourteen seminarians in monks' cells and "students and monks alike starved"); and finally drunkenness. In light of such grave accusations, the Holy Synod decided to ban Archbishop Vasilii *in absentia* from performing sacramental duties.[127] At the same time, the Holy Synod banned Bishop Mikhail Rubinskii of Kirovograd and Chigirin from service for six months and forced him into retirement for "lack of attention to his own appointment . . . due to a lack of general culture and elementary knowledge and due to his unusual development of criminal propensities and general immorality."[128] The Holy Synod was forced to take a series of steps to strengthen church discipline. Thus, it approved a special resolution in April 1946 banning "those levies" that bishops collected for ordination and for transfer or appointment of clergy to parishes. The Synod also declared invalid all awards bestowed by bishops on clergy without a written declaration to the patriarch. Another decision by the Synod cautioned certain clergy and bishops who had compromised themselves that they "must fundamentally change the character of their diocesan administrations." Some were forced into retirement—in 1946 alone, four bishops were removed from their positions.[129] While considering measures for strengthening ecclesiastical discipline, we should also mention the Synod's decision in early 1949 to set up its Department of Personnel for All Clergy.[130] However, upon the expiration of their terms of punishment, bishops were appointed anew to vacant dioceses. In the words of Patriarch Aleksii, the members of the Holy Synod "were forced to be tolerant due to the lack of personnel."[131]

Characterizing the episcopacy of the Russian Orthodox Church as a whole, Karpov informed the government that the vast majority of bishops exhibited loyalty to the Soviet regime. He added that, "In their actions, leaders of the Russian Orthodox Church and an absolute majority of bishops unquestioningly follow the proposals and recommendations of the Council and its local commissioners and often coordinate documents and issues with us on their own initiative."[132]

The type of ties that were established between the Council and patriarchate also allowed all problems and routine business to be decided "with com-

parative ease." These were usually discussed and resolved when the Council
for Russian Orthodox Church Affairs received church leaders and members
of the Holy Synod. Karpov directly instructed members of his staff, "You
can and should summon [Russian Orthodox clergy] to meet with you because you are senior inspectors of the Council, part of the state bureaucracy,
and you should not run to them concerning every matter."[133] The Council
received Patriarch Aleksii on twenty-eight occasions and members of the
Synod and other bishops 210 times in 1946. In 1947, the patriarch visited the
Council twenty-eight times, and other bishops made 143 visits.[134] Such one-
sidedness clearly attested to a "balance of power" that favored those struc-
turing church-state relations. But Karpov thought this communication was
justified and wrote, "Setting up such interaction with church leaders allows
the Council to move the church in the needed direction." Furthermore he
noted, "Such interactions also satisfy the church."[135]

It was impossible for certain connections between the two bodies—the
Council and the Moscow Patriarchate—not to form. While relations between
Karpov and Patriarch Sergii never ventured beyond official boundaries and
were appropriately reserved, generally warm and friendly ties formed between the Council chairman and Patriarch Aleksii (especially during the years
1945–48). The patriarch visited Karpov's home several times and was acquainted with his family—a wife and two daughters, the younger of whom
turned five in 1945. In the period from 1945–1948, Karpov received 180
letters and 65 telegrams from the patriarch.[136] In his letters, the patriarch
invariably conveyed his regards to members of Karpov's family, expressed
interest in their well-being, offered to help with medicine, and so forth, when
this was necessary. The two men exchanged traditional greetings, congratu-
lations, presents on holidays (Soviet and religious) and birthdays, and invitations to holiday meals and other celebrations.

One cannot rule out the fact, of course, that Karpov used these unofficial
relationships for his own purposes. As he later wrote to the government, "It
was possible to cultivate the patriarch's opinions when necessary."[137] In any
case, even descriptions of Patriarch Aleksii's personal characteristics in
Karpov's dry reports are filled with feelings of sympathy for the patriarch as
a human being.

A tradition of giving presents to leaders in the patriarchate began with
Stalin's new ecclesiastical policy. Various blessings fell on church leaders as
if from a cornucopia after the fall of 1943. They received apartments, automobiles, "presents," dachas, and permission to have vacations and get medical treatment at the best health resorts in the country. We do not know how
Patriarch Sergii, who was accustomed throughout his hard life to a much
more humble lifestyle, accepted gifts such as the ones he received on his

seventy-seventh birthday: a gold pocket watch, silken velvet for a patriarchal mantle, silken material for a cassock, silken linen for six pairs of underclothes, ten bottles of brandy, ten bottles of champagne, ten kilograms of fruit, caviar, and chocolate.[138] Patriarch Aleksii, however, did not shun life's comforts. The patriarch, Metropolitan Nikolai, and Protopresbyter Nikolai Kolchitskii accepted expensive presents with gratitude and pleasure, seeing these signs of attention as a unique expression of appreciation by the government for their work.

Russian Orthodox hierarchs also accepted state awards with gratitude. Patriarch Aleksii was awarded a medal "For the Defense of Leningrad," and Metropolitan Nikolai received a medal "For the Defense of Moscow." Evidence of the highest recognition for patriotic activity by the Orthodox Church during World War II was seen in the government's decision on "assigning places on the platform" to leading church figures during the military's Victory Parade on June 24, 1945. It is true that Karpov's motive for making this request was somewhat different: ". . . the presence of leading figures of the Russian Orthodox Church on the platform near diplomats and foreign guests should make a beneficial impression, especially in foreign countries."[139]

In general, issues surrrounding presentation of state awards to church leaders were Stalin's form of political gamesmanship, one that also characterized relations with his comrades-in-arms. The Council for Russian Orthodox Church Affairs in August 1945 petitioned for the order of the Red Banner of Labor to be presented to Patriarch Aleksii, Metropolitan Nikolai, and Metropolitan Ioann Sokolov of Kiev and Galicia. In response, the Kremlin issued instructions "to withhold approval (of the petition)."[140] The Council presented a second petition in July 1946, saying, "Until now, the patriarch has not been recognized in any way for his patriotic work during World War II . . . this is embarrassing . . . it is not to our advantage." In response, a decree from the Supreme Soviet of the USSR awarded Patriarch Aleksii the order of the Red Banner of Labor on August 16, 1946, "for the utmost organization and leadership of patriotic work during World War II."[141] The patriarch was awarded yet another medal that same month "For Devoted Service in World War II, 1941–45."[142]

A completely illogical episode (at least from the outside) occurred at the same time as these awards to the patriarch. His closest friend and former lay brother Daniel Ostapov was arrested on October 25, 1946. The extremely agitated patriarch wrote a letter to Karpov that "vouche[d] for Ostapov" and asked Karpov "to help speed up the investigation." With Karpov's assistance, Ostapov was soon released on November 6 by order of the minister of state security. The patriarch wrote a letter to Karpov that very day, expressing thanks "for intervening" and "for the unusually rapid resolution of the matter." The patriarch recognized that this matter irritated and depressed him very much.[143] Future relations between Patriarch Aleksii and Ostapov became subject to constant surveillance and attention from certain state organs and, of course, from the Council for Russian Orthodox Church Affairs.

Patriarch Aleksii himself, as head of the Orthodox Church, understood one of his main tasks to be preserving the status quo in relations between the government and the Russian Orthodox Church. The patriarch's messages and letters tirelessly appealed to more active bishops for restraint and caution in their activity. The most important thing in Aleksii's opinion was "not to overstep the limits of our rights." The patriarch even reproached Archbishop Luke in a letter in February 1947 for attempting to organize a Sunday school where children could "study the Word of God." The patriarch wrote, "It is a shame in relation to a government that has given the church such broad rights. . . . Let us assume the impossible, that Sunday schools are permitted. How many grounds will arise for accusations of counterrevolutionary deviation, for anti-Soviet speeches, etc.! How many new victims would there be! How much better that clergy are spared such danger."[144]

Fear of both new victims and a return to the horrors of the 1930s intensified the sense of self-preservation. It compelled church leaders not only to avoid overstepping the limits of permitted activity but also to continually thank the Soviet regime "for the freedom given to all religious associations" and to consciously spread an obvious lie by exaggerating the church's well-being in the country. Everything published by the Moscow Patriarchate in the 1940s provided evidence of this. An absolute majority of published material was aimed at foreign public opinion, and it goes without saying that the contents of such material were dictated by government interests—that is, how the Stalinist leadership understood those interests. As early as the fall of 1943, Molotov provided a lesson on how the church ought to understand "feelings of national pride" in the new era of church-state relations when he forbade a reciprocal visit to England by a delegation from the Moscow patriarchate. The head of the Foreign Ministry gave the following instructions to Karpov: "We should refrain from sending [the delegation] to England. Tell the patriarch that out of national pride we should not bow down and respond so quickly to their proposal since they still wage war so poorly. It is one thing when they come to us on their knees but another to go there. Very politely inform the patriarch of this."[145]

Precisely that perceived sense of national pride forced Patriarch Sergii to refuse foreign offers of assistance of money, theological books (that the patriarchate particularly needed), or church supplies. When a *Toronto Star* correspondent named R. Davis conveyed an offer of aid from Canada and America in January 1944, the patriarch answered, "The Russian Orthodox Church has sufficient means for its own needs. It also has the means to publish required theological books and to manufacture church supplies." Needless to say, Karpov was familiar with the contents of the interview and "approved of the patriarch's choice of words."[146]

This same feeling of national pride clearly motivated statements by participants in the National Church Council of 1945. Statements such as these were intended for broadcast abroad through TASS: "Russian Orthodoxy was never subjected to systematic persecution, and Christians were never killed as in ancient Rome. But slander is so tenacious that even now we hear rumors in protest. . . . Antireligious activity never received direct state support (that is another slander). . . . To speak about intolerance and persecution of religion in the USSR means opposing the truth."[147]

The contents of numerous appeals, messages, and appearances by leaders of the Moscow Patriarchate, the endless flow of doxologies both to the Soviet government and, of course, to Joseph Stalin, "the greatest friend of all believers"—all this should have been evidence of the willingness of the Russian Orthodox Church to fulfill its patriotic duty to the government and of its genuine desire to be useful to the state.[148]

Despite all the efforts by church leaders, the chill of past relationships began to be felt as early as the first half of 1947. The same factors that worried some staff members at the Council for Russian Orthodox Church Affairs—namely, the harshly critical interest of party ideologues in religion —also worried Patriarch Aleksii. Congratulating Karpov on the thirtieth anniversary of the October Revolution, the patriarch noted in a letter, "I would like to give you a present but have gotten signals that you do not desire such open signs of attention."[149]

The chill in church-state relations was not caused either by Stalin's whim or by his usual capriciousness. It resulted from a set of real causes. The fundamental reason for a halt in improved relations between the Russian Orthodox Church and the government was the shattering of hopes held by Stalinist leaders in connection with the church's international activity. These hopes were tied to a specific plan for creating an Ecumenical Orthodox Center in Moscow—or, as Patriarch Aleksii said, a kind of "Moscow Vatican."

As early as March 1945, the Council for Russian Orthodox Church Affairs proposed organizing a world conference in Moscow for all (non-Catholic) Christian churches as one means of struggle against the Vatican. Initiative for organizing the conference was expected to come from the Russian Orthodox Church.[150] Stalin undoubtedly supported this proposal, since its realization provided a possibility for exercising influence on countries throughout

the Christian world and not just those in Eastern Europe. However, this grandiose scheme was not to be. Claims by the Moscow Patriarchate to the role
of "the Third Rome" stirred up negative reactions from the Eastern patriarchs.* Leaders of Orthodox churches in Alexandria, Jerusalem, and Cy-
press declined the invitation to an all-Orthodox council, stating that authority
to call an ecumenical council "belongs to one person alone, the ecumenical
patriarch of Constantinople."[151] This change in political orientation by the
Eastern churches unquestionably reflected growing international tensions
due to the start of the Cold War between the former allies and the vigorous
policies of American and British spy agencies to gain influence over the
Eastern churches.

As a result, Moscow could not convene either an ecumenical council or
even a so-called preconciliar conference that was planned for September
1947. A conference for leaders of Orthodox churches was held in the summer of 1948 in celebration of the 500-year anniversary of autocephaly for
the Russian Orthodox Church.[152] The conference was sufficiency representative to adopt a minimal agenda for creating a European Orthodox bloc
under the guidance of the Moscow Patriarchate. On this basis, the conference was successful in the opinion of the Council for Russian Orthodox
Church Affairs.

But Karpov did not have a choice in evaluating the results of the conference
—responsibility for the patriarchate's failure in the international arena also
fell indirectly on his Council. As for the conference's significance to Soviet
leaders, Stalin no longer attached any political importance to a demonstration of unity by Eastern European Orthodox churches, because the countries
of Eastern Europe were already in the Kremlin's sphere of influence and
control. Thus, the Moscow Patriarchate faced the problem of finding a new
way to apply its strength in the international arena.

Pressure from ideological elements in the Party also influenced the nature
of church-state relations. Dissatisfaction grew among Communists in the
provinces who linked liberal policies toward the church only to the war and
refused to understand or accept the need to continue them in peacetime. Antireligious propagandists of the prewar years began working anew, although
timidly and with uncertainty for a while. Agitprop reflected these sentiments
and began to work out directives containing recommendations on antireli-

---

*In the early sixteenth century, about fifty years after the fall of Constantinople,
some in the Russian Orthodox Church advanced the claim that Moscow was "the
Third Rome." By this, they meant that Moscow was the new center of Christian civi-
lization, following in the tradition of the two former centers that had fallen (Rome and
Constantinople). Other Orthodox churches never recognized this claim.—Ed.

gious work and seminar topics for ideological activists at various levels. For a while these instructions and directives were sent to the regions marked "secret" and conveyed more a sense of being recommendations rather than direct orders. But the prevailing opinion among party-state activists in the vast majority of the country's regions was that the policy "of flirting with priests" had ended.

Advances in the development of relations between the Soviet government and the Russian Orthodox Church reached their peak by 1948. The state created "favorable conditions" for the church within the country so that the church could successfully fulfill its mission in the international arena. Considering that it was an atheistic government acting in its own pragmatic interests, the state did the maximum possible for the Orthodox Church between 1943 and 1947. The limitations set for the Moscow Patriarchate in foreign policy could not help but influence its domestic position. Leaders of the Russian Orthodox Church, in turn, understood the changed climate. Evaluating the climate that was taking shape in church-state relations at the start of 1948, Patriarch Aleksii noted with bitterness, "It seems that a new era has begun for us."[153]

By the second half of 1947, the general national mood was moving against liberal relations between the government and religious organizations. The country's population stopped expecting changes. The Stalinist leadership ended a period of wavering over the choice of a future political course. The first postwar campaigns—against the magazines *Zvezda* (The Star) and *Leningrad* as well as G. Aleksandrov's textbook, *A History of Western European Philosophy*—showed without a doubt that the choice had been made for severity in domestic policy. The ideological direction of this policy—a struggle against nonconformity for the purity of Marxism—had a direct connection with religion and clearly had an impact on the nature of church-state relations in the USSR.

Rebirth of the Russian Orthodox Church by Directive

The three metropolitans raised a set of issues concerning essential activity of the Russian Orthodox Church at their meeting with Stalin on September 4, 1943. These included the necessity of forming church administrative organs, organization of publishing activity for the Moscow Patriarchate, shortages of clergy and theological educational institutions, and matters related to opening churches and chapels. Stalin promised support from the Soviet government in the resolution of all these problems; however, the government could not avoid regulating the process of rebirth for the Russian Orthodox Church.

First, the traditional structure of the patriarchal church and the organs of its administration were restored. A council of Russian Orthodox bishops convened in Moscow on September 8, 1943. Its basic task consisted of selecting a patriarch of Moscow and All Russia. The sole candidate nominated for the patriarchate was the patriarchal *locum tenens*, Metropolitan Sergii. "The whole council" unanimously selected him to be patriarch of Moscow and All Russia, and he was enthroned in Moscow's Epiphany Cathedral on September 12. Patriarch Sergii received congratulatory telegrams from all the Eastern patriarchs and from the heads of some non-Orthodox churches. The Soviet government likewise congratulated Patriarch Sergii on his election.

The same council announced the formation of a Holy Synod under the patriarch with a membership of six men: three permanent members and three temporary ones. Metropolitan Aleksii of Leningrad, Metropolitan Nikolai of Kiev and Galicia, and Archbishop Sergii of Gorky and Arzamans were appointed as permanent members of the Synod. Temporary members of the Synod were to be summoned "for service" at the patriarchate for a term of six months. At the end of this term, they were to be replaced for the next six-month term by other bishops whom the patriarch appointed as temporary members of the Synod.[154]

Replenishing the episcopal ranks of the Orthodox Church began at the Kremlin meeting when the metropolitans handed Stalin a list of bishops who were in prison or exile along with a petition for their release. In the future, Patriarch Sergii and then Patriarch Aleksii petitioned the government repeatedly with requests to free clergy.[155] Bishops who received amnesty were immediately appointed to episcopal sees. Ordinations to episcopal rank were also frequent in this period. In the fall of 1943 alone, Metropolitan, and then Patriarch, Sergii elevated eleven men to the episcopate.[156] Nineteen hierarchs (three metropolitans, eleven archbishops, and five bishops) attended the council of bishops in September 1943. Four metropolitans, thirteen archbishops, and twenty-nine bishops (forty-six bishops in all) represented the Russian Orthodox episcopacy at the opening of the National Church Council in January 1945.[157]

Increasing the number of bishops was not an end in itself for the patriarch and Synod. This was primarily connected with the establishment of diocesan offices, the need to put local church life in good order—the basic problem of which was opening churches and chapels—and the organization of activity by church groups. That specific process of opening Orthodox churches and officially registering religious associations provided clear evidence for millions of the nation's believers of a turning point in relations between the Soviet government and the church.

During the years of war, in an atmosphere of immense suffering, deprivation, and the loss of relatives and loved ones, the popular need for religion and religious faith grew dramatically.[158] But real possibilities for satisfying the religious feelings of believers were almost nonexistent. Believers and clergy constantly submitted requests and petitions to both the patriarchal *locum tenens* and government institutions. The hierarchs mentioned this at their meeting with Stalin in the Kremlin. In response, the head of the government assured them, "The government will not place any obstacles relating to this matter." After the events of September 1943—selection of a patriarch, formation of the Holy Synod, and the organization of the Council for Russian Orthodox Church Affairs—the stream of petitions from believers increased. This forced the government to speed up development of instructions for a procedure to open churches. The Council for Russian Orthodox Church Affairs prepared several variations on these instructions, all of which were presented to Molotov for his review. Karpov and Molotov discussed the matter at a meeting on October 13, 1943, and drew up the system that Sovnarkom incorporated in its Decree No. 1325, "Procedures for Opening Churches," passed on November 28, 1943.[159]

The principle contained in those instructions was that local authorities (republic-level Councils of Ministers and regional executive committees) made decisions on opening a church or denying a petition from believers. In cases where the application was denied, a copy of the final decision and reasons for the refusal were sent to the Council for Russian Orthodox Church Affairs; but all documents remained in the files of the republic-level Council of Ministers or regional executive committee. If local authorities decided to grant a petition from believers, then the Council of Ministers or regional executive committee sent all documents and their final decision to the Council for Russian Orthodox Church Affairs. The Council, in turn, was expected to review the matter, reach a preliminary decision, and present the file to Sovnarkom for approval. After appropriate approval by the government, the Council informed local authorities of the final decision "for subsequent registration of the new religious community and arranging the transfer of a church building to believers." In addition, the republic-level Council of Ministers or regional executive committee had to coordinate matters with the diocesan bishop. During the same conversation on procedures for opening churches, Molotov remarked, "Churches will be opened in certain places, but the process must be contained. Decisions on such matters belong to the government."[160]

In October 1943 alone, the Council for Russian Orthodox Church Affairs received 517 applications to open churches from believers in thirty-two regions and seven autonomous republics of the RSFSR. The vast majority of petitions came from the following regions: Moscow (105 petitions), Ivanovo (63), Kirov (38), Gorky (36), and Kalinin (34). By March 1944, the number of applications that had been submitted totaled 1,215.[161] Molotov's recommendation on the need to contain the process of opening churches, however, meant that by March 1944 Sovnarkom gave orders to open only twenty-nine churches.[162]

A growing number of petitions, each of which included from 20 to 2,000 individual signatures, forced Molotov to reconsider his decision. He gave the following orders to Karpov at a meeting in May 1944: "Questions related to opening churches must be reviewed with greater boldness, so have your commissioners instruct local officials accordingly. In cases where it is necessary, talk with chairmen of republic-level Councils of Ministers or regional executive committees on Sovnarkom's behalf."[163] The Council sent an instructional letter to its commissioners that explained again and in detail the procedures for reviewing and resolving petitions from believers. In addition, the Council sent an instructional letter to executive committees and soviets of towns and regions that also laid out in detail the procedures approved by the government for opening churches. This second letter also gave details about all stages for handling materials and explained point-by-point the information that local authorities were obligated to present to the commissioner of the Council for Russian Orthodox Church Affairs, including data on applicants (e.g., ages, criminal convictions), condition of the church (a document of inspection by an engineer), and résumés for clergy "including all intelligence [collected by the secret police]."[164]

But little changed at the local level. In the course of three months (May to July 1944), regional executive committees denied 403 of 454 applications by believers to open churches and approved 51 only "in light of repeated and persistent petitions."[165] At the same time, Karpov noted in his reports the growth of unregistered, illegal chapels. In connection with this, the Council chairman sent a proposal to the government in October on the need to increase the number of active churches. He wrote, "For the purposes of fighting illegal church groups in areas where they have appeared on a large scale and where they persistently raise questions about opening churches, let us proceed to expand the network of active churches by two or three per region. We will not consider opening churches in regions with a significant number of active churches but in those regions where there are none."[166] Molotov supported this proposal.

All the same, despite decisions made "on high," the process of opening churches and chapels went slowly, and the number of favorable decisions by regional executive committees was immeasurably less than the number of applications and petitions submitted. As proof, we turn to statistics presented by the Council for Russian Orthodox Church Affairs to the government in January 1949 (see Table 1.1).[167]

Table 1.1

Year	Number of petitions to open churches submitted by believers	Number of churches opened
1944	6,402	207
1945	6,025	509
1946	5,105	369
1947	3,087	185
1948	3,174	—

Between 1944 and 1947, officials reviewed petitions by believers for opening 4,418 individual churches. More than 1,270 churches and chapels were opened during that same period.[168] This data from the Council shows that the number of churches for which believers petitioned was nearly four times greater than the number officially opened across the country as a whole. What were the precise factors that caused such a small percentage of petitions to be approved?

First of all, the Soviet government through its Council for Russian Orthodox Church Affairs regularly controlled the situation for opening new Orthodox churches. It approved only a set percentage (5 to 20 percent) of all applications submitted, although in the process it intended to take the complete domestic and foreign situation into account.[169] The procedure adopted for opening churches presupposed the drawing up of many documents, verification of data, and coordination among various levels of authority. Commissioners frequently complained that the majority of town and regional soviets acted in a perfunctory manner when documents were presented. The soviets gave incomplete and inaccurate information that resulted in requests for additional clarification. In addition, neither believers nor clergy had the right to become familiar with the contents of the decree on "Procedures for Opening Churches." All documents had to be completed "on the basis of oral explanations by the commissioner." As a rule, this led to mistakes in completing the documents—mistakes that required both the time and energy of believers to correct. It is interesting to note that Sovnarkom did not even give the head of the Orthodox Church the right to be familiar with "Procedures for Opening Churches." The Council's archives record, for example, these facts: "Notes on a conversation with Metropolitan Aleksii on September 29, 1944: . . . Aleksii asked me [Karpov] to acquaint him with the procedure for presenting applications from believers for opening a church, and I explained it."[170]

The Russian Orthodox leadership itself faced the problem of a clergy shortage. Growing numbers of churches made this problem more acute. For this reason, diocesan bishops themselves were forced to deny approval of petitions from believers. For example, in the first half of 1944 regional execu-

tive committees in Chelyabinsk and Sverdlovsk rejected petitions for opening eleven churches on the basis of decisions by Archbishop Varlaam of
Sverdlovsk, Chelyabinsk, and Irbit.[171]

In my view, the fundamental factor hindering the process of opening Orthodox churches was opposition by officials at the local level—by district,
town, and regional authorities. The most laconic expression of the position
held by representatives of the local state bureaucracy is found in a claim by
the deputy chairman for the city of Saratov, "The Soviet people do not need
churches!"[172] Certainly, at the heart of the negative reactions by local leaders to opening churches and, in general, to increasing church work lay the
conviction that the reversal in church-state relations was connected to specific political motives of the country's leaders and did not have any relationship to everyday work in their region or town.

Both commissioners and inspectors working under the Council for Russian Orthodox Church Affairs pointed out similar sentiments in reports and
documents that they sent to the Central Committee and the government. The
commissioner from Kirovograd complained in the spring of 1945 that, "He
[the chairman of the regional executive committee] and leaders of the regional party committee view this matter as temporary; the war will end, they
say, and we will quickly do away with churches for being centers of obscurantism."[173] Karpov pointed out the following incident in a memo of November 1, 1946, "Comrade Pugovkin, head of the regional party office of
the Pokrov district in the Kirgiz region, claimed in his antireligious report
that 'religion is temporarily allowed in the USSR in order to deceive America
and England.'"[174] And a senior staff member for the regional executive committee in the town of Borovichi told believers in plain terms, "We will not let
you open churches, because churches are being opened only in large cities
that need money and that are close to foreign embassies. We have money and
do not have any ambassadors in our region, therefore we will not open
churches."[175]

Local authorities tried in every way possible to stop attempts by believers
in their regions from raising the issue of opening churches. They withheld
documents needed for travel to regional capitals and threatened activists by
saying, "I will take away the garden plot near your house," or "I will fire you
from your job."[176]

In most cases, petitions from believers were denied at the regional level.
Motives for refusing them varied: "There is a church in a neighboring region," or "This group of believers does not represent the interests of the
majority of the region's population," or simply "It is inexpedient." The most
common reason for refusing believers' requests to open a church was use of
the church building for a storehouse, garage, granary, or other economic

need. Rejections based on that reason alone were so numerous that the Council for Russian Orthodox Church Affairs decided it was necessary to have its commissioners remind local authorities about a decision made by the Supreme Soviet of the RSFSR on December 16, 1938. The Council called attention to a section of that decision which said, "Former church buildings cannot be used for anything other than an institution's cultural needs. Using those buildings to satisfy economic needs or leaving them empty without appropriate supervision is totally impermissible and politically injurious." The Council indicated that such uses could not serve as a basis for refusing believers' petitions for opening that church building. Nonetheless, documents continued to arrive at the Council with refusals based on the reason that a church building was used for economic needs. Karpov warned local authorities in December 1944 that the Council would "present proposals to the government for reversing such decisions."[177]

Another widespread reason for refusing believers' requests to open churches was "the impossibility of utilizing [the building] due to dilapidation." In such cases the Council demanded that the case file include certification that an engineer had inspected the building and documents showing that believers refused to do needed repairs.[178] But, as will be made clear later, many written certificates did not correspond to reality. Believers' complaints "about fraudulent actions of authorities" came in large numbers to the Council. For 1947 alone, the Council received 2,033 complaints about opposition from authorities to opening churches.[179] Those who initiated petitions encountered officials who extorted bribes or made such demands as repairs of buildings before giving permission to use them or payment of "arrears in taxes" from prior years. On a suggestion from the regional executive committee for the village of Pavlovo in the Yaroslavl region, believers paid 27,000 rubles in taxes for the years when the church was closed and spent an additional 18,000 rubles to repair the building. Nonetheless, in July 1945, the church was not given to the group but was used as a granary.[180]

Local authorities tried to anticipate requests to give back church buildings to believers and asked the Council to permit the building to be used at their own discretion: to refit it as a social club (a use that was not "politically injurious") or to strip it for building material. The Council warned that attempts to tear down or refit a church building frequently engendered unity among groups of religious believers and stimulated petitions for opening a church in that building. Such an initiative by a district regional executive committee in the Riazan region led to a conflict with believers that dragged on for a whole year. On the basis of material submitted by the regional executive committee, the Council in June 1944 approved the dismantling of a church building in the village of Zatem' "because it is unsuited for the pur-

poses of prayer and is in danger of collapsing" (an engineer's building inspection certificate was included in the file). Twice, the Riazan regional executive committee attempted to begin demolition of the building but "met
with organized resistance from believers among workers at the 'Truzhenik'
and 'Bolshevik' collective farms" who simultaneously began to try opening
the church. Only in July 1945, however, did a new commission inspect the
building and decide that it was in "good condition." On the basis of a new
engineer's inspection certificate, the regional executive committee reviewed
its decision and "accepted the possibility of approving the believers' petition" in November 1945.[181]

The practice of dismantling vacant church buildings for building material
without the Council's permission became widespread in 1946–47. Karpov needed
to ask the general procurator of the USSR for help in resolving this matter.
On August 28, 1948, the general procurator sent circular letter No. 7/197s
to procurators of republics and regions. The letter directed them to protest
decisions and instructions by local authorities for refitting, demolishing, or
dismantling church buildings that were issued without the Council's consent.[182] However, this was already a belated measure.

Commissioners for the Council ran into yet another problem in a number
of places when they drew up documents for transferring church buildings to
religious communities. Boards of directors for collective farms and agricul-
tural cooperatives demanded that parish church councils pay money for the
buildings. At first, the Council categorized these incidents as "violations by
local authorities." Closer examination, however, revealed that such demands
were well founded from the perspective of collective farms. At some time in
the past, they redeemed church buildings from local financial organs, as
evidenced by deeds of sale and purchase. For example, the Krupskaia Agri-
cultural Cooperative in the Rostov region bought a vacant church building
for 22,000 rubles from the Miasnikov District Department for Financial Administration.[183] Thus, the buildings were already the property of collective
farms, and they thought they had a right to recover the money they had
spent.

The Council explained to its commissioners in an instructional letter of
September 14, 1944, that, in accordance with a Sovnarkom decree of April
17, 1943 (No. 404, "Procedures for Inventory and Use of Nationalized, Confiscated, Escheated, and Ownerless Property"), nationalized structures—a
category that included church buildings—could not be sold. Therefore, "sales
of church buildings by local soviets to collective farms, machine tractor stations, district consumer unions, and other enterprises were illegal, and corresponding transactions of purchase and sale were subject to cancellation."[184]
The situation did not change, however, and in November 1946 Council lead-

ers proposed to Sovnarkom's Council for Collective Farm Affairs that the two councils together solve the problem of church buildings purchased by collective farms. In a letter to G.B. Perov (president of the Council for Collective Farm Affairs), Karpov noted that the sales of buildings to collective farms and the inclusion of these buildings on their balance sheets were in fact illegal. Karpov wrote, "There is no reason to forbid the alienation of former church buildings from collective farms if a decision is made to transfer such buildings to communities of believers." The Council for Russian Orthodox Church Affairs proposed that, "expenses incurred by collective farms for purchasing and remodeling former church buildings that are alienated or proposed to be alienated should be refunded to the collective farms by those local soviets or organs that illegally sold those buildings to the collective farms, in accordance with Article 7 of the Decision by the Council of Ministers of the USSR and the Central Committee of the Communist Party on September 19, 1946."[185] But this did not resolve the problem. In August 1947, the Council again directed the attention of its commissioners to the fact that "it is forbidden to recover losses incurred by a collective farm from a religious community for this reason: A church building is given for use [by believers] without charge."[186]

Of course, it is impossible to simply state that all local leaders without exception regarded the initial process for opening churches negatively or tried to deceive believers by drawing up fraudulent documents. Reports from commissioners often included facts to the contrary. Representatives of local government, mostly at the district level, ranked a decision on opening a church in their region with other tasks of general governmental significance which they had direct responsibility for completion. At one of the collective farms in the Stavropol region, two members of the village soviet were placed on a church's auditing commission "for control." The chairman and party organizer of a collective farm attended a meeting held by believers for the purpose of opening a church in the village of Ushakovka in the Cheroiar district of the Stalingrad region and made recommendations for electing the church council of the religious community.[187] However, these were isolated cases and exceptions to the clearly emerging trend of opposition to activation of church life and an increase in the number of Orthodox churches.

Believers sent large numbers of complaints on the illegal activity of authorities to commissioners, the Council for Russian Orthodox Church Affairs, and the Moscow Patriarchate. Karpov noted in a memo to the government at the beginning of 1948 that petitions for opening approximately 1,200 churches had poured in nonstop since 1944. Envoys from these groups of believers presented complaints to every institution: the Supreme Soviet, the Council of Ministers, the Central Committee, Voroshilov, and the general procurator.[188] An opinion had spread among believers that "the center [central government] lies in its own instructions, churches in the USSR are being opened only on paper when in fact nothing is done. . . . Once again there is fraud and deception; it is impossible to trust official decrees."[189]

Groups of believers who lost hope of registering a community and opening a church by legal means occupied vacant churches without authorization. They resorted to bribing government representatives with presents and money, knowing that the offering of bribes was severely punished. The number of illegally opened chapels increased throughout the country. Between 200 and 300 illegal chapels operated in each of the central regions of Russia (Gorky, Ivanovo, Kalinin, and so forth) by 1948 according to the Council's data. These numbers were two or three times higher than those for registered churches and chapels.[190]

Leaders of the Council repeatedly offered the government their opinion that multiple refusals to approve petitions for opening churches only led to strengthening religious conviction and reinforcing religious fanaticism. Karpov saw greater evil in the appearance of illegal chapels than in larger numbers of officially registered churches, the activity of which was under control.[191] The Council informed the government that approving petitions had positive value—it sharply curtailed "illegal church activity led, as a rule, by hostile ecclesiastical elements" and "reduced the number of malcontents among the believing portion of the population."[192] Karpov at this same time reckoned, "Existing procedures for reviewing applications do not allow the Council operationally to regulate the opening of churches, since it is wholly dependent on the decision of local authorities; the Council does not have the possibility of reviewing the rejection of a petition. Bearing in mind that many local leaders see opening churches in a negative light, the Council considers it expedient that in the future local soviet organs preserve the right to express an opinion on a petition, but review and a final decision of the matter be given to the Council."[193] Karpov's proposals did not find understanding or support in the government.[194]

By the fall of 1947, positive decisions from localities became isolated cases. Local leaders justified "wholesale" refusals of believers' petitions by saying a new directive from the Central Committee on popular atheistic education gave them the right to think that opening churches was now unnecessary.[195] Karpov himself was worried by the waning attention that the highest structures in the party began to display toward religious matters and the activity of the Council for Russian Orthodox Church Affairs. In a memo to the government at the beginning of 1948 he asked, "Has the policy of the Council changed in connection with that directive? Are decrees that were adopted in relation to opening churches subject to change?"[196] And although the

Council's chairman did not receive a concrete answer, subsequent events showed that his concerns were not unfounded.

On March 18, 1948, the Council adopted its final decree for approving decisions made by local authorities that opened eighteen churches and chapels in twenty-eight populated areas around the country.[197] With this act, the government's policy of "unrestricted" growth in the number of Orthodox churches came to an end. The opposite trend began to gain momentum—the seizure of church buildings from religious communities.

This problem entered the Council's field of vision from the moment it received the first reports from its commissioners. It was essentially as follows. The Nazis did not restrict Orthodox Church work in occupied territory as they did with other confessions. In the 1920s and 1930s, former church buildings had been converted into clubs, apartments, and schools or given to various organizations and institutions. These buildings, newly restored and repaired under the occupation, regained their original appearance and functioned as churches. Chapels were also used as secular buildings. As the front line advanced toward the West, evacuated institutions and organizations returned, and Soviet authorities resumed their work. The process of seizing church buildings by administrative orders and closing chapels began, sometimes without any advance warning to church communities.[198] In a series of districts in the Ukraine and the Stavropol region, the process of seizing churches and chapels became mass campaigns. Thus, the chairman of Stavropol's regional soviet issued an order in the spring of 1944 to vacate all buildings that had been occupied and, if other opportunities were not afforded, to disband those religious communities.[199] Moreover, the campaign was conducted crudely in many places and was accompanied by insults to the religious sensibilities of believers that often led to clashes with church communities.

The Council tried to gain control of the situation through its commissioners by explaining in instructional letters the required process for how, in which cases, and in what sequence the seizure of church buildings should proceed. In addition, the Council sent a Directive (No. 48/s) in April 1944 to chairmen of the executive committees of soviets of workers' deputies, which specifically ordered that "you are not permitted to implement such measures as a campaign . . . this is wrong" and also explained in detail procedures for conducting this action.[200] Finally, Sovnarkom adopted resolution No. 1643–483s, "Procedures for Opening Churches and Chapels on Territory Freed from German Occupation" on December 1, 1944, in response to a petition from Karpov. In this resolution, the government specifically ordered that if the confiscated building had ever been used as an Orthodox church, then the matter of its seizure should be decided in coordination with the Council for

Table 1.2

Year	Total applications submitted	Number of churches requested to be opened
1944	910	266
1945	363	65
1946	279	33
1947	255	36
1948	121	18

Russian Orthodox Church Affairs. Also, believers were to be offered different premises (in the stipulations of an agreement) in exchange for the building subject to confiscation.[201]

As a rule, the building offered in exchange to believers had less floor space, was located on the outskirts of town, and sometimes was in such bad condition that the church community did not have the means to do repairs and was forced to refuse it. In such cases, the religious community was considered "disbanded" because the law allowed registration of a church association only under the condition that a building (church or chapel) was available for prayer. For example, Council Inspector Iakovenko reported the results of his inspection trip to the Sumy region. Out of twenty-two religious associations that had their buildings confiscated by decisions of the regional executive committee—decisions approved by the Council for Russian Orthodox Church Affairs, eighteen had "self-disbanded." Iakovenko commented, "All the decisions are striking due to their insufficient foundation . . . the written opinion of the bishop was ignored."[202]

According to the Council's data, religious organizations used a total of 1,701 public buildings in occupied territory for religious purposes. In the period from 1945 through 1947, a total of 1,150 buildings were confiscated from church communities; of that number, 324 were former church buildings and 826 were secular buildings.[203]

A paradoxical situation arose. Petitions from believers to open churches did not diminish, but in most cases they were not approved. Buildings belonging to active churches and chapels were confiscated, while at the same time 18,345 religious buildings under the control of local soviets around the country stood unused at the beginning of 1949.[204] Table 1.2 gives data from the Moscow region* through April 1, 1948.

Between 1944 and 1947, only fifty-eight churches were opened in the Moscow region (13.8 percent of the number of churches requested to be opened). The total number of active churches as of April 1, 1948, was 177.

*The Moscow region does not include the capital city of Moscow.—Ed.

Table 1.3

Date	Number of open Orthodox churches and chapels reported by the Council for Russian Orthodox Church Affairs
October 1, 1943	9,829
October 1, 1945	10,358
July 1, 1946	13,215
January 1, 1947	13,813
January 1, 1948	14,187

Five districts in the region did not have a single active church. Inactive church buildings totaled 1,070, of which 855 were used as storehouses, machine tractor stations, schools museums, or archives, and 215 were vacant and still held as religious property. From the beginning of 1947, the Moscow regional executive committee, having denied all petitions submitted, did not present a single decision to the Council for Russian Orthodox Church Affairs.[205]

Nonetheless, during World War II the number of Orthodox churches and chapels in the Soviet Union increased significantly; and, despite the complicated process for opening new churches, their total number also grew in the postwar period (see Table 1.3 above).

The total number (14,187) of churches open in January 1, 1948, included: 3,021 churches and chapels that had never been closed; 7,405 opened during the occupation; 2,491 former Uniate churches; and 1,270 opened by the Council for Russian Orthodox Church Affairs.[206]

A shortage of cadres became a serious issue in connection with the sharp increase in the number of Orthodox churches and the formation of new dioceses under the Moscow Patriarchate. Many episcopal sees remained unfilled. For example, seventeen out of eighty-three dioceses did not have their own governing bishops in 1946.[207] Some bishops had to take parishes from two and even three regions "under their leadership." Thus, in November 1943 the Holy Synod decided "to entrust his Grace Archbishop Varlaam of Sverdlovsk to temporarily settle church affairs in cases of appeals to him from believers in the Chelyabinsk region until the appointment of an individual diocesan bishop there."[208] This "temporary settling of church affairs" became permanent, but in March 1945 the Holy Synod entrusted jurisdiction over Orthodox parishes in the Kustanai region in Kazakhstan to Bishop Tovii of Sverdlovsk.[209]

The problem with cadres of rank-and-file priests was also serious. The patriarchate relied on government support for a solution. Former clergy who consented to return to church service were demobilized from active military duty. Former priests who left to work in government institutions were invited back to newly opened churches. Renovationist clergy who repented returned to the bosom of the patriarchal church (only those who had publicly renounced the priesthood were not restored to holy orders, in accordance with a special decision of the Synod).[210] "Devout laymen" wishing to take clergy orders and serve the church were also invited.

The Commission for Exemption and Deferment from the Military Draft, in a decree dated November 3, 1944, freed clergy from being called up for mobilization if they "held the office of priest or deacon with the conditions that they are registered under established procedures and serve in a church."[211]

The number of priests in the USSR on January 1, 1946, was 9,254 according to data from the Council for Russian Orthodox Church Affairs. On January 1, 1947, there were 9,617 priests. Priests and deacons together totaled 11,827 on January 1, 1948.[212]

During wartime and in the early postwar years, the senior parish priest became a suitably noticed and significant figure, especially in village areas. Karpov more than once reported to the government and the Central Committee that some clergy regarded their activity as having governmental significance, since they thought, "The church has become a component of the state." And they demanded appropriate treatment from local authorities in everything connected with the life of the parish community. The Council's chairman repeatedly cited instances where local representatives of the regime gave reason "for church activists" to be convinced of that opinion. Examples include:

> Chairman Stoliarov of the executive committee for the Pochek district of the Molotov region gave personal assignments to priests to deliver sermons in which they called on believers to sell grain to the government. Priests accepted orders from the executive committee's chairman and, in his words, managed to discharge their duties extremely well.
>
> The chairman of a collective farm in the Kiev region asked a local priest to make a report on "The Significance of May 1st"; the priest agreed and thanked the chairman for his confidence.
>
> Chairmen of several village soviets in the Stavropol region requested that priests deliver sermons related to increasing labor discipline.[213]

Quite frequently, village soviets asked priests to provide financial help, including funds "for budget needs." Another widespread phenomenon was sermons that urged believers to participate in the February 1946 elections for the Supreme Soviet of the USSR that were delivered on instructions from local authorities.

For their part, the Moscow Patriarchate and diocesan bishops worried about the low level of theological education among parish clergy. According to data from the Council for Russian Orthodox Church Affairs, only 305 clergy had higher theological education in 1946, while 3,289 had a secondary theological education; 468 had a secular higher education, 1,950 had a secular secondary education, and 3,418 possessed only a secular primary education. As of January 1, 1948, levels of education for clergy stood as follows: higher theological—1,359 clergy; secondary theological—4,816; secular higher—286; secular secondary—1,586; secular primary—3,780.[214] Lower levels of education were basically characteristic of village priests. Diocesan bishops in their reports to the patriarchate noted that due to "a lack of training for clergy in theological matters, the task of preaching in village churches is simply not being done." Bishops in the provinces also observed "deviations from liturgical norms" in the shortening of liturgical rites, wedding ceremonies performed on noncanonical days (Tuesdays, Thursdays, and Saturdays), the use of general confession, baptism of adults by pouring water over their heads [instead of immersion—Ed.], and so forth.[215] Some bishops tried on their own to raise the education level of parish clergy. They distributed so-called "Instructions for Pastors" in parishes, traveled around to the churches and chapels of their dioceses giving "exhortations," and organized short-term courses for raising the qualifications of clergy. The diocesan administration in Rostov, for example, formed a special commission in 1944 that examined the knowledge of those who expressed a desire to enter church service.[216]

Clergy conduct and amoral behavior by some priests brought complaints from believers. Most often conflicts arose between clergy and parish councils after the National Church Council of 1945 adopted regulations on church administration that gave senior priests access to the parish treasury. The Council for Russian Orthodox Church Affairs cited the following excerpts from complaints by parishioners about clergy: "They grab and grab, so I am now opposed to going to church" and "We haggled and haggled over how much he'd take for extreme unction [last rites—Ed.], and so the person died without the sacrament of repentance."[217] Despite an extreme shortage in the number of parish clergy, the patriarchate deprived some clergy of their holy orders. In 1947 alone, 105 priests were deprived of holy orders.[218]

Reports from diocesan bishops noted that the main disease afflicting church life was the large number of false priests who often did not have any form of ordination but still conducted religious rites in believers' homes and refused to recognize any ecclesiastical authority. For example, such "wild" priests in the Tula region referred to the patriarch as "the Bolshevik from the Church."[219] As a means of combating such priests, the Holy Synod proposed that laity who prayed with unlicensed priests would find themselves excommunicated from the church.[220]

Many commissioners for the Council for Russian Orthodox Church Affairs also worried about the activity of unregistered "sneaky" priests, as bishops were approaching commissioners with requests to stop the activity of such priests. Commissioner Tikhonov from Novgorod even ordered district executive committees and village soviets to investigate the performance of religious ceremonies and rites by men who were not registered in accordance with proper procedures. These men were to receive "a final warning that criminal proceedings would be instituted against them."[221] The Council labeled Tikhonov's actions "illegal and harmful" and pointed out that the legal codes of the republics in the RSFSR and the union republics generally did not contain any section that would allow prosecution of unregistered priests for performing religious rites. Karpov advised the Council to study this matter, "to present diocesan bishops with the issue of their taking steps according to church policy and to make the police aware of certain cases as needed."[222] The Holy Synod discussed this matter several times in 1945–46 and concluded that the only method for fighting against false priests was to have itinerant priests in dioceses "in order to meet the religious needs of all believers in attached parishes." In April 1946 the Synod adopted a resolution "to seek permission from the Council for Russian Orthodox Church Affairs to introduce the position of itinerant priest."[223] While the Council and the government discussed the matter, however, the Finance Ministry issued directions to local tax officials about levying taxes on the income that unemployed and other unregistered clergy received from performing religious rites. Karpov informed his commissioners about this plan in an instructional letter on November 1, 1946, and asked them to discover "how this measure affected religious life in Orthodox parishes and whether it alone entailed either an increase or decrease in the number of liturgies and rites performed by unregistered clergy."[224]

The Moscow Patriarchate placed its greatest hopes for solving the clergy shortage on institutions for theological education. Stalin and the metropolitans resolved the issue of opening a theological institute and courses for pastoral theological training in Moscow at their meeting on September 4, 1943. In the months that followed, Patriarch Sergii presented for the government's "agreement" a regulation for the institute, pastoral training courses, and an academic program. After Molotov approved them, Sovnarkom passed Decree No. 1324 on November 28, 1943, entitled "On an Orthodox Theological Institute and Courses for Pastoral Theological Training in Moscow." The December issue of the *Journal of the Moscow Patriarchate* contained an announcement stating that the institute would accept twenty-five students into its three-year degree program and thirty into its two-year course. The announcement said that study in both the institute and course would be free, with payment of stipends and provision of dormitory space provided to students who needed such support. The Moscow Patriarchate maintained educational institutions, but a motion by the Holy Synod suggested that dioceses contribute not less than 15,000 rubles every month, "and that wealthier dioceses [contribute] more."[225]

In a decision dated July 20, 1944, the Commission for Exemption and Deferment from the Military Draft issued personal deferments for seventeen students studying in the Moscow Patriarchate's Theological Institute.[226]

Karpov expressed the government's perspective on institutions for theological education in the Russian Orthodox Church. Addressing members of the Council, he stressed, "A refusal in this matter means that we are emphasizing the opposite and are not declaring freedom of conscience. The church needs cadres. Training new clergy renews the church to a certain degree and provides a young staff that was born and grew up under contemporary Soviet conditions. They did not experience the psychology, morality, and politics that existed under the monarchy." Karpov admitted the existence of yet another "limited" reason—"to use new cadres for the church's entry into the international arena."[227]

A network of institutions for theological education gradually spread throughout the country. In May 1944, a decree passed by Sovnarkom and signed by Stalin allowed the opening of courses for pastoral theological training in Saratov.[228] In March 1945, Sovnarkom approved a decision by the Council for Russian Orthodox Church Affairs to open courses for pastoral theological training in the cities of Kiev, Leningrad, Lvov, Lutsk, Minsk, Odessa, and Stavropol. In August of that same year, Sovnarkom approved the Council's proposal for starting such courses in the city of Vilnius. Executive committees for the Councils of Ministers in the Ukrainian, Belorussian, and Lithuanian Soviet Socialist Republics as well as regions in the RSFSR were required to provide premises and assistance in equipping these courses.[229] In 1946, the Soviet government agreed with a decision by the Moscow Patriarchate to return to a traditional structure for theological education. Sovnarkom's decree on May 29, 1946, authorized the opening of theological academies in Moscow, Leningrad, and Kiev; another decree on July 9, 1946, permitted the reorganization of courses for pastoral theological training as theological seminaries in Moscow, Leningrad, Kiev, Saratov, Lvov, Odessa, Minsk, Lutsk, and Stavropol.[230] The Moscow Patriarchate set up an Education Committee responsible for leadership "in matters of theological education." Committee members included Metropolitan Grigorii Chukov of Leningrad and Novgorod as chairman, Protopresbyter Kolchitskii, and Professor S. V. Savinskii. The Committee was required to seek the patriarch's approval and confirmation in all matters connected with the organization and activity of institutions for theological education.[231] Referring to a short-age of professors and instructors, the Committee and Patriarch Aleksii petitioned the government through the Council for permission to invite four or five Russian theological professors from abroad (from Paris and Prague) "to be used as instructors in theological academies." Karpov added the following point to this petition: "Require commissioners for issues of repatriation (under Sovnarkom) to take steps as proposed by the Council for Russian Orthodox Church Affairs to find bishops who fled abroad during World War II and repatriate them to the USSR."[232] The government did not, however, support this petition.

Not all regional officials obeyed Sovnarkom decrees on opening institutions for theological education. This was the result of the existing circumstances as well as the subjective opinions of local leaders who did not want to have "hotbeds of obscurantism" in their territory. Courses for pastoral theological training in Stavropol did not start as planned in 1945, because only five men showed up when classes began, although ten had passed the entrance exams and were admitted. A theological seminary opened in Stavropol the following academic year.[233] It took more than two years to settle the matter of opening an institution for theological education in the city of Saratov. Its executive committee appealed to the Council of Ministers of the RSFSR in November 1945 in a letter that "gives notice of our inability to fulfill the decree of the Soviet government on providing premises in the city of Saratov for courses in pastoral theological training and, in light of this, requests that these courses be relocated to another city within the RSFSR."[234] No seminary was ever opened in Lvov, and the governmentally approved theological academy in Kiev existed only on paper. A total of two theological academies and eight seminaries functioned inside the USSR during the 1946–47 academic year (see Table 1.4).

Students in the theological academies were for the most part mature people who had significant life experience; 78 percent of them were over forty years old. A majority of these students already had a higher secular education (62 percent), and 18.7 percent had a secondary theological education. Students in the theological seminaries on the whole were younger. As the Council for Russian Orthodox Church Affairs noted, one met representatives from all layers of society among those studying in theological schools.[235] Out of a total of 355 students, 31 studied in academies, and 324 in seminaries during the 1946–47 academic year.[236]

Patriarch Aleksii defined the programmatic targets and tasks that the Moscow Patriarchate set before its educational institutions in a speech given at the opening of the Leningrad Theological Academy. He said, "Prepare our pastors who, through spiritual leadership of their flocks, will lead believing

Table 1.4

Institution for theological education	Number of faculty (1946–47)	Number of students (1946–47)
1. Moscow Theological Academy	17*	14
2. Moscow Theological Seminary		130
3. Leningrad Theological Academy	10*	17
4. Leningrad Theological Seminary		57
5. Lutsk Theological Seminary	10	49
6. Odessa Theological Seminary	12	24
7. Kiev Theological Seminary	4	15
8. Zhirovit (Baranovichi) Theological Seminary	3	11
9. Vilnius Theological Seminary	4	23
10. Stavropol Theological Seminary	3	15
Totals	63	355

*Note: The Moscow Theological Academy and the Moscow Theological Seminary shared a single faculty. The same was true for the Leningrad Theological Academy and the Leningrad Theological Seminary.—Ed.

people to fulfillment of the same tasks toward which the government also strives, namely: teaching the people love for labor, leading them to moral perfection, and instilling devotion in them for the Motherland and her sacred, immemorial traditions."[237] Patriarch Aleksii thought that "religious fervor gradually died out" in the prerevolutionary seminary because it was not only a school for pastors but also an institution for general education. "Only those in whom beats a believing heart now come to teach and study in our seminaries."[238]

Questionnaires completed by those who entered institutions for theological education confirmed the patriarch's words. For example, applications received in 1946 listed motives for entering church schools such as religious education, the influence of religious literature, and experiences connected with the war. Middle-aged and older people went into institutions for theological education on the strength of "religious motivation." They saw the church as "a powerful, transforming force that could help influence and enlighten the people."[239] Among those who thought this way were: Ushakov, a mathematics teacher in a pedagogical institute in the town of Zaraisk; Epanechnikov, a former scientific researcher who had graduated from the Moscow Institute for Communications Engineers and the Plekhanov Institute for Economics; and Captain Ermolaev who had served as a battery commander during the war and was a member of the Communist Party. The student body of the Moscow Theological Academy even included P.P. Pronin, brother of the Minister for Labor Reserves and a former party member.[240]

Growth in the overall level of religiosity in the Soviet population during the 1940s can be explained (and was explained in the course of the decade) as the aftermath of World War II. Yet, part of the citizenry, born under the Soviet regime and educated by the Soviet system, not only turned to religious faith but also decided to dedicate themselves to outright church service. Explaining this exclusively in terms of suffering and experiences connected with the war was very difficult. The life experience of older people who submitted applications to theological schools allows us to discuss their consideration of that step and its realization. It demanded a great amount of courage at that time to assert that you were quitting the party—the Party of Victors—and relinquish your party card by laying it on the table. The desire of Soviet people to study in church schools was a completely new phenomenon in Soviet life. Yet, it also apparently reflected the country's postwar social atmosphere. Expectations of change and hopes for alterations in the existing order and for a return to the ideals bequeathed by the Revolution were characteristic of most of the population. For part of the intelligentsia, however, the conscious entry into institutions for theological education was probably a result of their disenchantment with communist ideals and a loss of faith in the ability of those ideals to mobilize people. In the Orthodox Church, they saw a force able to transform society.

Results of the fall 1946 entrance examinations for theological schools forced the Council for Russian Orthodox Church Affairs to direct intense attention on the activity of the Church's educational institutions. On November 14, 1946, the Council held a stormy debate on this matter. It heard a report by Senior Inspector K.G. Ivanov entitled, "Institutions for Theological Education in the Soviet Union." Ivanov supervised the activity of Russian Orthodox educational institutions within the Council's department for matters related to central church administration. The Council declared that Ivanov's work was unsatisfactory as a result of its debate. He was transferred to the Division of Inspectors, and control over activity of theological schools was assigned to Senior Inspector I. Kirillov.

The main shortcoming in Ivanov's work was the fact that he "overlooked" party members who had submitted applications and entered church schools. Karpov directly stated, "Pronin, the brother of a well-known government figure, a minister, is studying at a theological academy. . . . They are spreading this news in all languages. . . . He is compromising his brother. . . . Comrade Ivanov should have known this." Members of the Council as a whole acknowledged that the Council had practically ignored educational establishments of the church and that this important work was primitively organized. Council member I.I. Ivanov expressed the following views during the discussion:

"tolerated"

As workers on the Council and representatives of the party, we should know what kind of young people go there and why. It's very well that these people will be idealists and churchmen with their own worldview. But after all these people might relate to existing customs of Soviet power in a certain way. We should verify this. We should watch and observe. We should ensure that education of students is not directed against Soviet power. Christian ideology is tolerated because it is not waging war against Soviet power.

Council chairman Karpov expressed himself with even more determination: "We cannot overlook the question of how and whom they are training. And in certain cases we will directly correct, directly propose, directly forbid." In his remarks, Karpov also laid out aspects of activity by institutions for theological education that the Council needed to control:

- Composition of the student body. "We must study the background of students: their social background, nationality, education, where they came from, what they studied previously, and why they came to a theological institution. And we must inform the Central Committee if they are communists."
- Composition of faculty. "We must set many conditions on the composition of the faculty and have a file on each person. . . . The Education Committee must particularly examine the matter of qualifications for professor, holder of a master's degree, and senior lecturer at its meetings. We can then understand how they see this issue and then make our changes (consulting with them as necessary)."
- Educational curriculum of theological schools. "After they have prepared the curriculum, Comrade Utkin will review it and then speak to the Central Committee about this matter. . . . There is a question concerning important subjects like the history of religious and philosophical thought, Christian psychology, the basis for psychology, and metaphysics and logic. . . . I have spoken about these matters to the Central Committee. If they propose to exclude these subjects from the academic curriculum, we will not object and will comply with their request."
- Library collections. "We must check all libraries . . . we must examine all books, and not only those listed as anti-Soviet by the Central Directorate for Literature. It might be necessary to paste or paint over or cut out portraits of tsars, for example, in those books. All this will be done not by the Council but by the Central Directorate for Literature with assistance from the Council."

- Social life and leisure activities for students. "We should be interested in the leisure time of students and in their studies as a whole. . . . We must be interested in and support their social lives. This does not mean that we will approve all requests but will consider those we should approve since without us they cannot obtain anything."

The only matters that the Council chairman left directly under the church's authority were financial guarantees, student stipends, and faculty salaries. He said, "We have no right to be interested in the cash register."[241]

The fundamental points of Karpov's speech formed the basis of his instructional letter to commissioners dated December 3, 1946. It recommended that they collect data of interest to the Council, "while not creating the impression of control."[242]

Reports that commissioners submitted to the Council are staggering in the amount of informational minutiae they contain on the vital activity of institutions for theological education. They give characteristics and personal data for faculty and students. They analyze the general atmosphere in the collective. They note what and when students ate, what they wrote, and the questions they raised at lectures. Some commissioners attended oral entrance exams and even posed questions to the applicants. Individual commissioners displayed great energy during purges of seminary library collections. The commissioner from Odessa removed the book *Ivan Polzunov*, one in a series on "Lives of Remarkable People," from the library of the Odessa seminary.* The commissioner from Volyna wrote indignantly that he had confiscated from the Lutsk seminary "a brochure published in 1936 that attempts to refute materialistic teaching and establish that God really exists!"[243]

The Council developed recommendations based on the results of these first reports from commissioners. Commissioner Khodchenko from Ukraine was directed to devote "special attention" to the activity of faculty at the seminary in Kiev because the information he sent testified to "poisoning of the faculty's minds by undesirable elements."[244] Information about instructors at the seminary in Vilnius presented the Council with the unavoidable decision of "who to keep and who to fire," since practically all the faculty worked during the Nazi occupation.[245] A more "unfavorable" situation took shape at the seminary in Lutsk because eight of the ten instructors had lived and been educated in Catholic Poland and all had lived in occupied territory. The Council decided to recommend that the Education Committee of the

---

*Polzunov was a Russian scientist of the eighteenth century famous for his work on steam engines. He had no significant ties to religion or to the Russian Orthodox Church.—Ed.

Moscow Patriarchate offer a course on the history of the peoples of the USSR at the Lutsk seminary.[246] The Education Committee also received a recommendation that all institutions for theological education should observe Soviet holidays. Meanwhile, commissioners were instructed "to participate personally in observing these holidays (through lectures, reports, and the like)."[247]

Tighter control over functioning theological schools was not the only change that happened. Those "at the top" decided that the appearance of new educational institutions within the Russian Orthodox Church was inexpedient, although bishops repeatedly requested permission to open seminaries in their dioceses. Bishop Feodosii of Bukovina and Chernovtsy petitioned the patriarch from the beginning of 1946 to open a theological seminary in Chernovtsy (which had 365 churches but only 140 priests). The government of Ukraine reacted negatively to this request, and the Council for Russian Orthodox Church Affairs agreed with that opinion.[248] The patriarch's petitions for opening seminaries in the regions of Krasnodar, Yaroslavl, and Smolensk and in the Kazakh SSR also were denied.[249] The Council thought it possible to grant a petition from the patriarch and Bishop Serafim of Rostov and Taganrog for opening a seminary in Rostov-on-the-Don, but the government decided opening that seminary was "inexpedient."[250] The seminary in Vilnius was closed in 1947, and its students transferred to the seminary in Lutsk.[251] The government permitted a different form of theological instruction, however. Short-term courses for training new clergy were organized in Yaroslavl, Smolensk, Chernovtsy, and other cities.[252]

The first class of thirty-eight men graduated from Orthodox educational institutions in 1947. Twenty-six of these were sent to parishes. Out of fifty-three graduates in 1948, twenty-seven were sent to parishes, eighteen entered theological academies, two remained at jobs in seminaries, and six were listed as being in reserve.[253]

With such a small quantity of graduates headed for parish service, it was clear that institutions for theological education could not become the needed source for replenishment of clergy cadres. Nonetheless, the organization and activity of church schools was an event of major importance for the Russian Orthodox Church. The Moscow Patriarchate had the means to train a new generation of clergy and could guarantee continuity of personnel for Orthodox churches.

During World War II, the Moscow Patriarchate revived its publishing activity. The *Journal of the Moscow Patriarchate* began to be issued in the fall of 1943, with four issues published that year. Orthodox wall and desk calendars were published regularly starting in 1944, as were prayer books, other theological literature and *venchiks*,* and, at the request of Patriarch Aleksii, 30,000 copies of a theological book, *A Service for All Saints of Russia*, were printed in 1946.

Revival of publishing activity by the Moscow Patriarchate undoubtedly had significance for affirming the church's status and raising its authority domestically and internationally. One also cannot doubt that the quantity of published literature could not satisfy the church's needs. In addition, all material included in religious publications passed through strict, degrading censorship that started in the Council for Russian Orthodox Church Affairs and then moved to Agitprop. Thus, for example, the plan for the Council's work in February 1946 included this point: "Guarantee control over production of the February issue of the *Journal of the Moscow Patriarchate*."[254] In the decision-making portion of its meeting on May 27, 1946, the Council noted, "(1) Allow the Moscow Patriarchate to print the theological book, *A Service for All Saints of Russia*."[255]

Creation of the Moscow Patriarchate's own publishing house did not occur, although it received printing equipment in 1945. It stood idle until the beginning of the 1950s, when Patriarch Aleksii, in a futile attempt to create his own publishing house, requested that the Council take this equipment away from the patriarchate.[256] Religious literature was included in the general plan for the Association of State Books and Magazines Publishing Houses (OGIZ) on request from the Council and was printed using paper released through the Central Committee. Only limited quantities of paper were provided. In addition, production of religious literature always necessitated overcoming difficulties, as noted by Karpov himself. As a result, the actual press run of the *Journal of the Moscow Patriarchate* in 1943 stood at 3,000 copies per issue instead of the declared 15,000. In 1944, it was 6,000 copies.[257] A collection already completed, *Patriarch Sergii and His Spiritual Legacy*, was not published in 1946 as planned. It appeared only in the following year.

Karpov was forced to appeal to Voroshilov in December 1946 via a memorandum that asked him "to require OGIZ to include printing religious publications for the Moscow Patriarchate in its plan for 1947 and to speed up production of publications already prepared for printing" because the head of OGIZ (Grachev), "refuses altogether to include publication of religious literature in his plan for 1947."[258] Patriarch Aleksii presented a request to the Council in August 1947 on publication of a bimonthly journal called the *Theological Bulletin*. This was to have been a journal of theoretical theology to be used in institutions of theological education. However, G.F. Aleksandrov,

---

*The *venchik* is a paper band placed on the forehead of a corpse as part of the Russian Orthodox funeral service.—Ed.

then head of Agitprop, thought that "publication of the *Theological Bulletin* is not needed since the *Journal of the Moscow Patriarchate* also prints theoretical articles." Voroshilov "agreed with the conclusion of Comrade Aleksandrov."[259]

Constant "difficulties" in the publication of religious literature—combined with the fact that half of its press runs (including those for the *Journal of the Moscow Patriarchate*) were distributed abroad—did not permit the Moscow Patriarchate to provide adequate amounts of apologetic works either to Orthodox parishes or to institutions of theological education.

The state took a series of steps directed toward strengthening the financial situation of the Russian Orthodox Church during and immediately after the war. Resolution No. 801, adopted by Sovnarkom on June 30, 1944, supplemented its decision of April 17, 1943 ("Procedures for Inventory and Use of Nationalized, Confiscated, Escheated, and Ownerless Property"), with a point that transferred objects used for religious observance to religious communities free of charge.[260] Sovnarkom's instructions on August 24, 1944, officially allowed the State Bank of the USSR to open savings accounts for the Moscow Patriarchate, diocesan administrations, and parish church in order to safeguard church resources.[261] In August 1945, Sovnarkom adopted a resolution on giving "church diocesan organs, diocesan administrations, and parish communities juridical rights for: acquiring means of transportation; producing church equipment and objects used in cultic acts; selling these objects to communities of believers; renting, building, and purchasing private homes for church needs—all with permission from regional commissioners of the Council for Russian Orthodox Church Affairs."[262] A Sovnarkom resolution signed by Molotov lowered the rates for electricity used by religious institutions from 5.50 rubles to 1.65 rubles per kilowatt-hour, effective January 1, 1946.[263]

The state also changed its tax policies on religious organizations, including the Orthodox Church. I.V. Pokrovskii, legal consultant at the Council for Russian Orthodox Church Affairs, did important work in preparation of the decisions that were adopted. With his active participation, the People's Commissariat of Finance adopted a series of amendments to existing procedures for tax collection during 1944. In particular, the Commissariat forbade collecting taxes or insurance premiums from nonfunctioning churches.[264] It also established procedures for assessing income taxes on faculty at institutions for theological education and on persons employed by religious associations.[265] The commissariat decided to release clergy who lived in rural areas from the requirements to deliver meat and eggs if they did not have any cattle or chickens.[266] On a recommendation by the Council for Russian Orthodox Church Affairs, the government adopted Resolution No. 2215 on August 29, 1945 ("Procedures for Taxation of Income of Monasteries and

Enterprises Affiliated with Diocesan Administrations") that regulated tax
collection from monasteries, candle factories, monks, and nuns (in particular, monks and nuns were exempted from taxes assessed on people who were
not married).[267]

Resolving the issue of tax assessments on clergy proved to be especially
complicated. Its complexity, in the words of Council Legal Consultant
Pokrovskii, lay in the lack of "a single means for calculating the taxable
income of clergy." Proof of his point is found in an Order by the Supreme
Soviet of the USSR dated April 30, 1943 ("On Income Taxes from the Population"), which completely excluded the category of clergy. After a "Clarification" by the People's Commissariat of Finance in a circular of April 17,
1944, clergy began to be equated, for tax purposes, with independent handi-
craftsmen under Article 19 of the Supreme Soviet's Order of April 30, 1943.[268]
Local tax inspectors used their individual and personal discretion in calcula-
tions of clergy income. At the end of 1944, commissioners of various regions were ordered by the Council to investigate sixty-six Orthodox parishes
"in order to ascertain existing legal arrangements for levying income and
military taxes on the clergy." They uncovered many instances of double taxation of clergy by local finance departments. Taxes were assessed on casual
donations of food—tax inspectors included the cash equivalent at market
prices in the priest's income. Funds collected by the community to pay the
priest's taxes were included in his income and taxed anew. Sums of money
given to the superintendent of district clergy "for his expenses in traveling
around the diocese" were also taxed.[269] Tax inspectors in many areas chose
the month with the highest income, multiplied the income for that month by
twelve, and then collected taxes on the clergyman's annual income based on
that figure.[270]

The results of this study on clergy taxation became Circular Letter
No. 870 from the Ministry of Finance on December 13, 1946, entitled "Procedures for Collecting Taxes on Servants of Religious Cults."[271] It specifically indicated items to be included in a priest's taxable income. It also
stipulated those forms of income that could not be taxed.

In connection with consideration of this issue by the Council and government, Patriarch Aleksii repeatedly proposed switching or reclassifying clergy
tax rates from Article 19 to Article 18 of the Order "On Income Taxes from
the Population." Karpov's point of view on this is interesting and is clear
from his comments in the following excerpt from the stenographic record of
a Council meeting on clergy taxation, held on April 22, 1947:

> I think it is necessary not only to reduce the pressure found in Article 19
> but also to remove it completely. They are groaning under this pressure. Is
> this necessary now? No, this is now actually harmful. We should empha-

size that the government is building and restoring itself using revenues from industry and production, using revenues from the population that includes clergy who contribute to these revenues as citizens of the Soviet Union. . . . This is a minor matter but a political one. . . . We shouldn't think about picking on the clergy. It is possible to make concessions, to let go, to relax. . . . Therefore, we should present the matter to Comrade Stalin and request that clergy be placed in the category of employees. . . . We removed this pressure from Catholics; we must also remove it from the Orthodox.[272]

Those in the government decided differently, however. Despite the fact that in the future this matter was raised by clergy and discussed in the Council, procedures for taxation did not change.[273]

Bells in Orthodox churches rang once again in the 1940s. Instructions by Sovnarkom on August 22, 1945 included a proposal that local officials "not prevent church communities that already have bells from sounding them in towns and villages, and not to prevent the acquisition of bells."[274]

Acquiring bells was possible, however, only in those places where bells were available. It was possible to buy bells that factories had saved by some miracle or to negotiate with a business for their transfer. But, the Council told its commissioners that it was "absolutely forbidden" to cast new bells out of scrap metal collected by believers.[275]

The state even began a partial return of saints' relics to the Russian Orthodox Church in 1946–47, relics that had been seized as a result of a sensational propaganda campaign in the 1920s. According to the Council's data, a total of 245 saints' relics existed in the country and the majority of them were held at the Monastery of the Caves in Kiev. The rest were in local history museums and in the Museum of the History of Religion and Atheism in Leningrad. In 1946, officials decided "as exceptions" to transfer and install the relics of St. Sergius of Radonezh at the Holy Trinity Monastery of St. Sergius and the relics of the holy Vilnius martyrs to a monastery in Vilnius.[276] Karpov indicated in an instructional letter to commissioners on July 26, 1946 that, "no mass return of relics can take place, and commissioners should not show initiative in searching for relics in museums and other organizations."[277]

Karpov, however, was forced to present this matter to the government in light of repeated requests by Patriarch Aleksii to transfer famous relics of saints to the church. The Council's leader received the following instructions from Voroshilov: "You must tell the patriarch, without looking him in the eye, that this mysticism has become obsolete and it is time for the Russian Orthodox Church to renounce it."[278] Karpov himself reacted harshly and negatively to the idea of transferring relics of saints. He thought, "This could promote a revival of religious fanaticism and pilgrimages and also would increase income for clergy."[279] Karpov even presented a proposal from the Council to Sovnarkom on "the inexpediency of continuing to keep relics—about which petitions for transfer are not being submitted—in the Museum of the History of Religion and Atheism and other local museums. The Council for Russian Orthodox Church Affairs proposes to confiscate these relics, collect them in one place (preferably in Moscow or in the Museum of the History of Religion and Atheism), and destroy them. The Council will present its own views on the timing and methods of their destruction, if agreement from the government is given. We should preserve relics that have been the subject of petitions submitted by bishops and the patriarch, since representatives of clergy and laity have seen these relics. . . . They know their location and condition. A few of these relics might possibly need to be transferred to the church."[280]

Molotov probably decided that this proposal from the chairman of the Council for Russian Orthodox Church Affairs was too radical. In any case, he did not support Karpov's proposal. On instructions from Sovnarkom signed by Molotov, the relics for which Patriarch Aleksii repeatedly petitioned were transferred to the church. The relics of St. Anna of Kashin held in the Kalinin city museum were moved to the Church of the Resurrection, and the relics of St. Ioann of Tobolsk to the main cathedral in Tobolsk. Relics of St. Aleksii, Metropolitan of Moscow, were moved from the Assumption Cathedral in the Kremlin to Epiphany Cathedral.[281] According to information from Council commissioners, transfers of saints' relics did not influence believers and "took place without the revival that clergy counted on."[282] It is possible that it was precisely this circumstance that caused the remaining relics of Russian Orthodox saints not to be destroyed after all and to be preserved until the present time.

Overall, we can say that the years of World War II were a period of rebirth for the Russian Orthodox Church as an institution. Another factor helped strengthen its domestic position: antireligious propaganda, in all its forms and manifestations, ceased when the war began in the USSR. The League of the Militant Godless ended its active existence. From 1941 to 1947, practically no literature on antireligious topics was published in the USSR, even though nearly 2,000 titles of antireligious literature had been published every year until 1940, with press runs of over 2.5 million copies printed by both central and local publishing houses.[283] Ideas such as "antireligious struggle . . . atheist . . . obscurantist churchmen" that previously filled the pages of periodicals, completely disappeared from both newspapers and official documents.

Such an unexpected "lull on the church front" combined with the reversal of state policy toward the church in the fall of 1943 gave birth to utter dismay among champions of militant atheism. A lack of understanding of the reasons behind such fundamental changes evoked from many of these people not only bewilderment but also a desire to investigate and to receive clear and definite answers to such questions as why, how long, and for what purpose? A letter dated February 12, 1944, from P.P. Samokhin, chairman of the "Red Cornfield" Collective Farm, to the Agitation and Propaganda Department of the Tula Regional Committee of the Communist Party conveys the position of former agitators, propagandists, and antireligious workers so eloquently that it makes sense to cite it in full:

Memorandum

In this note, I am asking you to respond to me on the matter of religion in wartime. I request this because I have a social obligation and also a mission. I need this because I have been confronted with such questions and have difficulty answering them. My mission is as a political agitator for the village soviet.

First question: What are the changes relating to religion in wartime as opposed to peacetime?

Second question: What special departments under the People's Commissariat of Religious Issues* have been formed?

Third question: Which courses or seminars for the instruction of priests have been organized, and how are they set up?

Fourth question: Why are churches that previously did not function being opened in wartime?

Fifth question: Have these four questions arisen due to proposals by our allies or by our government? Or, is this simply a flight of fantasy and gossip of foreigners for undermining our government?

I put questions relating to religion to Comrade Gorbenki in the district party organization. He gave the following answer relating to opening churches: Priests have helped much and given their own resources to the task of destroying fascism; therefore our government made temporary concessions in order to direct religion for the purpose of destroying the common enemy. I did not agree with this and was not satisfied by his answer, since I have read V.I. Lenin's book on *Socialism and Religion* that says, "Religion is one of the forms of spiritual oppression which everywhere weighs down heavily upon the masses of the people, overburdened by their perpetual work for others, by want and isolation." Lenin characterized religion as "the opium of the people" and "the ruin of the poorer peasantry." Therefore, I ask you to give a more detailed explanation regarding religion in times of war and peace.

Chairman of the "Red Cornfield" Collective Farm
P.P. Samokhin[284]

---

*No such commissariat existed. One assumes the author was referring to the Council for Russian Orthodox Church Affairs.—Ed.

As if in answer to similar sentiments among some ideological activists in the Communist Party, a decree from the Central Committee appeared on September 27, 1944, entitled "On Organizing Scientific and Educational Propaganda." Pospielovsky thinks that this decree, "having called for strengthening antireligious propaganda through promotion of a scientific worldview," became "a precursor of the future attack on the church."[285] The idea of "antireligious propaganda" itself is absent, however, in that decree. The Central Committee set the task "for widespread promotion of natural-scientific knowledge in order to overcome the vestiges of superstition, prejudice, and lack of culture." According to the decree, the basic content of scientific and educational propaganda should be "materialistic explanations of nature and achievements of science, technology, and culture." In regard to basic forms for implementation of scientific propaganda, the decree recommended nothing more than holding lectures, discussions, and "public readings from popular brochures and articles on the formation of the universe, the origins of the sun and earth, and the emergence of life."[286]

Alekseev is right in my opinion in his conclusion that Stalin, by publishing this decree, "decided to perform a certain maneuver—to remind the party and Communist Youth League (Komsomol) about the importance of fighting prejudice and superstition and thereby to emphasize his own devotion to Marxist teaching. At the same time, by strategically avoiding specific instructions on the need for an antireligious struggle, Stalin continued his policy for "legalization" of church institutions within the country."[287] Stalin would indicate the subject and limits of activity in which agitators and propagandists could engage under the new conditions. Certainly, this maneuver was very subtle for the sluggish and dogmatic minds of state bureaucrats. The contents of the decree (if local officials could become familiar with it) did not dispel doubts and did not affect their conviction that "religion is one of the forms of spiritual oppression." During the war, many activists/propagandists continued to struggle against religion and the church according to their own understanding, using methods that were familiar and available to them. They forcibly expelled worshippers from churches. They set up placards by entrances to churches that read, "Religion is the opium of the people." On religious holidays, they organized dances and showed movies close to churches.

These facts worried the clergy, as did a quite widespread opinion about limitations of new church-state relations during the war. It was not coincidental that, during a meeting at the offices of the Council for Russian Orthodox Church Affairs with participants from the council of bishops in November 1944, Karpov especially noted:

Those phenomena that are now taking place . . . in relations between church and state are not presented as something accidental or unexpected. They are not temporary in nature. They are not a tactical maneuver, as some detractors are saying or as is sometimes said in narrow-minded debates. . . . These measures flow out of a trend that appeared even before the war and that developed on its own during the war.[288]

As a result of the implementation of state decrees and instructions, the economic and political positions of the Russian Orthodox Church strengthened significantly, and the vital activity of the church became a highly visible factor in the country's social life during and after the war. On the great Orthodox holidays, especially Easter, large numbers of believers always gathered at churches. Thus, according to the Council's figures, over 148,000 people attended Easter services in Moscow churches in 1944, with two to three times more people gathering around those churches in time for the Easter procession at midnight.[289] Throughout the country as a whole, an increase in the number of religious rites was seen every year. In only one church in the city of Kuibyshev, the number of weddings held in 1943 was 139. In 1944, there were 403 weddings; in 1945, there were 867; and for the first six months of 1946, the number of church weddings was 1,258. For that same church, the number of baptisms was: 20,403 in 1944; 22,045 in 1945; and 5,412 in the first three months of 1946.[290] Orthodox Church income also grew. For example, the income for all Moscow churches increased from 550,000 rubles in 1946 to 3,150,000 rubles in 1947.[291] The Russian Orthodox Church in these years also significantly increased its authority and position in the international arena.

Despite the external well-being of the Russian Orthodox Church during the war and in the postwar years, its position from a legal point of view had not completely changed. The April 8, 1929, decision "On Religious Associations" by the All-Russian Executive Committee and the Council of Ministers of the RSFSR still formed the basis for legal relationships between church and state, although this decision still did not have the force of law in the union republics. The new policy in relation to the Orthodox Church and other confessions was based on resolutions, instructions, circular letters, and so forth, that were adopted for specific matters. In 1946 alone, the government approved six decrees and thirty-three instructions.[292] Many instructions and decrees from the 1940s contradicted the 1929 decision. These included permission for the church to conduct charitable work (collections for the Defense Fund), active preaching activity outside the walls of a church (distribution of letters by the patriarch and members of the Holy Synod in the form of leaflets) and granting the patriarchate and religious associations the rights of juridical persons.

Leaders of the Council for Russian Orthodox Church Affairs believed it was essential to pass a new law to regulate church-state relations in new historical conditions. The following resolution passed at an early meeting of the Council on December 3, 1943:

1. Assign Comrade Pokrovskii: (a) to review the 1929 law overall . . . to study what needs to be changed completely, what needs to be altered, and what of its former contents needs to be preserved; (b) to draft of a new decree for Sovnarkom on the basis of this work.
2. To prepare for the issue of juridical rights of the church. To make changes in . . . the [1918] Decree "On the Separation of the Church from the State and Schools from the Church."[293]

In January 1944, Karpov presented a draft to the government for a national law "On the Position of the Church in the USSR."[294] Neither this draft from the Council nor subsequent proposals (written together with the Council for Affairs of Religious Cults) for developing and adopting a new Soviet law on religious denominations found support in the government. The refusal of the Soviet state to adopt a new national law on religious cults revealed, in my opinion, the underlying position of Stalinist leaders: in case of possible changes in the foreign and domestic political situation, they could easily return to the policies of the 1920s and 1930s in relations with the church.

Chapter 2

Church-State Relations Between 1948 and 1957

An Attempt to Revise Church Policy by the Party Central Committee and the Council for Russian Orthodox Church Affairs

After the end of the war, opposition to the increase in Orthodox churches became stronger and more vigorous in the provinces. Criticism of the state's new policy toward the church began to be heard more frequently, and talk about the need for a decisive antireligious struggle grew more active. The country's leadership could not avoid taking such attitudes into consideration. In fact, the Party Central Committee revived its work in the area of religion in early 1947. It discussed creation of an Institute for the History of Religion and Atheism, based on the museum of the same name, as part of the Academy of Sciences of the USSR.[1] Members of the League of the Militant Godless also reminded people of their existence at the start of 1947. Fedor Oleshchuk, president of that organization, requested permission from the Central Committee to name representatives from the League to the Council for the World Union of Free Thinkers.[2] But when Mikhail Suslov learned of this request, he sent a note to Alexander Kuznetsov, secretary of the Central Committee, expressing doubts about the expediency of the League's continued existence.[3] A decision by the Central Committee officially dissolved the League of the Militant Godless in the spring of 1947. Its functions were transferred to a newly created All-Union Society for the Dissemination of Political and Scientific Knowledge.[4]

The Agitation and Propaganda Department and of the Central Committee (Agitprop) turned its attention to the work of the Council for Russian Orthodox Church Affairs in the spring of 1947.

G.F. Aleksandrov, head of Agitprop, reviewed the following documents submitted by the Council: "Report on the Council's Work for 1946" and memoranda on "The Status of Institutions for Theological Education under the Moscow Patriarchate" and "Violations by Local Soviet Organizations and Workers of State Decrees on Cults." Aleksandrov sent his evaluation of these documents to Andrei Zhdanov,* secretary of the Central Committee. Aleksandrov criticized practically every aspect of the Council's work:

- "The Council clearly overestimates the degree of political reorientation by churchmen in our country, affirming that all clergy are loyal to Soviet power.[5] The Council does not see that many clergy also carry out anti-Soviet work under a very thin disguise."
- "The Council clearly exaggerates the degree of religiosity among our country's population, affirming that it continues to grow even now. . . . As is well known, behind the applications for opening churches very often are a small group of cunning operators hiding behind the names of believers."
- "The Council for Russian Orthodox Church Affairs takes the wrong approach in relations with churchmen. It very often exchanges greetings with them on various occasions and presents gifts to them. . . . All this is beneficial for churchmen, for it allows them to use such treatment for their own ends."
- "The Council seldom pays attention to its own cadres, least of all to its regional commissioners. Many of them are semiliterate and not reliable in either their political or moral attitudes toward people."
- "The Council follows an incorrect policy in its treatment of institutions for theological education. . . . It is difficult to distinguish where the functions of the Council end and those of the patriarch begin."
- "As is well known, there were several cases where people who were formerly members of the Communist Party entered institutions for theological education in 1946. Thus, the Moscow Theological Seminary accepted P.P. Pronin, brother of the current Minister for Labor Reserves,

---

*A.A. Zhdanov (1896–1948) played an important role in postwar Soviet politics. A member of Stalin's inner circle, he led a campaign for ideological purity (called the *Zhdanovshchina*) that began in 1946 by attacking the works of writer Mikhail Zoshchenko and poet Anna Akhmatova. His premature death provided an opportunity for his political enemies to conduct a purge of his supporters in the party that became known as the "Leningrad Affair."—Ed.

Captain Ermolaev, and others. The Council did not notice these abnormalities and did not react to them."

- "The Council for Russian Orthodox Church Affairs did not inform anyone about how the struggle against violations of government decisions on cults is proceeding or what the Council itself is doing in order to warn about the possibility of similar violations in the future. . . . The Council took the passive role of a recorder or neutral observer of events in this matter."
- "The Council for Russian Orthodox Church Affairs is required through its commissioners to track obedience by Soviet organizations of laws and decrees on cults and to lead a struggle against the violations of these laws. . . . The Council should organize appropriate educational work for its commissioners and especially for low-level Soviet bureaucrats."

Aleksandrov also made critical comments on the Council's reassessment of the international role for the Moscow Patriarchate. He concluded, "The Council does not completely or properly understand its task and must be corrected in this area."[6]

Zhdanov redirected these documents to Suslov with instructions to review the matter in the Secretariat of the Central Committee.[7] A hearing occurred on October 28, 1947. Council Vice Chairman Belyshev attended this hearing because Karpov was ill. All critical remarks by the head of Agitprop remained in effect. Officially, the Secretariat voted to: "Indicate to Vice Chairman S.K. Belyshev of the Council for Russian Orthodox Church Affairs that reports presented by the Council to the Central Committee for 1946 on conditions in institutions for theological education and on violations of state decrees on cults by local Soviet organizations and workers contain politically incorrect and mistaken positions."[8]

Leaders of the Council obviously did not expect such an evaluation of their work. The primary reason for their surprise was that the Council coordinated practically every step with the government. Numerous documents, letters, and proposals—distributed with the traditional ending, "We await your instructions"—testified to this.

Criticism voiced in the Secretariat focused on at least two main points. First, the Central Committee expressed mistrust of the information presented by the Council about attitudes of clergy toward the Soviet regime and about the level of religiosity among the population. Regional Council commissioners had direct responsibility for verifying signatures on applications from believers for opening churches. The Council's leadership had a solid basis for its conclusions that religiosity in the country was not falling but rather was tending to grow. Disregard for the Council's conclusions and mistrust of its reports by the Central Committee revealed an attempt by party leaders to force the Council to produce the results they desired. Second, the Central Committee insisted that the Council carry out the functions of control, prohibition, and punishment. It even required that the Council conduct educational work "especially for low-level Soviet bureaucrats." These demands in theory conflicted with the duties assigned to Karpov in the fall of 1943.

On October 14, the Council's chairman, probably having received information on the "opinion" of the head of Agitprop but before review of the matter in the Secretariat, sent Stalin, Molotov, and Voroshilov a proposal on "Directives to the Council for Russian Orthodox Church Affairs Concerning Its Future Work." Karpov outlined new tasks in this document in relation to the domestic and foreign policy activities of the Council, taking into account that its activity in fact went beyond the boundaries of the "Regulations for the Council" of October 7, 1943. For tactical reasons, Karpov anticipated elaboration of Stalin's orders on the Council's functions as Stalin expressed them at his meeting with the metropolitans in September 1943: "Report on everything and receive orders from the government. Do not harass groups of believers by finding fault over little things while you review requests to open churches; regulate but do not squeeze. Do not act like over-procurators of the past; your work should emphasize the church's independence." In his proposed directives, Karpov laid out a plan for the Council's future domestic agenda. On the whole, he upheld earlier policies on the Orthodox Church. Karpov did not propose changing the policies that had led to the Central Committee's criticism of the Council's activity. In this way, he emphasized his personal views on tasks that belonged to the Council and how it should resolve them:

1. Supervise and direct the organizational activity of the patriarchate, guaranteeing preservation of patriotic positions in Russian Orthodox activity.
2. Continue the same forms of contact that have been established and proven themselves.
3. Continue to approve petitions from believers for opening churches in those regions where this is required by actual necessity and expediency, carefully studying every application from believers. . . .
4. Supervise the work of institutions for theological education by controlling admissions, hiring instructors for the program for general education,* and providing assistance in selection of faculty for subjects in general education.[9]

---

*Students in seminaries and academies were required to take general education courses in nontheological subjects, such as Soviet history and law.—Ed.

Approval of the directives and the resulting show of government support for Council activity were important for its leadership in theory. Voroshilov, the vice chairman of Sovnarkom who was supervising the Council at the time, did not dare make an independent decision. He passed on the Directives to Molotov personally with a copy to Zhdanov in the Central Committee. Molotov was busy with other matters at this time; Zhdanov returned the directives, saying that the Central Committee would not review them.[10]

The Council was caught between criticism of its work by the Central Committee's Secretariat on one hand and disregard for the Directives combined with a lack of clear direction from the government on the other. As a result, Council staff members unofficially began to inflate the reality of a "new line" in relation to religious organizations. They said, "The work of the Council is unnecessary, it goes against the policy of our party. . . . We will be lucky if Comrade Zhdanov or Molotov is not in the mood to call people in, investigate, and take away party membership cards from Belyshev and others."[11]

The uncertain situation forced the Council's leadership to schedule a meeting with Voroshilov. He finally received Belyshev (Karpov was ill) and Polianskii, chairman of the Council for Affairs of Religious Cults, on February 18, 1948.

During this meeting, Belyshev stated openly, "By withholding approval of the directives, some members of the Council's staff feel that all our work in the current circumstances is not only unnecessary but even harmful." Voroshilov answered with his peculiar combination of straightforwardness and definite opinions. He said, "Those who think this way suffer from an inability to think things out politically, since the Council is doing necessary and useful business that will keep it busy for at least twenty or thirty years. You cannot let emotions guide your work. Reason should decide everything for you. But you must act with moderation and not cross the line. . . . You should not get carried away, and we think your work is essential." Voroshilov reminded them that the councils were created to enable communication between the government and religious organizations. In his opinion, the councils had a valve in their hands that they should open or close, depending on specific conditions of place, time, and circumstances. Simultaneously, workers for the councils should not think of their work as a game because national religious leaders would then form the impression that the Soviet government was insincere with them. Voroshilov also stated with certainty that the job of educating the population in a scientific worldview did not fall within the scope of commissioners for the Councils. The party, Komsomol, and other social organizations were expected to be engaged in that task.[12] Belyshev was impressed by Voroshilov's words and held a conference for leading members of the Council on February 21, 1948. At this conference, the vice chairman assessed the mood of his coworkers as slander against the Central

Committee: "Certain comrades have shown revisionist tendencies toward decisions by the government. This is an environment of disorder that leads to a loss of Bolshevik vigilance."[13]

Later events, however, showed that their reasons for concern over the Council's future were not groundless. Reactions of *apparatchiks* in the bureaucracy served as a kind of litmus test. From their reactions, one could judge the smallest changes in the state of affairs in the corridors of power during the Stalinist era—in relation to both individual officials and the organizations that they headed. An expressed "opinion," even if it was still only floating in the air and had not been enacted through appropriate instructions, was picked up by bureaucrats and at a moment's notice reverberated in the "Table of Ranks"* of the affected system.

This truth was reflected in the Council for Russian Orthodox Church Affairs by a series of measures that limited the rights and privileges of its chairman, staff members, and commissioners—rights and privileges given earlier and that were proper for that body's status. Thus, a request from the Council for salary increases was not approved in 1948, whereas previously such requests had been approved annually and in full. Only ten of the fifty salary increases requested that year were approved.[14] For unexplained reasons, Karpov's shortwave radio transmitter was disconnected, thereby causing him to lose personal contact with regions throughout the country. He had a right to such a radio as did all the officials who headed state committees and commissions.** In February 1948, the Commission for the Kremlin Cafeteria refused access to leaders of the Council who had previously used the cafeteria's services.[15] Beginning in the summer of 1947, a host of regions in the RSFSR stopped paying the so-called "social livelihood" (salary supplements of 200 rubles per month) to Council commissioners. Instructions from the Council of Ministers of the RSFSR on February 13, 1948 ("Norms and Procedures for Disbursing Temporary Monetary Allowances"), did not even include such categories as commissioners for the Council for Russian Orthodox Church Affairs or for the Council for Affairs of Religious Cults.[16] Despite multiple petitions by leaders of both Councils about the dissemination

---

*The Table of Ranks was a legally established order for promotion (and therefore prestige) for government bureaucrats, the military, and courtiers in Imperial Russia. Established by Peter the Great in 1722, the Table of Ranks was officially abolished after the October Revolution of 1917.—Ed.

**A shortwave radio transmitter (in Russian, a "high-frequency" radio—*apparat vysokochastotnoi sviazi*) was given to high-ranking government officials (*nomenklatura*) whose appointments were ratified by the Party itself. This radio gave officials the ability to hold private conversations with important local officials throughout the country, such as chairmen of regional executive committees.—Ed.

1948-57 *(handwritten)*

of these instructions related to their commissioners (who were equal in rank to heads of departments in regional executive committees, according to the 1943 Regulations), payment of monetary supplements ended everywhere at the beginning of 1948.

Conflict arose with the Ministry of Cinematography of the USSR in June 1948 over financing the film "The Moscow Conference of Heads of the World's Autocephalous Orthodox Churches in 1948." Based on past experience, the Council planned to make a documentary about the conference. Films about church activity previously had been issued without delay, and therefore the question was never raised about who should bear the expenses for their production. In June of that year, V.S. Bolshakov, minister of cinematography, directed the Central Studio for Documentary Films to charge expenses to the Council for Russian Orthodox Church Affairs. Karpov asked Voroshilov to intervene in the situation. But even after such "high-level" intervention, the minister of cinematography did not reverse his decision and agreed only that the ministry would refund the Council's expenses if the film were shown in wide release.[17]

In August 1948, the Ministry of Finance rejected a petition from the Council on disbursing payments from a fund for awarding bonuses that year and refused a stipulation for such a fund for the Council in 1949.[18]

Local party organs that earlier had disapproved of actions by the Council and its commissioners sensed changes in the higher echelons of power in *Stalin?* *(handwritten)* relation to "church policy." They began to openly express displeasure and criticism not only toward the work of commissioners but also toward the Council itself. Memoranda and reports from local party-economic activists to central organs of the Communist Party characterized the Council's activity as "supporting church influence" and reinforcing the church and "reactionary actions of priests." They expressed the opinion that such work was not beneficial to the government in any way but was only detrimental, since the government was forced to pay for "politically harmful work that undermined the people's well-being." Theses were once again circulated about blunted political vigilance and "harmful and dangerous" antiparty practices of indifference to religious activity.[19]

A demand from the Council to dismiss men who were unsuited for the duties of a commissioner brought a harshly negative reaction from N. Gusarov, secretary of the Party Central Committee in Belorussia. The Council tried to dismiss commissioners in three regions of Belorussia "due to their low level of education, poor health, and unsatisfactory work." Karpov's critical pronouncements on the personnel policy of leaders of the Belorussian Central Committee and Council of Ministers also angered Gusarov. In a memo to the Party Central Committee in Moscow, Gusarov attacked Karpov by saying that many of his personal instructions to commissioners (in particular, "return public buildings to religious organizations") led to "distortions of the party's policies regarding religious cults." Gusarov assessed Karpov's instructions for allowing clergy to serve attached parishes as nothing less than "anti-Soviet agitation."[20]

The Central Committee supported and encouraged the position of local party organizations. That position was used by Agitprop as a powerful argument for the need to adopt a special resolution relating to religion. Under Suslov's leadership, Agitprop began to draw up a draft resolution in the fall of 1948, later entitled "Measures for Strengthening Propagation of Scientific-Atheistic Knowledge."

The Council's chairman actively sought a way out of the increasingly complicated situation. Having worked in state security organs since the 1920s and reached the rank of major general, Karpov was well aware of how such a campaign might end. A cascade of ideological resolutions would turn into public persecution of representatives of the creative intelligentsia. The problem of "purging cadres" would once again be on the agenda. The machinery of repression would spread anew in the country. In conditions of bitter struggle against both nonconformity and "penetration of bourgeois influence into the consciousness of Soviet people," activity in such a "slippery" area as control over religious organizations could receive a completely unpredicted assessment "from above." Receiving support for the work of the Council, in other words, was literally a matter of life or death for its leaders.

Voroshilov could not give such support. He had long ago lost political clout and the possibility to influence government policy. His meetings with Council leaders usually were reduced to discussions of unimportant problems or passing on directions from higher-ranking officials. On the majority of Council documents presented for Voroshilov's approval, he wrote these types of notations: "I agree with the Council's opinion," "Ask for an opinion from the Ministry of Foreign Affairs," and "You must discuss this with Comrade Molotov."

In the crisis situation facing the Council, Karpov tried to enlist support from the highest person in the land. On November 5, 1948, he wrote a memo to Joseph Stalin.

In the memo, Karpov noted that an opinion had taken hold among party and Soviet leaders to the effect that, because the social roots that gave birth to religious ideology in the USSR had been destroyed, religious ideology had lost its foundation and it was finished. But their opinion ignored the fact that believers whose petitions had been rejected organized underground chapels served by questionable and suspicious people.

Karpov noted that reviving antireligious work was directed not so much at a struggle against religious prejudices as against the church and was accompanied by political attacks against clergy. The patriarchate and Council were receiving many letters from clergy and believers who cited antireligious articles in newspapers and asked why they conflicted with statements made on behalf of the government during the National Church Council of 1945.

In the opinion of the Council's chairman, the time was not right to artificially worsen relations between church and state or to arouse dissatisfaction in masses of believers. Karpov wrote to Stalin, "The Council suggests that the position adopted by the church in relation to the state, and especially its patriotic work carried out in World War II, cannot be disregarded in the present circumstances."

Karpov recognized emergent "opinion" and remarked that the work of the Council was temporary in nature. Still, Karpov insisted on strengthening the Council's structure and prestige to ensure its success. Pointing out underestimation and misunderstanding by certain regional party leaders on the significance of work being done by Council commissioners, Karpov asked Stalin to approve a series of proposals in support of the employment and legal positions of commissioners and Council members. These included: "refreshing" cadres in the central offices of the Council and in the ranks of regional commissioners; establishing that "appointment to and release from the position of regional commissioner can take place only in coordination with the Council; prohibiting the use of commissioners for other work"; and increasing staff in the central offices by fifteen people and funds for Council salaries.[21]

Stalin's answer, however, did not come. And a decision on "Directives" for the Council was never made.

Meanwhile, a draft resolution on "Measures for Strengthening Propagation of Scientific-Atheistic Knowledge" was prepared at the start of 1949 and awaited approval by the Politburo.

The draft resolution noted that in many regions "revival of religious ideology and rebirth of prejudices, superstitions, and barbaric ancient ceremonies are taking place. . . . All this testifies to the intensification of activity by churchmen who have expanded religious influence on backward segments of the population." The Central Committee criticized a variety of groups (regional party organs, national and local newspapers, institutions for cultural education, organs of popular education, Komsomol organizations, and the All-Union Society for the Dissemination of Political and Scientific Knowledge) for slackening off, passivity, and in some cases for stopping work in propagating scientific-atheistic knowledge.

The draft took a totally negative attitude toward the activity of the Council and its commissioners. It especially stressed that an "incorrect line" in the

Council's work "enabled a revival of activity by churchmen. . . . The Council for Russian Orthodox Church Affairs exceeded its mandate, began to give orders to local organs of power . . . illegally expanded the rights of its commissioners, gave them an improper mindset that favored the growth of church organizations and religious activity. . . . Instead of carrying out the government's line on matters of religion, the Council's commissioners began to see their main purpose as giving aid to church organizations."[22]

The Central Committee decided "to end the neglect of scientific-atheistic propaganda" and proposed a concrete program for all sociopolitical associations and organizations related to public education aimed at eliminating the deficiencies that were listed.[23]

Specific decisions were also made relating to the Council for Russian Orthodox Church Affairs. The Central Committee decided to limit the Council's activity to establishing communication between the state and the church. It required Karpov to bring new "Regulations for the Council for Russian Orthodox Church Affairs" to Sovnarkom for review. The Central Committee also decided to eliminate the network of Council commissioners throughout the country. Finally, it decided, "to reprimand Comrade Karpov, chairman of the Council for Russian Orthodox Church Affairs, for gross violation of directives from the party and government in relation to the church and for exceeding rights granted to him."[24]

Important points of the draft were the Central Committee's requirement that Karpov present new "Regulations for the Council" and its reprimand of him (something that was generally uncharacteristic of party resolutions). The Council had equal status with other committees and commissions under the Council of Ministers of the USSR. The very criticism of the state-approved Regulations from October 7, 1943, and a demand to draw up new regulations testify, in my view, to a claim by the party's ideological structures on direct administrative control over the work of the Council.

Those who framed the resolution needed a specific example of "church obscurantism" to give it more intensity and reality. A propaganda campaign around that example would help shape suitable public opinion and would receive support from local ideological activists. This background work in turn would help win approval for the proposal and its final ratification by the Politburo. Such an example was found. A powerful antireligious propaganda campaign was launched in connection with the so-called "Saratov Affair."

In the city of Saratov on January 19, 1949, on the Orthodox holiday of the Baptism of the Lord (Epiphany) in accordance with age-old tradition, a ceremony called a Procession to the Jordan River took place for blessing the water. Bishop Boris Vik of Saratov, in accordance with procedures at the time, received permission from the executive committee for the city's Volga district to conduct the celebratory rite. Representatives from the district's Lifeguard Patrol (*Obshchestvo Spaseniia na Vodakh*, or OSVOD) cut holes in the Volga's ice in advance and set up fences. Clergy and the majority of believers returned to town at the end of the ceremony. A group of some 300 people (or 500, according to other sources) stayed behind, and began to plunge into the icy, blessed water over the course of thirty-five to forty minutes (according to other sources, for five hours). This caused a bit of a stir among those who stayed behind. A photographer appeared and took pictures of the "bathers" (later he sold the photos for "a large sum").[25]

Events in Saratov became the subject for an investigation by the Secretariat of the Central Committee in February 1949. At this time, the ministry of State Security (on instructions from Georgii Malenkov) gave additional information about the "bathing." In particular, the ministry gave the last names and ages of those who participated, established that the air temperature in Saratov that day was −10°C, and confirmed that there had been no outbreak of infectious diseases in the city.[26]

The Council immediately sent Vice Chairman Belyshev to Saratov. The results of his visit were put in a memo to the Central Committee with information on the status of the church in the Saratov region, clergy in the diocese of Saratov, the number of baptisms and weddings in the region for prior years, and the work of Council Commissioner Polubabkin (the commissioner himself was not in the city on January 19 because he was on a business trip "to verify shipments of grain" at the region's collective farms). The Council particularly stressed in the documents it submitted that the religious rite took place without any violations of public order; the bishop had received permission for the religious procession three days in advance, in accordance with instructions from the Council and directions from the government; and the proper organizations took steps to guarantee security, with police present during the rite itself.[27]

The "Saratov Affair" was given new impetus by publication of a feature story in the newspaper *Pravda* on February 19, 1949, entitled, "The Saratov Font"* written by a certain I. Riabov. We do not know why this exact form for presenting the incident was chosen. Contents of this feature story had little similarity to that genre, and the article soon appeared by itself in an overtly political pamphlet. Besides describing the rite in a tone offensive to believers—"pornographic acts . . . mockery over the people . . . a rite dictated by idiocy of the old life"—the "feature story" listed specific names of "victims of the rite": Nikolai Semenovich Oreshkin stricken with pneumo-

---

*Font is an ecclesiastical term referring to a vessel or body of water used for baptisms.—Ed.

nia and Liubov Ivanovna Molokanova turned into an invalid when she became deaf after "bathing." In addition, local officials, whose full names were also given, were directly accused of assisting "the wild rite." "The fellow countrymen of Chernyshevskii* should be ashamed to go to an event for foolish, hysterical women and obscurantists, helping them to resurrect wild rites from the time of paganism and the god Yarilo."** The author also instructed workers in party committees for the city and region, "Do not disregard the lesson given on January 19."[28]

Indeed, the lesson did not go unnoticed.

"The Saratov Font" became the signal for a series of militantly antireligious articles and administrative measures against clergy and laity. Officials in Saratov also were punished. I.D. Pribytok, chairman of the Volga district's executive committee, and I.K. Karamyshev, chief of OSVOD in Saratov, lost their positions and had harsh penalties imposed on them. P. Komarov, deputy chief of the city's police administration, received a strict reprimand. The Central Committee noted the political carelessness of the Volga district's party committee.[29]

The Moscow Patriarchate also took administrative measures. A worried patriarch immediately called a meeting of the Holy Synod on February 22. In his speech concerning events in Saratov, the patriarch stressed that, "Bathing by a few hundred people . . . did not amount to a church rite but was spontaneously connected to it and resulted in an article that accused the church of 'obscurantism' and 'paganism.'" The Synod decided on its own to issue a strong rebuke to Bishop Boris.[30] Soon, however, even stricter measures were taken against Bishop Boris. He was demoted by a transfer to the Chkalov diocese and removed from a patriarchal delegation sent to Harbin.[31]

Yet another draft resolution for the Central Committee emerged as a result of the investigation into "The Saratov Affair." Agitprop developed a proposal on "Mass Observance of a Religious Rite on the Church Holiday of 'Epiphany' in the City of Saratov."

The new draft resolution placed practically all the blame for events in Saratov on the Council and its chairman. "Abusing his official position, Comrade Karpov on December 6, 1948, sent Instructional Letter No. 34 to commissioners of the Council for Russian Orthodox Church Affairs in regions and republics. He oriented local authorities on widespread conduct of 'religious processions' to bodies of water, prayers, and 'Epiphany water blessings.' In a host of regions Comrade Karpov's improper directive was

---

*The writer N.S. Chernyshevskii (1828–1889), whose works helped inspire the Revolution and were therefore revered in the USSR, was from Saratov.—Ed.

**Yarilo is a fertility god from pre-Christian Russian mythology. His cult was known for its carnival games and dances.—Ed.

passed on by local Council commissioners to all district executive committees and village soviets, although commissioners did not have the right to
give instructions to local authorities."

The Central Committee decided anew, "We issue a reprimand to Comrade Karpov, chairman of the Council for Russian Orthodox Church Affairs
under the Council of Ministers of the USSR, for sending an improper instructional letter to the provinces and exceeding his established rights. We
revoke the instructional letter of the chairman of the Council for Russian
Orthodox Church Affairs under the Council of Ministers of the USSR,
No. 34, dated December 6, 1948, as harmful and aimed at the revival of wild
customs that have brought serious harm to the health of the population."

Aside from this, the draft included a point that did not have any connection to events in Saratov but was directed against the increasingly complex
relations between the Council and the patriarch. It read, "We consider it improper that Comrade Karpov gave presents to high-ranking clergy and propose that the Council for Russian Orthodox Church Affairs end this practice
in the future because it is unworthy of the Council."[32]

An extensive amount of material was attached to the draft: reports compiled by the Ministry of State Security on events in Saratov, excerpts from
government decisions and instructions compiled by Karpov on procedures
for conducting religious processions, and a selection of responses sent to
Pravda about its feature story "The Saratov Font" (including letters from
both militant atheists and defenders of religion). These materials on "The
Saratov Affair" supplemented the Central Committee's draft resolution on
"Measures for Strengthening the Propagation of Scientific-Atheistic Knowledge" as well as the draft of the new "Regulations for the Council for Russian Orthodox Church Affairs under the Council of Ministers of the USSR."[33]
All these documents awaited approval.

Council staff worked out a draft for new Regulations for the Council on
the "recommendation" of the Central Committee. A special point in the new
draft regulations stipulated that the Council did not have the right to give
instructions to local authorities. According to the draft, all instructions on the
application of laws and decrees related to the Russian Orthodox Church should
come only from Sovnarkom.[34] The Council's proposed changes in the Regulations of October 7, 1943, were also presented for government review on
February 24, 1949.

Although written along the lines demanded by Agitprop, the draft still did
not propose totally eliminating the network of regional Council commissioners. Council leaders introduced a proposal to eliminate 26 of 104 commissioner positions, preserving them in those regions where bishops lived
and where the total number of churches was higher than 115.[35]

Karpov personally and unexpectedly introduced new proposals to the Central Committee four days later on February 28. He proposed fundamental changes in the sphere of activity and structure of the Council for Russian Orthodox Church Affairs. Only four commissioners would remain in the USSR: in Ukraine, Belorussia, and the two regions of Carpathia and Lvov. Karpov also presented a new version of the draft "Regulations for the Council." According to this version, registration of religious communities was transferred to the competency of councils of ministers in republics and regional executive committees. The Council's work was limited to reviewing matters raised by the patriarchate, doing preliminary work on drafts of legal acts, and informing the government on domestic and foreign activity by the church's central administration.[36]

The Council also sent a proposal to Sovnarkom, which developed ideas from Agitprop on limiting activity by the Russian Orthodox Church. These included planned steps for reducing the number of Russian Orthodox institutions for theological education and limiting the volume of publications by the Moscow Patriarchate, as well as initiatives for the complete elimination of the nation's monasteries. In addition, the Council held out the possibility of confiscating public buildings without any formal legal investigation in cases where the buildings were used as chapels by religious organizations. Council leaders took positions on all these points that were diametrically opposed to those they held earlier.[37]

The situation had obviously become very serious if leaders of the Council were forced to endorse such radical changes in the structure of the staff and the Council's activity. Karpov was frightened, and one of the reasons for such a metamorphosis had to be that he was in an unknown position "with the highest level of authority"—Joseph Stalin—despite his constant use of Voroshilov as a sounding board and the information he received through his own channels.

The matter ended on May 13, 1949. This date appears on the first page of materials attached to the draft resolution with these instructions: "Do not adopt these decisions. Comrade Malenkov reported the matter to Comrade Stalin personally."[38]

Forward momentum of the steamroller was stopped.

This business concerning the Council for Russian Orthodox Church Affairs probably never would have turned into such a public and dramatic event as the "Leningrad Affair" that was being investigated during the same months. But it was impossible to be sure of one's future when only the word of a single man decided people's fate.

What prompted Stalin to make such a decision? We can only guess. Maybe Stalin liked the fact that the Moscow Patriarchate praised him to the skies.

Maybe, as Alekseev suspects, eleven years of study in church schools and seminary left in the depths of Stalin's heart "a carefully concealed trembling before a church that also could preserve the image of 'the greatest leader of all times and all peoples' in the memory of generations over centuries."[39] It is difficult to read a dark soul.

Still, in my view, reasons for stopping the campaign go back to the national social and political situation shaped in the second half of the 1940s.

The Russian Orthodox Church was a repository of national traditions and served in its own way as an ideological buttress to the state in the unfolding battle against cosmopolitanism and "servility in the face of foreign culture" in the late 1940s. By openly expressing faithful sentiments for the leader, the church served as an additional source of legitimacy for the Stalinist regime. In addition, the church at the end of the 1940s took an active, patriotic stance just as it did during World War II, yet still did not lose its ability to fulfill many international assignments, doubtlessly within the lines of Stalinist foreign policy. Adopting the proposed draft resolutions would also have entailed changes in relations with the church. Perhaps it was precisely that this did not suit Stalin. The attempt to revise church policy in the USSR was repulsed.

ROC

The same fate befell the campaign organized in 1948–49, leaving traces of Agitprop's handiwork. In July 1949, the Council for Russian Orthodox Church Affairs was attached to the newly formed Cultural Bureau of the Council of Ministers of the USSR. Voroshilov headed this new body and continued to direct the work of the Council for Russian Orthodox Church Affairs on behalf of the government. This action without a doubt bore witness to the Council's reduced status in the general hierarchical system of government organs. The Cultural Bureau reviewed Karpov's radical proposals of February 28. Characterizing them as "untimely and inexpedient," the Bureau issued a resolution saying, "The Council for Russian Orthodox Church Affairs should adhere to the 'Regulations for the Council' of October 7, 1943."[40]

The Central Committee also reviewed the Council's activity, including the question of "The Council's Work with Its Cadres of Commissioners" in July 1950. It decided that the Council had accepted people who did not meet the demands of the job and who carried out their responsibilities carelessly. The Council had not provided needed leadership and control over the work of commissioners and did not make enough demands of their work. For these reasons, the Central Committee required the Council to strengthen the ranks of commissioners with politically mature workers, to establish "new procedures" for appointment and dismissal of commissioners, and "to rebuild the Council's work through a plan for more precise and critical discussion of the work of its regional commissioners."[41]

Carrying out instructions from the Central Committee, Council leaders acted quickly to implement organizational changes. Four men were fired from the central Department of Inspectors. Eight regional commissioners were replaced in the course of three months. Thirteen positions across the Soviet Union were eliminated. A new procedure was set up for working with commissioners. Every month, three or four commissioners presented reports at Council meetings. The Council heard thirty-three such reports in 1949 alone, and another forty-one during the first ten months of 1950.[42] It held group instructional conferences for commissioners in November and December 1950 for the purposes of gaining detailed familiarity with the work experiences of commissioners and providing them with practical help.[43] A separate brochure dated March 8, 1951 entitled "Instructions from the Council for Commissioners for Russian Orthodox Church Affairs," was issued that month. It was devoted solely to laying out fundamental principles for relations between commissioners and religious organizations. Hereafter, the Instructions of March 8, 1951 became the sole guidebook for the work of commissioners. An accompanying letter instructed commissioners to request guidance directly from the Council on all practical matters. Commissioners were given a list of instructional letters issued before 1950 and ordered to hand over those letters to special departments of republic-level councils of ministers and regional executive committees.[44]

The campaign of 1948–49 was not only reflected in the staff and structure of the Council and its machinery in the provinces. These years were crucial moments in the work of the Council and defined a qualitative change of duties and functions in the years that followed.

From this time forward, the Council's activity moved steadily out of the sphere of control of governing organs and into the orbit of ideological structures—specifically, of Agitprop. The Central Committee formally increased this influence through a resolution of its Secretariat on December 15, 1950. In accordance with this resolution, the positions of not only the chairman but also his deputy, assistant, and even the other three members of the Council were included in the *nomenklatura* of the Central Committee.[45] This meant that appointments to these positions and also dismissals from them took place only by action of the Central Committee. Issues that had formerly been resolved as part of the government's exclusive prerogative in the 1940s were ultimately settled from the beginning of the 1950s through "instructions to the Council for Russian Orthodox Church Affairs" passed by the Central Committee. These instructions primarily concerned problems of relations between the Council and patriarchate. Thus, the Central Committee "agreed" with the Council's opinion in February 1952 "not to take any steps at this time for separating Ostapov" from Patriarch Aleksii.[46]

A change in the Council's status could not help but tell on its relations with religious organizations of the Orthodox Church. Under pressure from Agitprop, the Council's work after 1948 distinctly veered away from previous positions of basing relations with the church on constitutional law and toward basing them on ideology.   *Post 1948...*

Conflict Between Believers and Local Authorities and the Severity of Control over Clergy

The "new line" toward religious organizations was clearly revealed in the way local authorities treated petitions from believers for opening churches. Beginning in early 1948, every single petition was denied in the regions of Moscow, Gorky, Tula, and the Tatar ASSR. Regional executive committees in Sverdlovsk and Ivanovo requested that the Council reverse its earlier resolutions to allow the opening of churches. Executive committees that made these requests referred to the "opinion" of their regional party committees.[47] The Council commissioner for the Tatar ASSR decided to confirm personally the opinion of the regional committee and received the following instructions from Muratov, secretary of the party's republic committee: "There should be no decisions or agreements whatsoever. Keep this in mind for the future."[48]

Council leaders informed the government about these facts in the winter of 1947 and during the first half of 1948 and asked Voroshilov to give them instructions and "orientation" on this matter. Karpov noted, "The situation of regional commissioners . . . is extraordinarily difficult since they cannot explain the motives for denying applications to believers."[49] The Council itself during this period continued to defend its previous position, namely, that denial of absolutely all petitions from believers "is politically inexpedient" and even "harmful" and that the refitting and alteration of church buildings "is intolerable without the Council's agreement." In the spring of 1948, the Council gave Voroshilov the draft of a government resolution that agreed with the resolution still in force on "Procedures for Opening Churches" of November 28, 1943. The draft made one important change: Councils of Ministers of union republics and regional executive committees could make a final decision on petitions only in agreement with the Council for Russian Orthodox Church Affairs.[50] However, as mentioned previously in this chapter, the government did not issue official instructions on the further work of the Council in 1948.

A discussion of the problem of opening churches did not take place until August 7, 1948 during a meeting between Voroshilov and the Council's chairman. Voroshilov expressed this opinion on the draft resolution: "It is badly drawn up, since the government cannot agree to be guided solely by a resolution. If [local officials] transgress, we need to investigate every specific case."[51] This moment clearly illustrates the Soviet government's attitude at the time toward the law in general and toward the existing legal framework for church-state relations in particular. Current political interest determined the expediency for using either an official document or official instructions in every specific case.

Voroshilov also expressed the government's opinion on opening new Orthodox churches and chapels. "We should open fewer churches and regulate them, but of course it is not right to deny all petitions. . . . Look, it's possible to cure a small wound on the hand quickly and to localize it. And just the opposite, it's also possible to cause an infection by inflaming a wound. So it is with the church: its position and its relation to the government directly depend on our attitudes toward it." Voroshilov recommended that Karpov review applications only in those cases where they were signed by 200 to 300 believers instead of by 20 to 30 as required by the decree on "Procedures for Opening Churches." Voroshilov complained, "We certainly did not foresee this moment in 1943!" He instructed Karpov "to carefully investigate" cases of unauthorized refitting of buildings in the Moscow, Riazan, and Sverdlovsk regions. "This is counterrevolution! Aiding and abetting counterrevolution! Or, at best, hooliganism."[52]

But subsequent events showed how little weight Voroshilov's opinion and word carried. Intrigues and internal party struggles "at the top" also touched those of lower rank. This process came to include the Council for Russian Orthodox Church Affairs and, through it, all matters connected with national church policy.

As has already been noted, in March 1948 the government confirmed a decision by the Council to open eighteen churches and ten chapels in various regions of the country. On October 28 of that year, however, the government issued instructions revoking its March order. One detail served as formal grounds for such a step—the March document was not signed by Stalin, the chairman of Sovnarkom, but by his deputy Voroshilov, although previously all documents signed by Stalin's deputies had been valid.[53]

Revocation of the government's March decision and the complex situation taking shape around the Council in the fall of 1948 did not influence the attitudes of the Council's leadership toward the problem of opening churches. In a letter to Stalin dated November 5, 1948, Karpov insisted that a fixed number of believers' applications must be granted ("for the sake of expediency"). In December, the Council twice asked the government to ratify documents for opening twenty-three churches and five chapels.[54] Additionally, the Council petitioned the government to keep in force part of its decision from March 18, 1948, and open four religious buildings from that list (three churches and one chapel).[55]

Table 2.1

For year ending	Number of petitions submitted for opening churches	Resolutions to open churches from regional executive committees presented to the Council for Russian Orthodox Church Affairs
January 1, 1949	3,174	28
January 1, 1950	2,297	0
January 1, 1951	1,143	0
January 1, 1952	729	0
January 1, 1953	818	0

This may have been the sole issue on which Karpov's position remained unchanged during his long tenure in leading the Council. It is possible in this case that Karpov did not speak as the chairman of a governmental institution but as a secret policeman. After all, his main argument for the necessity of opening churches was the fact that the number of illegally operating chapels where "suspicious people with anti-Soviet sentiments" preached was increasing. Controlling the activity of underground communities was difficult in his opinion. Methods for fighting them had not been developed, and "chairmen of district executive committees [did] not even know about their existence."

Between 1949 and 1951, the Council tried to receive instructions on "the line that must be followed" on the issue of opening churches. They finally arrived on June 6, 1951 in the following formulation: "You correctly raise the question about the need for established procedures for opening a number of churches—twenty to thirty per year—in order to fight chapels opened without authorization and eliminate unhealthy attitudes among believers. But it would help if the Council would attempt to reduce the number of active churches by closing them."[56] Yet when the Council presented a resolution in May 1952 to open five churches and chapels, the government did not send any reply. Moreover, these documents were returned to the Council a year later without any resolution.[57] The government's position remained "unclear" for the Council. Meanwhile, petitions from believers for opening churches continued to be received (see Table 2.1 above).[58]

Over half the applications received for opening churches came from the same central regions of Russia that had sent them during the war: Moscow, Ivanovo, Kalinin, Voronezh, Gorky, and Yaroslavl. The Council continued to receive applications with not just a few signatures but with hundreds or even thousands of signatures. For example, the Council received thirty-nine petitions from the village of Mitsino in the Kalinin region between 1944 and 1955. The applications for 1951 included 850 signatures of residents from

Mitsino and thirteen neighboring villages (200 of these signatories were between the ages of 18 and 25). Believers from the town of Pavlov in the Gorky region first petitioned to open a church in 1944; their application in December 1950 included signatures from 2,600 people.[59]

Paradoxical situations resulted. In a workers' settlement called Vorsma in the Gorky region, a fully equipped chapel had operated since 1945 and was served the whole time by an unregistered priest named Bratanov. The commissioner from Gorky indicated in his report for 1952 that, for this whole period (i.e., since 1945), believers of the settlement regularly drew up petitions to register the church, and the executive committee regularly denied them as "inexpedient." Even more remarkable, the chapel's priest over the course of six years had submitted income declarations to local financial organs and annually paid between 10,000 and 17,000 rubles in income taxes.[60]

It would be possible to continue listing similar cases. Grounds for rejection besides the widespread formulation of "it is inexpedient" often referred to other open churches nearby or to falsified conclusions that the building did not meet requirements for fire safety. Notwithstanding, the Council's statistics for June 1953 counted over 3,000 inactive church buildings in the USSR that "preserved their religious furnishings and keys, which were held by church activists."[61]

Local Soviet authorities resolved the problem of vacant churches on their own initiative. Starting at the end of the 1940s, they began widespread refitting whereby those buildings became clubs, schools, storehouses, and granaries or were simply dismantled for building materials. The Council was required to approve decisions by regional executive committees on refitting twenty-two Orthodox churches in 1948–49, fifty-two in 1952, twenty-six in 1953, and ten for the first half of 1954.[62]

The Council's leaders tried to hold this process in check. They understood that widespread refitting of vacant churches, combined with 100 percent denial of petitions for opening them, angered believers and led to local conflict. Prior experience in the Council's work showed that believers did not become angry when buildings of inactive churches remained vacant or even were used as storehouses or granaries, provided that no attempt was made to refit the building either inside or outside. Instructional letters from the Council intentionally and persistently asked commissioners to take these facts into account.

Still, the whole process began to spin out of the Council's control. Decisions on refitting and demolishing buildings were frequently made without its consent even at the district level. A total of 292 Orthodox churches and chapels were demolished, dismantled, or refitted between 1948 and 1955.[63]

Pravda's publication of the feature story "The Saratov Font" served as a pretext for making administrative decisions in relation to religious organizations throughout the whole country. In the spring of 1949, the city soviet of Saratov passed a resolution suspending activity at the theological seminary. The electricity was shut off, and food deliveries were discontinued.[64] Only two small cemetery churches were open in Sverdlovsk; both of them found their electricity, water, and heat disconnected on instructions from the regional party committee. The diocesan administration in Sverdlovsk also lost its lights and water, its telephones were disconnected, and license plates from its automobiles were confiscated.[65] Six Orthodox churches in Kiev were closed between March and June 1949.[66]

Some regions seized Orthodox churches and chapels by officially citing a Sovnarkom decree of December 1, 1944. This decree indicated that if the building had been a church at any time, its confiscation needed approval from the Council for Russian Orthodox Church Affairs. The Council received petitions from regional executive committees for confiscating 280 Orthodox churches between 1949 and 1954. After events in the winter of 1948–49, the Council's basic position changed in regard to buildings confiscated from religious communities. Such decisions were infrequent prior to that crisis; afterward, the Council approved the seizure of 263 churches between 1949 and 1954 (205 in Ukraine, 14 in Belorussia, and 44 in the RSFSR) and ruled that such decisions were inopportune in only seventeen cases.[67]

Confiscation of churches provoked natural opposition from believers. According to the Council's data, "attempts to save buildings have been made by all religious communities."[68] Refusing to vacate churches, believers set up guards around-the-clock, collected signatures in defense of the church, organized human chains to prevent government representatives from entering buildings, and hampered the removal of crosses and icons. The process of confiscating churches in a few cases provoked believers to "anti-Soviet attacks." For example, during the closure of a cathedral in the town of Nikolaev, shouts rang out from a crowd of 500 people. They yelled, "Bandits!" and, "Don't trust the Constitution!"[69] Believers from the village of Khoteichi in the Moscow region wrote a letter that said, "It's clear to all collective farmworkers that our leaders speak only at roundtable discussions abroad about freedom of religious belief in the USSR, when actually they suppress it."[70]

Over eight months in 1949, the Council received 127 applications from parishioners who requested that their buildings be returned.[71] Its statistics showed that out of 280 communities that lost their buildings, 273 sent a total of 761 complaints to the Council alone—this number did not include those sent to other authorities. Representatives from 236 organizations went directly to the Council's office.[72]

Conflicts between believers and local authorities were so severe in some districts that the Council for Russian Orthodox Church Affairs was forced to instruct its commissioners to go before the regional executive committee and raise the issue of repealing a decision to confiscate a church.[73]

Churches were also closed for other reasons. In some cases, the church was labeled a "dilapidated building." In other cases, the parish council had not fulfilled a requirement to install a standard fire alarm, or local officials claimed a shortage of space for "temporary grain storage."[74] The last of these reasons was most common at the beginning of the 1950s. On January 1, 1952, 130 churches were inactive "due to filling up church buildings [with grain] on orders of village authorities."[75] By March 1955, 298 churches were not functioning for this same reason.[76] In eighteen districts in the Kamenets-Podolsk region alone, grain storage "temporarily" occupied seventy-six active churches in 1951.[77]

Only a total of five churches and ten chapels functioned in the Kemerovo region, and five of the chapels were closed between April 1949 and April 1950. Comrade Gusev, chairman of the regional executive committee in Kemerovo, did not reverse his decision despite complaints from believers, a petition from Patriarch Aleksii, and an appeal by the Council for Russian Orthodox Church Affairs to the office of the public prosecutor for the purpose of influencing the regional executive committee. Gusev informed the Council in a letter of December 6, 1950, "Executive committees for these towns have not found it possible to rescind their decisions because social organizations and broad sections of workers respond negatively to a revival of activity by chapels in these towns."[78]

Leaders in the Kazakh SSR said, "Soon we will report to the Central Committee that religion in our republic has generally ceased."[79] The chairman of the regional executive committee for Izmail in March 1951 demanded that the Council's commissioner close all functioning churches within 130 days.[80] Novikov, chairman of the regional Soviet of Workers' Deputies in the city of Stavropol, gave a speech at a session of the executive committee in which he publicly demanded "the absolute closing of all churches in the region" by Council Commissioner Chudin.[81]

Activity by churches and chapels in many regions became directly linked with the work of the Council's commissioners. The results were not only criticism as in Stavropol but also administrative measures against them, as in the Krasnoyarsk region. The regional party committee in Krasnoyarsk removed Commissioner Gusev from his position on July 19, 1950, despite his protection by Karpov. The basic reason for Gusev's removal was that, as Council commissioner, he "stood for a mistaken position of defending and aiding churchmen."[82]

Characteristic reactions to activity of commissioners at the district level, especially in the period of grain requisitions, are seen in the following examples. When the commissioner for the Gomel region visited a district and called on the district party committee, the district party secretary Novikova told him, "I know what kind of person you are. You loaf around the district for a whole week and have suspicious conversations with priests?! Are you a member of the party? Why are churches opening here? Get out of this district right now, and don't show your face around here again!"[83]

Commissioners for the Council certainly could not disregard the position of local party leaders. The Council ever more frequently began to receive complaints from believers about the actions of commissioners ("we will not only open but also will close all your churches for you"). Decisions about "the haste of commissioners in cases of closing churches and revoking registration of clergy" frequently appeared in minutes of the Council sessions. At the end of 1950, the Council changed procedures for striking active churches from the register. A commissioner could not make a final decision on this matter by himself but now had to present the documents to the Council for ratification.[84]

However, at the beginning of the 1950s leaders of the Council themselves developed different tasks that regional commissioners should decide:

a. Deeper study of the status and activity of churches so as to improve the quality of the Council's information to the Central Committee and the government.

b. Further limitation of church activity, while not failing to account for local conditions and the general situation and not permitting rudeness, uncontrolled administrative actions, or poorly-thought-out measures.

c. Intensification of the struggle against mystical charlatanism ("miracles" and "self-renewing icons"*).

d. Unabated control over the maintenance of legality in church matters, *mainly on the part of clergy*,** and struggling against violations.[85]

The Council sent an instructional letter in June 1949 that indicated if a church building was not used for six to twelve months due to lack of a priest, the regional commissioner could revoke the church's registration.[86] This letter in fact untied the hands of those commissioners who saw the main significance of their work as an active struggle "against the remnants of capitalism

---

*A "self-renewing icon" is one that suddenly becomes bright, as if it had just been cleaned or freshly painted, but without human intervention.—Ed.

**Emphasis added.

in the common consciousness by placing maximum limitations on activity by religious communities." Waiting for the expiration of the set minimum period of time for an inactive church, some commissioners delayed in every way possible the registration of priests appointed by the bishop in order to tell the patriarchate, "Officially, that church does not exist."[87] In an instructional letter in November of that same year, Karpov expressed bewilderment, "Why are all commissioners sticking to the period of six months . . . haste . . . a strict approach. . . . Such work in many regions has led to this: Clergy are forming the opinion that the Council is following a new policy in its work that aims at limiting church activity."[88]

As a rule, churches and chapels were closed demonstratively during the Divine Liturgy and accompanied by rudeness, insults to the religious feelings of believers, and outrages against sacred objects. Bells were pulled down; icons were broken off and trampled on, sometimes with shooting and profanity.[89]

All this could not help but evoke a multitude of complaints from believers. Indignant and confident that they were right, envoys traveled from the depths of the country to the Council for Russian Orthodox Church Affairs. Thus, the Council received 897 people with complaints about the illegal activity of local officials in 1951; in 1953, 878 people; in 1954, 1,171 people.[90]

Neither efforts of believers nor appeals from the Moscow Patriarchate could change the situation—the number of Orthodox churches steadily decreased after 1948 (see Table 2.2 below).[91]

One must note that it is impossible to consider the problem of church closures in the late 1940s and 1950s solely as an aggressive policy of state authorities or as a policy directed toward nothing less than destroying the church. Reduction in the number of Orthodox churches occurred mainly through the closing of rural parishes. The reason for this lay in the socioeconomic conditions that gripped the Soviet countryside in the 1940s and early 1950s. Economic hardships—excessive taxation, extorting all the "surpluses" from the collective farms, symbolic pay in "gold stars"* for work done by collective farmers, and finally the drought of 1946 that caused famine in regions of Russia, Ukraine, and Moldavia—brought the countryside to the edge of catastrophe. Escape from collective farms, despite existing passport restrictions, became a mass phenomenon. Between 1949 and 1953, the number of able-bodied workers on collective farms decreased by 3.3 million people.[92]

---

*The Russian phrase "*za palochki*" (translated here as "gold stars") is colloquial and ironic. It means to work without pay or as a gift. Collective farmers in the Soviet era often provided a day of free labor in exchange for a vertical mark (*palochka*) by their names in the work registry.—Ed.

Table 2.2

Year ending	Total number of churches	Number of churches removed from registration	Number of rural churches removed from registration
January 1, 1949	14,445	186	no data
January 1, 1950	14,323	443	no data
January 1, 1951	13,913	410	379
January 1, 1952	13,786	127	111
January 1, 1953	13,555	264	255

An Orthodox parish church could not survive under such economic conditions. Parishioners basically provided labor for its vital activities, but the priest's income depended on parish revenues. Reports from commissioners to the Council and from diocesan bishops to the Synod gave evidence on the disastrous condition of rural Orthodox churches. Bishop Tovii of Sverdlovsk, Irbit, and Chelyabinsk acknowledged at the beginning of the 1950s that rural parishes "had reached the end of their rope." Having studied the financial reports of seven rural churches in the Chelyabinsk region, the bishop concluded that it was impossible for them to continue functioning because "the aforesaid parishes currently are unable to maintain the church building in proper order, much less to guarantee even a minimal standard of living for their parish clergy."[93] Archbishop Antonii of Stavropol "came away with painful impressions" during his travels around the diocese in 1951 and said, "There is desolation and poverty in the villages."[94]

Many diocesan bishops tried everything possible to preserve active churches and support religiosity within the population. Rural parishes in many dioceses were freed from support payments to their diocesan administrations, which in some cases provided financial assistance to these parishes. Clergy often transferred from one parish to another for the purpose of improving conditions in the community. Diocesan administrations took steps to strengthen discipline among the clergy. For example, the agenda of a diocesan congress in the Chelyabinsk region in 1951 included only one issue, clergy discipline. Many bishops and priests preached more frequently.

On the one hand, this irritated local authorities. On the other, it worried the patriarchate. The Synod adopted a resolution in August 1948 in which it reminded clergy that, according to the Regulations on the Russian Orthodox Church, "The structure and routine of church life should not prevent parishioners from fulfilling their duties as citizens. . . . Episcopal leaders should not permit the performance of liturgical acts in public places (prayers for rain, religious processions), because this is a clear violation of legislation on the separation of church and state."[95] Under pressure from the Council,[96] the

privatization

Synod passed a resolution on November 16 of that year placing limitations on preaching by clergy, saying, "Sermons should be free of any interference in politics and have a purely ecclesiastical character." The Synod also recommended that clergy read sermons only on Sundays and church holidays.[97]

These conditions attracted new attention to the practice of using attached priests. From the viewpoint of church leaders, this allowed them first to keep churches open and second to battle successfully with illegal priests and religious sectarians. Apparently not recognizing the seriousness of the situation surrounding religious issues, the Synod decided in February 1949 to introduce the use of attached priests and petitioned the Council for Russian Orthodox Church Affairs "for permission to register them in the provinces."[98] Despite the Council's negative reaction, the Moscow Patriarchate's Department of Management distributed a letter to the dioceses that recommended the introduction of attached priests.

Karpov in turn instructed commissioners, "The Council does not endorse or accept this decision. . . . Do not allow the introduction of attached priests."[99] In July 1949, the Cultural Bureau already reckoned it was necessary to recommend that the patriarch "temporarily rescind" the Synod's decision.[100]

During a meeting in the Council's offices on March 8, 1949, Karpov recommended to Patriarch Aleksii, "Generally, the Synod and the Moscow Patriarchate should think about comprehensive measures that would limit activity in churches and parishes." When the patriarch referred to the resolutions already adopted in 1948, Karpov remarked, "These measures are not enough. I would hope that the Synod would think about what can and should still be done in this direction." The patriarch answered, "Very well. A small circle of us will think about this further, and I will tell you later."[101]

Indeed, the Synod ratified a message from the patriarch "To All Bishops" on March 17. Touching on events in Saratov, Patriarch Aleksii wrote, "Are the clergy guilty? Yes. They should have foreseen [the need] . . . to give a warning to the people who were praying and by this to guard themselves from any reprimand." The patriarch demanded vigilance from diocesan bishops and the most serious attitude to their duties as archpastors because, "An abundance of negative aspects in the activity of both ordinary clergy and bishops causes great temptation in all circles of society and demands that church authorities adopt measures for putting church life in order." Among the immediate measures named was a revision in the number of dioceses.[102]

Patriarch

The patriarch adopted a key measure at the end of 1949. He issued a message to bishops that forbade organizing religious processions to "the Jordan River" (a rite that had existed for centuries in the Orthodox Church). Instead, the blessing of water was to be conducted within "the fences surrounding church grounds."[103]

State organs tightened control over clergy activity. The Council required its commissioners to include information in their reports on preaching by clergy and to revoke the registration of priests who organized religious processions or outdoor prayer services.[104] Twelve clergy were removed from the registry in the first six months of 1949.[105] Local authorities in many areas of the country acted on their own initiative at the beginning of 1949 and forbade the performance of religious rites in homes. In a host of regions in Ukraine and Belorussia, large fines were imposed on priests for baptizing children in homes at the request of believers. As a result, not a single home religious rite was recorded anywhere in the country during the first quarter of 1949.[106]

Authorities tried to eliminate undesirable activity by clergy. Tightened passport procedures in 1948 and a system of restricted regions proved to be convenient instruments for attaining this goal. Karpov openly wrote in an instructional letter to commissioners, "An established procedure for using passport rules against clergy gives you an option both now and in the future to send away those whose presence in a given place is undesirable."[107] Commissioners were required to review all lists of clergy and to ask for information from police organs (the MVD and MGB). Commissioners then were to deny registration to clergy for whom the police provided the necessary data. Priests were sent out of restricted regions and into new areas that permitted their residence. They remained unregistered for long periods of time, which meant that they could not earn money to live. A wave of complaints to the Council forced its leaders to send out supplemental instructions that said passport rules should not be used to send away masses of churchmen.[108]

The Council conducted a census of members of church councils around the country in the second half of 1948. This census, in Karpov's opinion, provided the possibility to expose persons among church activists who did not inspire confidence. Measures followed to replace these persons gradually. Offering this process as a feasible contribution to the struggle against enemies of the people, Karpov reported to the government that the initial stage of the census had already led to a certain weeding out of persons who did not wish to provide their personal information.[109]

A new wave of repression broke over the ranks of Orthodox clergy, although arrests of churchmen were not so widespread as in the 1930s. A peculiarity of 1948–49 was an increase in the number of "repeat offenders," that is, clergy who prior to the war did time in prison for the same crimes of "anti-Soviet propaganda and agitation" or "concealed counterrevolution." For example, Archbishop Manuil Lemeshevskii of Chkalov and Kurgan was arrested for the fourth time in 1948.

1948-49

The Moscow Patriarchate tried to help families of those repressed and presented "Regulations for Pensions and Extraordinary Financial Assistance to Clergy of the Russian Orthodox Church" for the government's approval. This proposal envisioned establishing a special fund for widows and minor orphans. The regulations were approved by the Council of Ministers on February 21, 1948.[110] The Council for Russian Orthodox Church Affairs, however, adopted a "Supplement" to these Regulations on December 25, 1948. This supplement can only be regarded as an antihumanitarian act, since it recommended that the Moscow Patriarchate not provide pensions to families of clergymen who were serving prison sentences, had been "disenfranchised" [because of criminal convictions—Ed.], or who had died during incarceration.[111]

As the public campaign against nonconformity gained momentum, official pressure increased for limiting institutions for theological education. Suffice it to say that 189 faculty members and students from theological seminaries and academies were arrested in 1948–49 on the standard charge of "anti-Soviet agitation."[112]

In response to comments by the Central Committee on increasing control over admissions to and the activity of institutions for theological education, the Council's Department of Inspectors developed new instructions in October 1948 for commissioners, which outlined procedures for supervising the activity of the institutions.[113] At the same time, a conference of commissioners from regions in which theological seminaries were located adopted a new way of tracking recruitment of students. The conference recommended that commissioners use various sources for receiving information on the internal life of seminaries and academies as well as on attitudes held by the student body and faculty.[114]

The patriarch was informed of the opinion of the Council (and, as it came to be, of the government too) on the undesirability of expanding the network of institutions for theological education. Thus, neither the seminary in Lvov nor the academy in Kiev was opened,[115] despite requests from the Archbishop of Lithuania and a petition from the Synod.[116] The seminary in Vilnius was also not reopened, and the Council considered it "inexpedient" to open a theological seminary in Novosibirsk as requested by the patriarch and the Synod.[117] Pressure was so strong, it seems, that in June 1949 Patriarch Aleksii expressed his intention to review some seminaries and "possibly close a few of them in order to enlarge others." Karpov approved these intentions.[118]

Patriarch Aleksii announced his intention to close the departments for the history of Russian religious thought at the theological academies in Moscow and Leningrad under pressure from the Council in the fall of 1948. A lack of textbooks and qualified personnel served as the official reasons.[119] Meanwhile, the Ministry of Higher Education of the USSR approved a document entitled, "Changes to the Regulations on Institutions for Theological Education." As a result, the curriculum for theological academies excluded the study of logic, Christian psychology, the history of philosophy, and Christian pedagogy. The curriculum for theological seminaries also excluded such disciplines as the foundations of psychology and a survey of philosophical studies.[120]

The Leningrad Theological Academy introduced the practice of recording lectures in shorthand starting in the 1948–49 academic year. On one hand, this innovation resolved the problem of providing textbooks to students; on the other, it offered a means for controlling the contents of lectures. Karpov persistently recommended that the patriarchate also introduce shorthand recording in Moscow's academy.

A change in the rules concerning the military draft for students in seminaries and academies complicated the work of the institutions. The change reversed state resolutions in force since 1944 that granted draft deferments to those students. The Council instructed its commissioners to inform bishops and leaders of educational institutions about this change in January 1949.[121] Adoption of this decision threatened the whole educational process. Hoping to somehow rectify the situation, the Moscow Patriarchate petitioned for the granting of deferments, if only to students in their final year to allow them to complete their studies.

But in March 1950 Karpov opposed granting deferments, "because church institutions can become a distinctive base for sheltering unstable elements among men eligible for the draft."[122] Nonetheless, numerous petitions from the patriarch and members of the Synod had an effect. On instructions from Sovnarkom on October 18, 1950, the Ministry of War was allowed to grant draft deferments to all students in theological academies and to students in their final year at theological seminaries.[123]

Control over personnel policies of the Moscow Patriarchate also became stricter. Members of the Council for Russian Orthodox Church Affairs—not the patriarchate or the Synod—made the final decisions on appointments to episcopal sees and transfers for the senior hierarchy. Karpov shed his former mask as an observer on the sidelines who made cautious resolutions such as "I do not oppose," and "This is an internal church matter." He now openly directed the patriarchate on whom to appoint and where. Three examples of this were:

Record of a conversation between the Council's chairman and Patriarch Aleksii on February 17, 1949:

Karpov: "I now have a proposal for a dismissal. The person is Vladimir Andreevich Sretenskii who, if he is not dismissed, might be subject to the same fate as Archimandrite Veniamin. He incorrectly interprets the Stalinist Constitution to young people at the academy."

Patriarch: "This is disgraceful! Sretenskii is a completely useless person to me. He teaches English poorly. . . . How can there be people who still do not understand all the benefits of the treatment that the church receives from the state!"[124]

Record of a conversation on June 12, 1951:

Karpov: "When and how does the patriarch plan to carry out my recommendation for replacing Archpriest Razumovskii with Citizen Shishkin in the Department of External Relations?"

Patriarch Aleksii: "This would be most useful, but a conflict is possible with Metropolitan Nikolai."[125]

Record of a conversation on March 8, 1949.

Patriarch Aleksii: "The episcopal sees in Saratov, Nikolaev, Kirovograd, and Petrozavodsk are vacant—they are not occupied by anyone."

Karpov: "Isn't it possible to assign them to bishops in neighboring dioceses in order to delay bringing new men into the episcopal hierarchy for now?" Dissatisfied and confused, the patriarch agreed.[126]

Descriptions of representative bishops that Karpov compiled for the government and the Central Committee became harsher and sometimes insulting ("sanctimonious and a windbag," "a decrepit old man") and clearly filled with propagandistic clichés ("an extreme obscurantist," "a secret reactionary"). Karpov informed the government that "a small group of six to eight men stand out for their religiosity and are very demanding." Those named in this group included Archbishop Luke of the Crimea, Archbishop Antonii of Stavropol, Archbishop Nikolai of Alma Ata, and Bishop Gurii of Ulyanovsk.[127] In Karpov's opinion, however, most bishops were "people whose personal qualities made them inclined to careerism—money-grubbers and troublemakers. Most bishops are not distinguished by particular religiosity and observe monastic vows of celibacy only on paper."[128]

Karpov formulated the Council's position on the higher clergy of the Orthodox Church as follows: "The Council is not interested in having diocesan bishops in the USSR who would be energetic and theologically educated men. A certain number of cultured and theologically educated hierarchs is necessary, however, for the church's work abroad and to represent the church [to foreigners]."[129]

An openly discriminatory policy was followed in treating more active and independent-minded bishops. They were forced into retirement or transferred to distant dioceses through actions of the Holy Synod and the patriarch. The fact that many bishops were in their declining years made resolution of the problem easier. Five metropolitans, twenty-two archbishops, and thirty-three bishops were dispersed across the country in 1953; two-thirds of them were over sixty years old.[130]

Three bishops were arrested between 1948 and 1952.[131] Archbishop Luke also remained under threat of new arrest. The situation that developed around him in January–April 1949 best illustrates the mechanism for removal of undesired bishops.

In January 1949, Secretary Soloviev of the regional party committee for the Crimea accused Luke of the following crime: "He openly and systematically preaches sympathy for tsarist autocracy and hostility toward the Soviet regime and its leaders. . . . He rallies all reactionary forces in the Crimea around him."[132]

The Council verified this information and concluded, "The anti-Soviet nature of the archbishop's preaching has not been established." The MGB also conducted its own investigation. Karpov wrote to D.T. Shepilov on January 29, 1949, "If MGB USSR does not have grounds for arresting Archbishop Luke for counterrevolutionary activity, it is inexpedient to remove him from the Crimean episcopal see. He is seventy-two years old and has stopped practicing medicine due to failing eyesight."[133]

In a letter written after discussion of this matter with the patriarch, Karpov laid out a proposal from the Council to the Central Committee concerning Archbishop Luke. "The Council proposes the following: The patriarch will invite Luke to Moscow. Then Metropolitan Nikolai will present the patriarch's grievances and warn Luke that the patriarch intends to force him into retirement and strictly censure his activity through a decision of the Synod. Nikolai will recommend that Luke himself request retirement. If he does not agree to do this, he will be dismissed by decision of the Synod that will give reasons for his dismissal. But, the patriarch thinks it best if Luke retires 'at his own request.'"[134] The archbishop did indeed arrive in Moscow on March 28. After a conversation with the patriarch, Luke agreed to preach at only three regular church services each week and then cut back to only two services a week.[135] He was not dismissed.   *Patriarch*

Karpov did not exaggerate when he told the government two things: "Patriarch Aleksii holds steadfast positions more than loyal ones in terms of the domestic and foreign policies of Soviet power," and, "the patriarch accepts and implements all recommendations from the Council."[136] Still, Karpov repeated with unwavering sympathy the positive personal characteristics of Patriarch Aleksii: sincerity ("by which he clearly distinguishes himself from all other bishops"), sociability, and simplicity. The patriarch's crippling arthritis required him to devote much time to treatment. By his own admission, he relieved the compulsory solitude by "regularly watching television—an activity concealed somewhat from the clergy."[137] Karpov mentioned, "The patriarch devotes more attention to domestic issues of church life and activity and shows little initiative in issues related to church activity abroad." Despite the depths of his loyalty to the state, the patriarch reacted harshly and painfully to cases of crude administrative measures in the provinces and to the reality that not a single church was opened in the whole Soviet Union after March 1948.[138]

Indeed, Patriarch Aleksii experienced a crisis in 1948–49. The discontinuation in opening churches, combined with the strengthening of antireligious propaganda that led to political attacks against clergy and laity, caused the patriarch to ask the Council repeatedly about the possibility of a meeting with Stalin. Aleksii mainly wanted to clarify the attitude of the state toward the church.[139] The patriarch endured delays over this matter with difficulty. Even in March 1949, he awaited a meeting with Stalin and said, "Undoubtedly, our meeting with I.V. Stalin will not take place as long as the painful impression of the incident in Saratov has not abated."[140]

In the winter of 1948–49, the patriarch became depressed over the sudden end to unofficial and official meetings with leaders of the Council and personal meetings with Karpov. In accordance with orders "from above,"[141] the Council did not send gifts or greetings to Patriarch Aleksii on his name day (the anniversary of the day that he took monastic vows and received his monastic name). Nonetheless, Karpov thought that it was essential to present a gift to Aleksii and offered the following justification for his views: "We have noticed that national church leaders, for a variety of reasons, are obviously uncertain about continued stability in church-state relations. If there are no gifts or official meetings, the patriarch will regard this as a setback."[142]

Karpov also declined an offer to accompany the patriarch on a steamboat cruise along the Volga and Oka rivers and refused an invitation to travel to the patriarch's summer home in Odessa. Reporting to the government, Karpov noted that the patriarch suffered "emotional outbursts" and "frustration" because his invitations were refused. Karpov then proposed to send Aleksii a congratulatory telegram on his birthday in November 1949.

Metropolitan Nikolai kept Council leaders informed of the patriarch's mood and utterances (strictly speaking, not only about the patriarch's utterances and health but also about the state of affairs in the patriarchate and about Russian Orthodox bishops in general).[143] It is impossible to pretend that Nikolai did so under duress. This practice without a doubt revealed his personal characteristics. At meetings in the Council's offices, the metropolitan often expressed dissatisfaction with the activities of the patriarch. "The patriarch does not make decisions independently." "He often changes his mind." "He forgets instructions that he has given." In the opinion of Nikolai and other members of the Synod, the reason for the patriarch's lack of independence was found in the influence of his former lay brother, Daniel Ostapov. Ostapov's interference in all affairs of the Moscow Patriarchate provoked indignation from many bishops.

Karpov himself pondered the unanswered question, "What exactly connects them (the patriarch and Ostapov)?" An "unsubstantiated rumor" even circulated to the effect that Ostapov's son Leonid was really the son of Patriarch Aleksii and Ostapov's wife. People said it was no coincidence that the patriarch in 1951 issued an order for accepting students from the graduating class of the Moscow Seminary (one of whom was Leonid) into the Moscow Theological Academy without requiring them to take entrance exams.[144]

Whatever the truth, Karpov knew how to use intrigue among church leaders, the personal qualities of bishops, and existing disagreements among them in order "to channel the activities of the church's national leadership for the interests of the state," as he expressed it to the government.[145] Karpov gave a totally accurate characterization of Metropolitan Nikolai:

> He is very proud and vain. He is greedy for money and presents, cunning and reserved, and sometimes a liar. Outwardly, relations between Patriarch Aleksii and Nikolai are normal; in reality, they hate one another. The patriarch justifiably thinks Nikolai is a hypocrite and capable of any intrigue within the patriarchate for the sake of personal glory. Other metropolitans and bishops in general also do not like him. By attracting attention to himself (through participation in national and international conferences in defense of peace) and through his oratorical skills, Nikolai promotes himself through the church press as an important person in society.[146]

Karpov was able to abolish the sermon section that Nikolai edited for the *Journal of the Moscow Patriarchate* by using the metropolitan's peculiar qualities against him. During a meeting at the Council in August 1952, Nikolai and Karpov had a conversation that was recorded in shorthand and reported to the Central Committee. Karpov said, "The Council has several statements from various groups (in fact, the Council did not have even a single such statement, since it had never received any).* These statements say that Metropolitan Nikolai's sermons are bewildering because they often refer to the 'sinfulness' of this life and the 'purity' of the afterlife." Nikolai was troubled and demanded to see these statements but did not agree with them, since he

---

*The remark in parentheses was added by Karpov.

always exhorted people in his sermons to love and labor for the Motherland.[147]

As a result, Metropolitan Nikolai stopped publishing his sermons in the *Journal* and thus—as Karpov underlined—"no one wrote any more, so the sermon section of the *Journal* was abolished."[148]

Following the crisis of 1948–49, relations between the state and the Moscow Patriarchate stabilized at the beginning of the 1950s. They followed their previous course in many ways. Various forms of relations between the Council for Russian Orthodox Church Affairs and the patriarchate were restored, thanks to a letter written by Suslov and Karpov that listed procedures for relations between the Council and the patriarch. The government approved the letter in February 1952.[149]

Patriarch Aleksii was awarded his second Order of the Red Banner of Labor in November 1952 on the occasion of his 75th birthday, and his name was included in the *Great Soviet Encyclopedia.*[150] Episcopal ordinations resumed at the end of 1949, and nine men had been consecrated as bishops by the middle of 1952. A representative of a new generation was ordained bishop in 1953—Mikhail Chub, who had graduated from the Leningrad Theological Academy.[151] Starting in April 1949, the Russian Orthodox Church actively participated in the fight for peace. Metropolitan Nikolai was chosen as a member of the Standing Committee of the All-World Council for Peace. The Moscow Patriarchate from this time on played a leading role in the international peace movement.[152]

The church's status inside the country stabilized at the beginning of the 1950s. The patriarchate and diocesan administrations took steps to strengthen parishes financially and to secure cadres of clergy in parishes. Demands from bishops that priests hold more than one position and serve vacant neighboring churches yielded results. The number of churches where services were conducted on an irregular schedule declined from 3,671 in 1952 to 1,525 in 1953.[153] Cadres of priests were replenished from men who had retired from civilian jobs, had a "deep religious persuasion, and knew church reading and singing." Bishop Veniamin Fedchenkov of Rostov alone ordained twenty-eight men into holy orders at the end of 1951.[154]

Statistics on Orthodox clergy for these years are given in Table 2.3 (below).[155]

Parish income throughout the country remained constant, although it was significantly lower in rural churches compared with urban ones. An increase in the number of religious rites, especially baptisms, was seen beginning in 1950. The number of people participating in major religious holidays did not decrease. Church attendance on these days continued to be high, according to estimates by the Council for Russian Orthodox Church Affairs.

Antireligious propaganda subsided after the commotion of 1948–49.

Table 2.3

| Date | Total number of priests | Towns | Number of priests in: | |
			Worker's settlements	Rural areas
January 1, 1950	13,235	3,013	647	9,575
January 1, 1951	12,374	2,903	652	8,819
January 1, 1952	12,254	3,011	629	8,614
January 1, 1953	12,031	3,174	626	8,231

Articles on this subject moved from the pages of national publications to the regional and large-circulation mass media, primarily those intended for young people.

Material on antireligious topics rarely appeared in print at the beginning of the 1950s and turned up mostly in the form of feature stories, signed with pseudonyms such as Zorkii and Strogii.* The stories generally contained only fabrications and anecdotes from the lives of clergy. Far from any scientific understanding of religious matters and atheistic propaganda, articles of this type insulted the religious sensibilities of believers and resulted in a multitude of complaints.

Orthodox clergy at the beginning of the 1950s reacted strongly to the appearance of such publications and regarded them as violations of the legislation on religion. They sent newspaper clippings to their regional commissioners and even directly to the Council. The leadership of the Council, in turn, informed the government and Central Committee about these facts. For example, on July 3, 1952, the Council sent Suslov excerpts from a feature story published in *Okulovskii kommunar* [Member of the Okulovka Commune], a newspaper published in the Novgorod region. Karpov noted in the accompanying cover letter that contents of this article ran contrary to the Constitution of the USSR.[156]

The struggle against religion did not cease in many regions of the country. Ideological activists in the party, however, were unable to lean on directives "from above" in their "struggle."

In reality, the party had not adopted a single resolution on antireligious propaganda since the 1930s. Even the party congress of October 1952 did not set goals for the struggle against religion. Delegates did not use the phrase "religious worldview" in their speeches. They replaced it with neutral terminology such as "remnants of a lack of culture" or "superstitions" or "preju-

---

*These fictitious names are a play on Russian adjectives that mean "vigilant" (*zorkii*) and "strict" (*strogii*).—Ed.

dices."[157] The new Charter for the Communist Party of the Soviet Union that was adopted at the Nineteenth Congress did not list the struggle against religion as one of the obligations of party members.[158] Lacking support even from the Central Committee, members of the state bureaucracy continued to fight against religion and its supporters using weapons borrowed mainly from the arsenal of the 1930s. D. Erofeev, division head of the district party committee for Gavrilov Posad [suburb] in the Ivanovo region, summoned ten men to meet with him. They were all workers in Soviet enterprises who had relatives serving on parish "twenties."* Erofeev threatened to fire them unless they exerted influence on their relatives.[159] A college student named Klius, daughter of a priest, lost her place at the conservatory in Lvov because she refused to renounce her faith at a public student meeting.[160] Complaints about persecution of believers who lost their jobs came from Molotov, Ivanovo, Kemerovo, and other regions. In the Chuvash ASSR, authorities in one district conducted a general "census" of all believers (as a result, most rural residents appeared on the lists).[161]

Crude and illegal administrative measures were used against clergy; at times, these bordered on hooliganism. Authorities from the village of Verkholes in the Brest region prevented a priest from conducting Easter services in 1952 with threats of fines, while in the Zhiromir region "they held a priest under armed guard overnight in order to disrupt Easter services."[162] The most widespread and effective method for fighting the church was levying excessive taxes on parishes and their priests. N.A. Negreiskii, party organizer for the village of Molodov in the Rovno region, expressed the views of supporters of this method quite well, "We must levy such taxes on the church so that it gives up and goes bankrupt. The church does not have any rights in our eyes. The church is the enemy of the state because it preaches capitalism. I am tsar and God and military commander in Molodov. I speak—and my will is obeyed!"[163]

Conducting antireligious work through such methods was a consequence of generally low competency in the nation's party, government, and propaganda bureaucracies.[164] Local activists displayed complete incompetence and a lack of basic culture when it came to understanding the nature of church-state relations. Karpov corroborated this point in particular through memoranda that he sent to Agitprop. The following questions were posed to student propagandists in a course organized by the Central Committee in the Kirovo-

---

*Soviet law required every religious community to sign an agreement on maintaining the church building given for its use. The agreement had to be signed by twenty people from that community who then assumed continuing responsibility for oversight of the parish. This group was called "the twenty" (*dvadtsatka*).—Ed.

grad region in September 1951: "Can the secretary of a Party organization enter a church for control purposes? Does the chairman of a collective farm have the right to drive people out of church on Sunday? Can a member of the Communist Party be a priest or other employee of a church? Can a priest conduct wedding ceremonies and baptisms without permission from his village soviet? Is it a crime for the chairman of a collective farm to give an automobile or cart to a church for use in weddings? Is it possible to appear at a funeral for a distinguished foreman or team leader that is being conducted by a priest?"[165] The contents of these documents hardly require additional commentary. However, the very fact that Karpov had to send such memoranda to Agitprop attests to the minor position of religious issues on the radar screen of the highest party structures. Although official documents avoided the topic of atheistic education, it occupied a more prominent place in the work of Agitprop.

Regular reports from the Council for Russian Orthodox Church Affairs to the Central Committee became traditional and provided information on the condition of religion in the country, the status of the Orthodox Church, and characteristics of its senior clergy. Leaders of the Council also required commissioners at the beginning of the 1950s to give a more detailed and complete analysis of activity by parish clergy and to inform the Council immediately of evidence of manifestations of religiosity among the general population. The Central Committee used the Council's data to inform Central Committee secretaries, secretaries of regional committees, and Central Committee instructors who taught party seminars at various levels.[166]

Accumulation of this material was no simple matter. Agitprop reviewed issues related to establishing antireligious propaganda in various regions of the country, checked on progress, and made decisions. Thus, in November 1949 Agitprop reviewed the matter of "The Status of Atheistic Propaganda in the Tatar ASSR and Other Republics and Regions."[167] On instructions from the Central Committee's Secretariat, Agitprop verified the status of antireligious work in Moldavia in January 1950. The verification found, "Neither the Moldavian Central Committee nor district party committees nor institutions for cultural education had led an adequate struggle against the activities of churchmen." Agitprop required the Moldavian Central Committee to develop practical measures for strengthening large-scale party and cultural-educational work in the republic.[168]

Decisions made by the Central Committee itself in the early 1950s usually came in response to cases where communists participated in religious rites. Material did not only come from the Council for Russian Orthodox Church Affairs. During this period, information about those cases became part of reporting by staff correspondents for the newspaper *Pravda*. The Central Committee quickly created investigating commissions to verify material submitted by correspondents to their editors at *Pravda*. These commissions operated in Moldavia, the Kuzbass, Kemerovo, and other regions of the country.[169] Through Agitprop's verification of "the use of churchmen by communists," the regional party committee for Ivanovo on June 20, 1950, adopted a secret resolution with the lengthy title, "On Shortcomings in Establishment of Scientific-Atheistic Propaganda and Facts Concerning Distortion of the Party Line Relating to Religion on the Part of Certain Local Party Leaders and Soviet and Social Organizations."[170] In Kuibyshev, participation by communists from the regional automobile trust in the May 1953 Orthodox funeral of its senior engineer resulted in measures that were influenced not only by ideology. After a commission from the Central Committee verified the work of the party organization in Kuibyshev, a series of resolutions were adopted on deficiencies in scientific-atheistic propaganda and on measures for improving it at the regional, urban, and district levels. Four senior staff members in the regional automobile trust were expelled from the party, fired from their jobs, and received numerous reprimands "for loss of political vigilance."[171]

In accordance with Central Committee policies, measures were also taken in cases where communists committed gross violations of legislation on religious cults. Thus, the Central Committee demanded an explanation from Novikov, chairman of the regional executive committee in Stavropol, for making "baseless accusations" to Council Commissioner Chudin in January 1950 concerning insufficiently energetic work against churchmen. Novikov gave his "explanation" to the Central Committee in writing.[172] Steps were also taken, per Central Committee policies, on the above-mentioned complaint from the Brest region. A severe reprimand was recorded in the permanent files for the party organizer and the chairman of the Verkholes village soviet "for permitting rude conduct and illegal administrative action." Comrade Los´, secretary of the Ukrainian Party's district committee in Iarun, was singled out for "weakness in political work and in selection of cadres."[173]

Agitprop also took steps relating to the organization of propagandizing atheistic work. So-called brigades of lecturers specializing in antireligious propaganda formed at Suslov's initiative within the framework of the Central Committee's lectureship group. The brigades traveled for extended visits to regions where the religious situation was unacceptable. Per materials presented to the Council for Russian Orthodox Church Affairs, brigades of lecturers were sent "to provide help to district party committees and to conduct educational work." In the first half of the 1950s, lecture groups from Agitprop worked from two to four weeks in Moldavia, the Tatar ASSR, Buriat-Mongolia, and the regions of Kursk, Smolensk, Voronezh, and Stanislav (western Ukraine).[174]

Thus, the government "distanced" itself from the problem of church-state relations. As a consequence, the transfer of initiative for solving problems in the religious sphere to party structures (which characterized the second half of the 1950s in Odintsov's opinion)[175] appeared complete by the end of the 1940s. Agitprop eagerly sought control over the country's religious life in the first half of the 1950s. I believe this attests to the fact that Suslov (who headed Agitprop from the beginning of 1949), D.T. Shepilov, and others continued to hold views expressed in the draft resolution presented to the Central Committee in 1949, "Measures for Strengthening the Propagation of Scientific-Atheistic Knowledge." Of course, the Central Committee took into account its experience related to the 1949 resolution. It could not ignore Stalin's orders prohibiting adoption of that resolution or any general decision in the area of church-state relations. Therefore, there could be no discussion around developing and adopting such a document at the national level during Stalin's lifetime.

Party ideologists, leaders of the Russian Orthodox Church, and state authorities all understood that the duration for sufficiently "calm" church-state relations at the beginning of the 1950s was completely dependent on the length of one person's life—that of Joseph Stalin.

From Propagandistic Attacks to Stability in Relations with the Church

Stalin's death in March 1953 and the emergence of new faces among the country's leaders naturally caused anxiety within the Council for Russian Orthodox Church Affairs and the Moscow Patriarchate. How would the transfer of power and subsequent changes in political policy affect church-state relations?

Patriarch Aleksii expressed concern over measures for strengthening government ministries. "Will the Council for Russian Orthodox Church Affairs exist in the future? What will its status be? . . . . Will there be a change in the existing regulations on communication between the church and the state?"[176] Although Karpov calmed the patriarch in a letter sent to him in Odessa in April 1953 ("I do not see any basis for your concern, since no changes in Regulations for the Council have been introduced"), leaders of the Council were highly anxious. What would attitudes "at the top" be toward their agency and the policies that it carried out?

Over the course of a year—through June 1954—the Council asked both the government and the Central Committee "to give instructions to the Council for its future work" and sent a detailed list of problems about which it wanted to know the opinion of the government and Central Committee.[177] These included the following issues: new regulations for the Council, a new law on religious cults, opening new churches and chapels (the Council thought it was "expedient to open from ten to twenty churches per year in places where this is necessary"), activity of unregistered communities (the Council proposed that "functioning churches should be registered, thereby legalizing their activity"), monasteries ("so that tonsuring of monks takes place only with the patriarch's approval"), the activity of priests, and the status of the church in western regions of Ukraine.

In addition, the Council for Russian Orthodox Church Affairs together with the Council for Affairs of Religious Cults repeatedly sent the government and the Central Committee proposals for uniting the two Councils. Their chairmen—Karpov and Polianskii—justified this proposal by saying unification would allow a reduction of staff of the two structures, improve the quality of work, eliminate redundancies in their work, and, finally, end official inequality of religious confessions in the Soviet Union.[178] In May 1954, Karpov wrote the Central Committee asking them to provide him with help and support and stressed, "I can get them [help and support] only from the Central Committee."[179]

But the government seemed to have forgotten about both Councils.[180] No "instructions" came to the Council in either 1953 or 1954. It was not clear who was now personally supervising the Council's work for the government. Voroshilov's name disappeared from the list of addressees for memoranda in April. After that time, they were formally directed to Malenkov as head of the Council of Ministers. The absence of any reaction to the Council's letters by the government forced Karpov to appeal to Nikita Khrushchev, first secretary of the Central Committee, in April 1954. In taking such a step, Karpov certainly considered previous cooperative work with Khrushchev— decisions on a host of matters connected with Russian Orthodox activity in Ukraine, primarily connected to liquidation of the Uniate Church—and thought it possible to direct Khrushchev's attention to the Council's problems and to receive his support. The letter's informal tone testifies to this, as does its confiding character and unofficial greeting to the first secretary: "Much esteemed Nikita Sergeevich! . . . Dear Nikita Sergeevich! . . . With great esteem." Karpov again listed the main questions that "must be discussed" and for which "I must receive instructions." He especially emphasized that, "I am not being guided by any personal motives and am concerned only to preserve for now our government's interests in this complex ideological field."[181]

The bureaucracy of the Central Committee sent this letter back with instructions "to reformulate and address [it] to the Central Committee." As a result, the revision turned out impersonal, dry, and lacking a specific addressee.[182] It also remained unanswered.

Continuing to direct "proposals for its future work" to the government and the Central Committee, the Council essentially followed its own views in relations with Russian Orthodox organizations in 1953–54, as formulated in memoranda. The Council's position did not exceed the limits of ecclesiastical policy that had been set during and after the war. If the Council's position did not promote a revival of religious life, at least it did not prevent such a revival around the country in the conditions existing in the mid-1950s.

Actually, a revival of the country's religious life clearly took place in the second half of 1953, assisted in no small measure by the energetic activity of clergy. The number of petitions from believers for opening churches increased sharply. In 1953, the total submitted was 990 (most of these arrived in the second half of the year); in 1954, there were 1,361.[183] Actions taken by many diocesan bishops to strengthen parish churches and establish order in them led to a decrease in the number of churches where services were held on an irregular schedule. As noted earlier, that number dropped from 3,671 (in 1952) to 1,525 (in 1953).[184]

A severe shortage of clergy in the Russian Orthodox Church forced it to intensify "recruiting" work of parish priests to persuade young people to enroll in institutions for theological education. The Education Committee of the Moscow Patriarchate took concurrent steps to strengthen the financial base of those institutions and to raise the levels of education and training. Considerable credit for this belonged to Metropolitan Grigorii Chukov, chairman of the Education Committee. On his initiative, and for the first time in the ten-year history of the church's new theological schools, a seminar was held in July 1953 for rectors, vice-rectors, inspectors, and instructors from institutions for theological education. The seminar developed and authorized a common curriculum and a charter for theological seminaries. Overall, it reached a consensus on matters of education and training.[185] Finances and living conditions for students improved. Their stipends were raised, a schedule of four meals per day was introduced, and the number of excursions to museums, theaters, and movies increased. The patriarchate replaced rectors, vice rectors, and inspectors in several seminaries. Institutions for theological education became stronger by recruiting young theologians from the new generation of graduates.[186] As a result, after some decline in the 1948–49 academic year, the number of those wishing to study in institutions for theological education increased each year. In 1950, the number of applicants was 269; in 1951, 400; in 1952, 496; in 1953, 560.[187]

The Moscow Patriarchate increased funds for loans and financial assistance to dioceses for use in helping clergy in weak parishes and in repairing and restoring monasteries. It also raised appropriations in support of institutions for theological education.[188]

Beginning in the fall of 1953, Patriarch Aleksii petitioned for a meeting with Malenkov through the Council. Karpov passed this request to the government and stressed that the patriarch "by means of this [meeting] wants to check up on attitudes of the state toward the church and, at a minimum, to enhance his own prestige."[189] Using this document, Karpov enumerated those issues that Patriarch Aleksii might raise at a meeting and the Council's positions on them:

1. . . . buildings in the Holy Trinity Monastery of St. Sergius that are currently occupied by tenants.
2. . . . construction of a five-story house in Moscow for the patriarchate.
3. . . . tax obligations of clergy—to request that taxes be collected not according to Article 19 but according to Article 18, as with other professional persons.[190]
4. . . . opening churches and chapels. The Council thinks it expedient to open not more than ten to fifteen churches and chapels annually in those places where there is a real necessity.[191]
5. . . . the Cathedral of the Smolensk Mother of God, located in the former Novodevichy Convent. The Council opposes this, since new petitions will follow on opening a convent there."[192]

Karpov himself "would consider it essential to grant the patriarch's request to be received by Comrade Malenkov."[193] The Council chairman, it seems, believed that setting up a meeting between the heads of government and the church would finally force the government to pay attention to the problems of church-state relations and to establish basic directions for the Council's activity from the perspective of state interests.

The meeting did not take place, however, either in the fall or winter of 1953 or in May 1954. Quite different events forced Malenkov to agree to a meeting with Patriarch Aleksii. On July 7, 1954, *Pravda* published a resolution of the Central Committee entitled, "Serious Shortcomings in Scientific-Atheistic Propaganda and Measures for Improving It." Adoption of the resolution by the Central Committee must be seen as a logical consequence of the very position taken by those who drafted the 1949 resolution and on the very work conducted by Agitprop at the beginning of the 1950s. The possibility for approving such a document at the national level became a reality after Stalin's death. This document was completely unexpected by Russian Orthodox clergy. Relatively stable relations with government authorities and the overall success of the church in recent years did not, it seems, foreshadow anything reminiscent of prewar times.

The tone and nature of the Central Committee's resolution of July 7 had an essentially aggressive character. The document as formulated once again revived traditional stereotypes from the 1930s. Religious organizations and believers supposedly were opposed to the rest of society—they were "consciously and energetically" against citizens who were building communism. The resolution noted particularly, "Churchmen and sectarians search for various tricks to poison the consciousness of people with a religious narcotic. The church and various religious sects have intentionally revived their activity, strengthened their cadres, and increasingly spread religious ideology among other segments of the population through flexibility in adapting to contemporary conditions."[194] Critically evaluating the state of atheistic work by party organizations, the Central Committee called for "a decisive end to passivity in attitudes toward religion, and exposure of its reactionary essence and the harm that it brings by distracting a portion of our country's citizenry from conscious and active participation in building communism."[195]

This document, although it touched exclusively on issues of ideological work, clearly demonstrates the authoritative and governmental functions of the party. First of all, it shows that the Central Committee required atheistic work be done not only by party organizations but also by the All-Union Central Soviet of Trade Unions, the Ministry for Enlightenment and Culture, and central and local state publishers.[196] Therefore, fulfillment of the resolution's instructions had to reflect church-state relations as a whole around the country. Metropolitan Nikolai primarily directed attention to this exact point. While being received at the Council for Russian Orthodox Church Affairs, he said, "If antireligious propaganda was previously part of the party's work, in this new era it has taken on a governmental character since the state demands that students depart from schools as atheists, that army officers force their soliders to reject religious belief, and so forth. One concludes that all believers are lumped together with people who oppose state policy."[197]

The Council itself was forced to react to publication of the Party resolution that directly related to its area of responsibilities. At the end of June 1954, the Council compiled and sent to its regional commissioners, with approval by the Central Committee, a so-called "Orientation" entitled "Current Forms and Methods of the Church's Ideological Influence on Believers."[198] This document followed the spirit of the party's resolution and regarded all forms of Orthodox Church activity—including preaching and policies on cadres—as marking time with "the goal of delaying the inevitable end of its [the church's] existence."[199] First and foremost, opinion changed about the clergy. The Council recommended that commissioners view clergy as ideological opponents instead of as subjects of legal relations. The Orientation noted, "Clergy actively disseminate religious ideology and must be seen only from this perspective."[200] The Council required its commissioners to study clergy activity in depth and called on them to refrain from "a harmful and overly emphasized practicality in our work, as when we were completely absorbed by practical matters and did not draw political conclusions." While recognizing a new turn in attitudes toward religion, Council chairman Karpov, who signed this document, established clear limits for a commissioner's duty: "When fulfilling assignments from party and Soviet agencies, Commissioners should confine their practical assistance to providing urgent operational information on issues connected with the status and the activity of the church."[201]

Leaders of the Council repeatedly stressed this position at Council meetings while hearing reports from commissioners. The Council described the work of certain commissioners as being unsatisfactory if they thought their primary task was to reduce the number of churches in their regions on their own using every possible means. During discussion of a report by the commissioner from Kursk at a Council meeting in October 1954, Karpov stated, "We are all communists, and as communists we would like to participate actively, not passively, in antireligious propaganda. But how would it look if today we give a lecture on the topic 'Religion is the Opium of the People,' but tomorrow we approve the production of candles. Let's influence things some other way."[202]

A broad campaign for propagating "scientific-atheistic knowledge" began in the mass media after publication of the Central Committee's resolution. It is very likely that not a single newspaper, from national ones to those published in regional editions, avoided this subject. As usual, in time this campaign took the form of a struggle against religion and the clergy. Its basis lay in a theoretical position, the heart of which was contained in the slogan, "Socialist reality does not give rise to religion." Consequently, religion does not proliferate because of objective sources but rather due to individual shortcomings, as do vestiges of bourgeois morality such as drunkenness and hooliganism.[203] Thus, in newspapers during 1954 the theme of drunkenness by clergy and believers was widespread.

A feature story that appeared on October 10, 1954, under the byline "Strogii" in the newspaper *Znamia kommunizma* [Banner of Communism]—a publication of the regional party committee in Kemerovo—alarmed Patriarch Aleksii, who until this time was reasonably calm about similar published accounts. The article insulted and ridiculed Metropolitan Varfolomei Gorodtsev of Novosibirsk and All Siberia. The author described his own fantasy of a "drinking bout" in which allegedly "Varfolomei drank like a fish."[204] Not only was the article a pure fabrication, but it also described someone in the highest ranks of the Orthodox Church, not an ordinary clergyman. There were only five bishops with the rank of metropolitan in the Soviet Union in 1954, and Metropolitan

Varfolomei at eighty-nine was the most senior among them. Still, publications on the topic of clergy drunkenness were so numerous that the patriarch as early as August 1954 asked the Synod to approve an appeal for clergy to intensify preaching on the struggle against drunkenness.[205]

The antireligious struggle moved off the pages of the press and into the arena of sociopolitical practice. Again, churches were closed by fiat. Holy springs were filled up with dirt. Instances of administrative pressure on believers and clergy became common once again. In September 1954, the Council prepared a broad summary for presentation to the Central Committee and government on "Violations of Legislation on Religious Cults and Instances of Gross Illegal Administrative Measures against the Church and Believers."[206] In addition, the Council directed the attention of Soviet leaders to new, previously unobserved phenomena, to wit: cases of hooligan escapades and foul language, mostly by young people, against clergy; destruction and arson in churches and chapels; and breaking church windows while services were being held.[207] In one instance, a group of young people organized a pogrom, broke lamps, and defiled icons in catacombs connected with Kiev's Monastery of the Caves.[208] Large numbers of complaints pouring into the Council and other offices of the government and party were the first result of the antireligious campaign unfolding around the country after publication of the Central Committee's resolution on July 7, 1954. Rumors began to spread about possible mass closures of churches and arrests of priests. As a result, the number of religious rites done at requests of believers, especially baptisms of children, sharply increased across the entire territory of the Soviet Union. Demand also grew dramatically for crosses worn around the neck. The Council informed both the Central Committee and the government about this rise in religious activity among the population.[209]

Russian Orthodox bishops reacted extremely negatively and issued a protest in response to events. The style of publications and methods of antireligious struggle in the provinces served as topics of heated discussion during the Synod's meeting in August 1954. The patriarch was forced to calm down the "agitated" Metropolitans Grigorii and Nikolai by saying, "These articles cannot influence our old women. . . . Only we, the clergy, might suffer. But, I do not see this happening at this time."[210] The style and content of publications especially annoyed Metropolitan Nikolai.[211] He repeatedly expressed his opinions about this at meetings with the Council, stressing that atheistic propaganda in its present form (aimed at "chewing up priests") lowered the prestige of the USSR abroad and would damage the fight for peace.[212]

Metropolitan Grigorii of Leningrad and Novgorod thought it necessary to present his own report on the actual status of the Orthodox Church. He gave this report to the patriarch in September 1954 so that the patriarch, in turn, could deliver it personally to Karpov. Analyzing "the true state of affairs and not what is being told to foreign delegations," Metropolitan Grigorii concluded that, "there are violations of the law and limitation of the church's interests by organs of state power." Grigorii appealed to the chairman of the Council: "Instead of trying to solidly unify all citizens of our multinational state, is it in the government's interests to divide citizens artificially? Should the state encouage religious discrimination that portrays sincerely religious citizens as 'a harmful class that must be restricted in every possible way'?"[213]

The Council received information that Metropolitans Nikolai and Grigorii had persuaded the patriarch to present an official protest to the Soviet government.[214] But the patriarch limited himself to personally giving Karpov a note on October 4 entitled, "Opinions of Patriarch Aleksii on Antireligious Propaganda." Karpov correctly deduced that this handwritten note was passed on to the Council for a specific purpose—to inform the government about the feelings and misgivings of the Moscow Patriarchate.[215] The patriarch simultaneously made requests through the Council to Malenkov. Karpov wrote to the Council of Ministers, "Now the goal of this reception was not simply to have a meeting between the head of the state and the head of the Russian Orthodox Church. The patriarch insisted on meeting for the purpose of clarifying the government's real position on ever more complicated church-state relations."[216]

The new wave of Soviet antireligious propaganda also worried foreign Orthodox churches. A member of a delegation from the Finnish Orthodox Church who was in Moscow in August 1954 expressed his own attitude toward current events in this way, "The year 1924 is happening to you all over again. Hard times are beginning anew."[217]

Patriarch Justinian, head of the Romanian Orthodox Church, expressed his personal concerns during Metropolitan Nikolai's visit to Romania in August 1954. While being received by the Council for Russian Orthodox Church Affairs in September 1954, Patriarch Alexander III of Antioch asked Karpov to pass along a request that the Soviet government instruct local officials to stop harsh treatment of the church.[218]

Belyshev reported to the Central Committee in September, "For the past three or four months, interest in the status and activity of the church in the USSR by individuals and delegations from abroad has grown stronger. People from various professions are expressing a desire to visit church services in Moscow, Zagorsk,* and other cities." Belyshev also relayed the questions

---

*The Holy Trinity Monastery of St. Sergius is located in Zagorsk (now renamed Sergiev Posad). This monastery had been a center of Russian Orthodoxy spirituality since its founding in the fourteenth century by St. Sergius of Radonezh. After World War II, it housed the Moscow Theological Seminary and Academy and hosted numerous foreign delegations that visited the USSR.—Ed.

that foreigners were posing and cited a sample answer by Kolchitskii: "No, the church is not being persecuted. The church enjoys total freedom."[219]

For its part, the Council did not restrict itself to merely informing the government about violations of legislation on religion. Council leaders also issued memoranda that expressed their opinions about publications on antireligious themes in national and local newspapers. At the beginning of November, the Council sent out letters to the Central Committees of the Komsomol and Communist Party and to the regional party committee in Chelyabinsk. These letters highlighted mistakes made by the author of an article entitled, "Greater Aggressiveness in Antireligious Propaganda," published in the newspaper *Stalinskaia smena* [Stalin's Successors], the Komsomol press organ in Chelyabinsk. The letter remarked, "The article incorrectly interprets V.I. Lenin on the attitudes of communists toward religion. Some statements in the article are insulting to the religious feelings of believers. It violates the basic principle of freedom of conscience in the USSR by including names of people who are not party members and who are still not free from religious prejudices."[220]

An article in *Literaturnaia gazeta* [Literary Gazette] also did not go unnoticed. Its authors proposed that the catacombs attached to Kiev's Monastery of the Caves be confiscated and scientific-atheistic propaganda be presented on the monastery's grounds.[221] In response to this publication, the Council sent the Central Committee and the Council of Ministers a summary of the monastery's history, at the conclusion of which Council Vice Chairman Belyshev expressed the opinion that currently discussion about closing the monastery was untimely because, "This will provoke a strong reaction from church leaders and will be used against the USSR by ecclesiastical and anti-Soviet circles abroad."[222]

The nature of antireligious propaganda in the press forced Karpov and Polianskii to send a joint letter to the Central Committee in October 1954. In this letter, they indicated, "Many national and local newspapers—especially *Komsomol'skaia Pravda* [Komsomol Truth], *Leningradskaia smena* [Leningrad Successors], *Kalininskaia Pravda* [Kalinin Truth], *Literaturnaia gazeta*, and others—have gone too far in broad, uncontrolled, antichurch and anticlerical propaganda and by publishing fables, caricatures, and simple slogans. These mistakes and distortions have angered not thousands but millions of Soviet citizens who draw inflammatory conclusions from these mistakes. Individual church leaders from Eastern Europe also draw such conclusions. Leading national religious representatives in the USSR, who daily receive almost all foreign delegations that arrive in our country, and church officials who travel abroad, are placed in a difficult position."[223]

Thus, the reaction of believers to the forms and methods of local antireligious propaganda, the negative reaction of the Moscow Patriarchate, the international response, and the position of leaders in the Councils for Russian Orthodox Church Affairs and Affairs of Religious Cults all led to the need for a new resolution by the Central Committee. These very factors prompted publication of the Central Committee resolution on "Mistakes in Conducting Scientific-Atheistic Propaganda Among the Population" on November 10, 1954. The Central Committee officially acknowledged at the time that the resolution was required to correct mistakes and "repeated use of unsatisfactory propaganda methods" by "local organizations" and "individuals" in "certain places."

Party leaders took stock of all the negative factors that resulted from the July resolution. They approached the preparation of "Mistakes in Conducting Scientific-Atheistic Propaganda Among the Population" more carefully and professionally. This is also evident in the fact that members of both councils were included in drafting the resolution.

A comparative analysis of comments submitted by the Council for Russian Orthodox Church Affairs and the final resolution speaks to the fact that the Central Committee took those comments into account. For example, the Council recommended that the Central Committee remove the more odious expressions and terms—such as "so-called 'holy places,'" where the use of quotation marks offended the feelings of believers in the Council's opinion. The Council's comments also increased the emphasis on criticism of mistakes in local antireligious propaganda and added the phrase "and distortions."[224] In addition, the Central Committee agreed with Karpov's idea to send a telegram on behalf of N.A. Tikhonov, chairman of the Soviet Committee for the Defense of Peace, inviting Metropolitan Nikolai to participate in the October session of the World Council for Peace and requesting he speak at the session.[225]

The Central Committee's resolution on "Mistakes in Conducting Scientific-Atheistic Propaganda Among the Population" was published in *Pravda* on November 11, 1954. The document itself made a distinct impression on the lives of laity and clergy from all religious confessions. Odintsov distinguishes three basic attitudes in the resolution as it related to church-state policy.[226] First, it promoted a new theory on the church's place in socialistic society as opposed to its place in a state founded on economic exploitation. Second, special attention was paid to the overwhelming majority of Soviet believers who were devoted to society and conscientiously fulfilled their responsibilities. Therefore, attempts to place activity of religious organizations under "political suspicion" and to express "political distrust" toward clergy and laity were declared intolerable. Third, the resolution indicated that religion was a private matter from the government's perspective, although it recognized the party's right to conduct scientific-atheistic propaganda as long as it was scientific and free of any form of politicization. Ideological struggle could not be allowed to include administrative measures or insults to the religious feelings of laity and "servants of the cult" [the official Soviet term for the clergy—Ed.].[227]

Publication of the resolution coincided with a regular session of the Holy Synod and the traditional reception of senior bishops by the Council for Russian Orthodox Church Affairs to mark the anniversary of the October Revolution. During the Synod's session, its members expressed their unanimous opinion that, "it is a very good and necessary resolution . . . adopted at the proper time." According to Kolchitskii, Patriarch Aleksii responded enthusiastically to the Central Committee's action and on his own initiative proposed that the Synod approve a statement to the government. The statement passed and was presented to Karpov during the reception.

This document, "A Resolution of the Patriarch and Synod" dated November 12, 1954, said, "The Holy Synod of the Russian Orthodox Church, gratefully learning about the Central Committee's resolution of November 10 that gives instructions on the proper treatment of clergy and religious sensibilities of believers, consider it our duty to ask the chairman of the Council to express our thanks to our government for its unwavering benevolence toward the Orthodox Church."[228]

Churches in Moscow and Leningrad were filled on Sunday, November 14, 1954. Clergy announced to their parishes that the Central Committee had adopted the resolution. It was also read aloud in all classes at the theological academies and seminaries.[229] As early as November 17, commissioners from Belorussia, Ukraine, Moldavia, Georgia, and Kazakhstan sent information to the Council on reaction by local laity and clergy. The reaction was unanimous ("The resolution was greeted positively and with gratitude") except for some examples of skeptical remarks from believers ("Time will tell if it will be implemented").[230] Ambassadors for the Eastern Orthodox churches also expressed their favorable impression of the resolution.[231]

Malenkov received Patriarch Aleksii on December 11, 1954.[232] The results of their conversation were insignificant from the perspective of fundamental issues regarding church-state relations.[233] The head of the Soviet government did become personally acquainted with the head of the Orthodox Church. The very fact that they met reflected favorably on the tone of those relations.

In December 1954, the Council once again presented a proposal to the Central Committee for awarding Metropolitan Nikolai with the Order of the Red Banner of Labor. The Council made several arguments,

. . . In the period when he (Metropolitan Nikolai) was finishing his work on the Extraordinary State Commission for Investigating Crimes by German fascists, they promised to decorate him but did not. . . . For the last two to three years, he has awaited the conferment of the International Stalin Prize "For strengthening peace among peoples." . . . Despite his negative personal qualities, he has accomplished important patriotic work and will long remain useful in this arena. For the purpose of reversing the negative mood of Metropolitan Nikolai and bearing in mind his forthcoming trip in 1955 to the capitalist countries of England and West Germany, it would be expedient in the Council's opinion to recognize his patriotic activity and to time the award to fall on January 13, 1955, in belated recognition of his sixtieth birthday on January 13, 1952.

Metropolitan Nikolai was awarded the Order of the Red Banner of Labor by the Presidium of the Supreme Soviet of the USSR on August 6, 1955.[234] The Central Committee in January 1955 approved publication of *We Will Defend Peace*, the second volume of Metropolitan Nikolai's speeches and public statements.[235]

The Council held a series of group conferences for commissioners between December 1954 and February 1955 in Moscow, Leningrad, Minsk, and Kiev. The purpose of these conferences included warning commissioners about mistakes in their work, explaining the Central Committee's resolution of November 10, 1954, and setting practical tasks flowing from that resolution. Conference speakers stressed that all practical work of the Council and its commissioners should be directed to this important task: "Keeping the church loyal to the state—a position that the church gradually moved toward and finally reached during World War II—while at the same time restraining expansion of the church's religious influence."[236]

In their policy toward the Russian Orthodox Church between 1955 and 1957, leaders of the Council closely and consistently maintained the course that the Council followed during and immediately after the war. The Council could do this thanks to a unique situation that formed in the country for this brief period.

Two factors—an internal struggle for party leadership and the complexity of domestic and foreign policy problems that faced the Soviet government in those years—pushed issues related to both church policy and the agencies responsible for implementing that policy to the back burner. The Councils were unsuccessful even in promoting their own cause and taking part in the multiple reorganizations of the administrative bureaucracy, although at every opportunity the Council for Russian Orthodox Church Affairs and the Council for Affairs of Religious Cults developed plans for merger and presented them to the government.

The general atmosphere of the country, known as the "Thaw," set in motion the process of spiritual liberation of the people. Authorities at both the national and local levels began to think about "public opinion,"[237] which included the opinion of believers in the population. Not by chance, the Council for Russian Orthodox Church Affairs noticed a sharp decline in this period in the number of violations of the laws on religion by governmental agencies around the country.

The new foreign policy of the Soviet leadership found a demonstration of complete freedom of conscience in the USSR very useful. It promoted increased authority for both the country and its new leaders.

Meetings were arranged between church leaders and the heads of state, with Malenkov in 1954 and Nikolai Bulganin* in 1955 and 1956. Although official in nature, these meetings did take place, and that fact served as a strong argument from the Council for the need to resolve the matters that were discussed. As a consequence of these circumstances, the Russian Orthodox Church experienced a new renaissance, similar to the one in the mid-1940s but not as complete.

Responding to a draft presented by both religious councils, the Council of Ministers adopted resolution No. 259, "Changes in Procedures for Opening Buildings for Prayer," on February 17, 1955. The resolution stated that a final decision on opening a church or chapel, after getting the agreement of one of the councils, belonged to governments of union republics and became their prerogative. The most important point of the resolution (Point 2) gave the Councils the right to register religious communities that were in fact active and using buildings for prayer.[238] Despite the fact that only ten churches were officially opened in the USSR in 1955–56,[239] the number of Orthodox churches increased specifically through registration of these buildings.

Numbers of clergy in the Russian Orthodox Church also increased. They began to return from imprisonment and exile—at first through amnesty and then through rehabilitation. At the end of 1955, the Council sent a letter to its commissioners rescinding the section of instructions dated February 2, 1949, that prohibited the ordination of men who had been convicted. Now, with permission from offices of the Ministry of Internal Affairs, commissioners had the right to register priests who had formerly experienced political repression.[240] By the end of the 1950s, the portion of clergy who had either served prison sentences or been released early from prison was 30 percent in Latvia and Lithuania, 45 percent in Belorussia, and 80 percent in Ukraine (see Table 2.4).[241]

---

*N.A. Bulganin (1895–1975) was a Soviet military and political leader who served as chairman of the Council of Ministers of the USSR from 1955 to 1958.—Ed.

Table 2.4

Date	Number of registered Orthodox churches[a]	Number of registered Orthodox clergy[b] (total including bishops, priests, and deacons)
January 1, 1954	13,423	11,912
January 1, 1955	13,376	11,993
January 1, 1956	13,416	12,185
January 1, 1957	13,430	12,288
January 1, 1958	13,414	12,169

Notes:
a. See Odintsov, "Pis'ma", 34. Reports from the Council for various years (owing to more exact figures and submission of supplemental information from commissioners), give different figures. For example, on February 4, 1956, the Council reported to the Central Committee, the Supreme Soviet, and the Council of Ministers that, as of January 1, 1956, the number of churches was 13,463, with 10,844 being of the usual type. With this data, the Council stressed, "These figures, as absolutely precise data from the Council, are not to be published and should not be used for propagandistic purposes, because we and the church always (since 1944) give totally different figures abroad and in general for use in propaganda." GARF, f. 6991, op. 1, d. 1331, l. 58.
b. GARF, f. 6991, op. 1, d. 1648, l. 33.

Graduates of theological schools also entered church service. New clergy differed qualitatively from representatives of the older generation, who were in Pospielovsky's estimation "timid and demoralized by having lived through the Stalinist terror."[242] According to reports from commissioners, young clergy in particular were energetic and "ecclesiastically active." In 1955–57, all the seminaries and academies of the Russian Orthodox Church that were opened in the earlier period (with the exception of the seminary in Vilnius) were operational. However, the number of students and consequently the number of graduates increased noticeably. The number of applications received in 1952 was 401. In 1956–57, that number rose to 750–800. Theological schools accepted 368 men in the 1957–58 academic year, while only three to four years earlier annual admissions had not exceeded 250 to 275 students, according to information from the Council. In more than ten years of operation, institutions for theological education had sent out 1,203 graduates; 208 of these came from the academies and 995 from the seminaries. One quarter of the faculty at theological schools in the 1957–58 academic year (out of a total of 133 faculty members) were "not over thirty years of age."[243]

Press runs of religious literature published in the country increased during the second half of the 1950s. The Council supported requests from the patriarchate to publish additional religious literature (Gospels, Prayer Books,

Psalters, etc.) and passed along reasons for these requests: "1) The need for religious literature in the Russian Orthodox Church has remained unsatisfied for nearly forty years. 2) The Russian Orthodox Church thinks it undermines its authority to use church books from American religious publishers. The church itself should have the means to give its members essential books. It should even supply books to other Orthodox churches and not be an object of their concern."[244] The Central Committee approved printing the Gospels and Psalter (50,000 copies), Prayer Book (250,000), and Bible (25,000) in 1955.[245] In 1956 for the first time during Soviet rule in the USSR, Bibles were printed in Russian; moreover, the Central Committee agreed to increase the press run from 25,000 to 28,000 copies.[246]

The Council also supported requests made by Patriarch Aleksii during his meeting with Bulganin on March 26, 1956. These requests related to: opening Orthodox churches, for which believers continued to submit numerous petitions (the Council received a total of 1,309 petitions in 1955; 2,258 in 1956; and 2,043 in 1957);[247] relocating institutions out of buildings in the Holy Trinity Monastery of St. Sergius to new quarters in the town of Zagorsk; opening the Trinity Cathedral in the Alexander Nevsky Monastery in Leningrad;[248] extending labor legislation to cover workers and employees to church organizations;[249] and changing procedures for assessing income taxes.[250]

The Council informed the Central Committee that stable church-state relations in the years 1955–57 allowed Orthodox clergy to become more active in significant ways by using "various forms and methods"—repairs and beautification of church buildings, establishment of professional choirs, active preaching and personal work among the population, special attention to young people, and charitable activity in various forms.[251] Despite the small growth (according to the Council's data) in numbers of participants in religious rites in comparison with the beginning of the 1950s and the small proportion of donations from believers, the Church's income "increased substantially each year." The Council attributed this mainly to sales of candles and other religious objects in parish churches.[252] In 1948, the annual income of the Russian Orthodox Church stood at 180 million rubles, but in 1957 its income had reached 667 million rubles.[253]

Availability of resources allowed the Moscow Patriarchate to direct large sums of money in support of parishes, monasteries, and institutions for theological education, as well as to improve the financial condition of the clergy.

The status and character of church-state relations in 1955–57 engendered a certain amount of euphoria among Russian Orthodox bishops and a belief by some of them, Metropolitan Nikolai being the leader, that it was possible and essential to expand church activity. Metropolitan Nikolai repeatedly expressed dissatisfaction with the results of Patriarch Aleksii's meetings with both Malenkov and Bulganin, saying, "The patriarch did not raise any issues at the meeting, he mumbled something and limited himself to trivialities."[254]

The patriarch's illness and Daniel Ostapov's influence over him provided Metropolitan Nikolai with an excuse to carry on intrigue among other bishops. Indeed, Nikolai imparted to the Council "opinions of members of the Synod" on such issues as who would become patriarch after Aleksii and who would be exarch of Ukraine.[255]

In April 1957, Karpov learned the medical diagnosis regarding the state of Patriarch Aleksii's health and sent the following "Informational Report" to the Central Committee and Council of Ministers:

> This document gives the medical diagnosis regarding Patriarch Aleksii's health. The Council reports that, in addition to disease of his legs, he began to complain about pains in his chest. A medical commission said that he showed changes in the region of his heart and vascular illness. Because of this, Patriarch Aleksii left for rest and treatment at his summer home in Odessa at the beginning of May of this year. On November 9, the patriarch will be eighty years old.
>
> For the Council, this circumstance raised the question of possible candidates for the future head of the church in the event of the patriarch's death. According to Regulations that govern the Russian Orthodox Church, in the event of death or other condition that prevents the patriarch from governing the church, the metropolitan of Krutitskii and Kolomenskoe becomes *locum tenens*—at the moment that is Nikolai.
>
> In such a case, it would became much more difficult for the Council to exercise the necessary influence on the church's activity and guide it in the direction we require, since Metropolitan Nikolai's personal qualities are diametrically opposed to those of Patriarch Aleksii. . . .
>
> Despite the fact that he conducts important work in defense of peace and in maintaining ties with foreign churches, Metropolitan Nikolai is insincere in his relations with the Council. Proof of this has come in many instances of deception that bordered on abnormal pride and ambition. His lively participation in foreign affairs can best be explained only as a desire to satisfy his ambition. He is devoid of a sense of modesty. . . .
>
> Unlike Patriarch Aleksii, if Metropolitan Nikolai comes to govern the church, he will make a series of serious demands for strengthening the church and expanding its activity without regard to recommendations from the Council. His goal will be to increase his personal prestige in the eyes of foreign religious leaders, especially those from capitalist countries who repeatedly have said that the Russian Orthodox Church does not use all available legal means to expand its work.

Under these conditions, we desire that Patriarch Aleksii remain head of the Russian Orthodox Church for as long as possible. Therefore, the Council requests that the Fourth Directorate of the Ministry of Health for the USSR give greater attention to overseeing the condition of his health.[256]

The situation in the religious sphere could not remain outside the attention of national party leaders. It was also impossible for ruling elites in the party and government not to become concerned by the growing strength of the Russian Orthodox Church. One fact became obvious to them. The forms and methods used by the party to exert ideological influence on the population through the mid-1950s seemed powerless in the struggle against the religious influence of the church.

1. The council of Russian Orthodox bishops held on September 8, 1943. This council elected Metropolitan Sergii Stragorodskii as Patriarch of Moscow and All Russia.

2. Patriarch Sergii Stragorodskii at the December 1943 session of the Holy Synod.

3. The building at 5 Chistyi Pereulok in Moscow that housed the Moscow Patriarchate from the 1940s to the 1980s.

4. A religious procession in 1943, part of a prayer service for rain held by villagers in the fields of the Rostov region.

5. His Holiness Aleksii Simanskii, Patriarch of Moscow and All Russia.

6. Reception held by patriarchal *locum tenens* Metropolitan Aleksii Simanskii (center) in 1944 for a group of senior priests from Moscow who had been decorated with state medals "For the Defense of Moscow."

7. Metropolitan Nikolai Iarushevich,
Doctor of Theology.

8. National Orthodox church leaders at the 1945 enthronement ceremony
for the newly elected Patriarch Aleksii of Moscow and All Russia (left
to right): Patriarch Alexander of Antioch, Patriarch Christopher of
Alexandria, Patriarch Aleksii, and Catholicos Kallistrate, Patriarch of
Georgia.

9. An undated photograph from a session of the Holy Synod showing (left to right): Patriarch Aleksii, Metropolitan Nikolai, and Archbishop Luke Voino-Iasenetskii.

10. Metropolitan Grigorii Chukov of Leningrad and Novgorod casts his vote during a Soviet election in Leningrad, 1946

11. Georgii Karpov (left), chairman of the Council for Russian Orthodox Church Affairs, extends greetings to the opening session of the Moscow Conference for Leaders of Orthodox Churches in 1948 celebrating the 500-year anniversary of autocephaly for the Russian Orthodox Church.

12. A plenary session of the 1948 conference for Leaders of Orthodox Churches.

13. The Russian writer Nikolai Tikhonov addresses a conference on world peace for Soviet religious leaders at Zagorsk in May 1952. A large portrait of Joseph Stalin hangs in the background alongside his words, "We stand for peace and set aside the affairs of the world."

14. A delegation from the National Council of Churches of Christ in the United States sits in on a class for third-year students at the Moscow Theological Academy on March 16, 1956.

15. An Orthodox wedding being held at the Moscow church dedicated to the Icon of the Mother of God, the Joy of All Who Sorrow (1957).

16. Patriarch Aleksii (center) receives a delegation from the Exarchate of North America on August 30, 1960.

17. Metropolitan Nikodim Rotov of Leningrad and Lagoda speaks with members of a delegation of theological students from the World Federation of Christian Student Associations of the World Council of Churches (no date).

18. Brother Aleksander in his cell at the Monastery of the Caves in Pskov in the 1960s.

Chapter 3

The Soviet State and the Russian Orthodox Church, 1958–61

The Council for Russian Orthodox Church Affairs Responds to Changes in Political Priorities

The vulnerability of the Council for Russian Orthodox Church Affairs became obvious after the Twentieth Congress of the Communist Party of the Soviet Union. An environment developed in the country that allowed for criticism of Stalin's "cult of personality" and a struggle to restore socialist legality. In that environment, at least two questions unfailingly appeared as topics for discussion among those who worked on the Council:

- How to assess the Council's work from the moment the Council was formed, which Stalin directly oversaw and controlled?
- In a situation growing more complex, how to deal with the demand to adhere to the law in its strict interpretation on the church, whose ideology is alien to the ideas of socialism?

Discussion of these issues at planning conferences, party meetings, and informal conversations revealed differing viewpoints, a divergence of opinion, and likely conflicts between members and staff on the Council. Evidence of this appears in letters* dated December 15 and 18, 1956, to P.N. Pospelov of the Central Committee from two members of the Council—I.I. Ivanov, head of the Division of Inspectors, and his deputy V. Spiridonov.[1]

---

*Contents of the letters convince me that these were not the first requests by staff members of the Council for advice from the Central Committee.

In my view, there is no basis for seeing these letters as evidence of a "struggle" within the Council between supporters of "a war against religion" and "advocates of normal relations between the state and the church."[2] Ivanov's point of view was no different from the position of Council chairman Karpov on the Russian Orthodox hierarchy or toward opening churches in the Soviet Union. Ivanov thought that the Council had "the means and resources to limit the activity of the church and clergy." Most important among these resources was the policy relating to the episcopate: "Send the more obscurantist and reactionary [bishops] into monastic retirement and assign others who are more loyal and less fanatical in their place. . . . The old saying, 'Like priest, like parish,' is used for a reason." Ivanov did not suggest reducing the number of bishops but only proposed replacing them—and the Council pursued that exact policy during the whole course of its existence. Ivanov thought that instructions given by the Central Committee in establishing the line followed by the Council were correct: "Do not do anything that in any way would assist in strengthening the church or in broadening its activity. Yet, at the same time, the Council should not permit illegal administrative measures in its own work or by local officials." Beside this, Ivanov thought that refusing believers' petitions was "a violation of Article 124 of the USSR Constitution that guarantees civil freedom in performing religious rites." Ivanov wrote, "When an unhealthy mood is created by refusing petitions from a significant group of believers, we must provide a safety valve. That is, we must register the religious community."

The only area of the Council's work that Ivanov criticized and the only area where he did not see a clear mission was the foreign policy of the Russian Orthodox Church. "We expend a large amount of hard currency to support reactionary clergy abroad . . . without any useful results."[3]

Ivanov's deputy Spiridonov expressed leftist-liberal views, so to speak, on relations between church and state. In his opinion, "The Council should not become headquarters for a political war with religion. It should not do anything that would disturb normal relations between church and state or that might damage the political line of the church, as expressed in actively fighting for peace and support of domestic measures by the party and government—all of which are favorable toward us." Spiridonov wrote, "Comrade Ivanov proposes to shake up the episcopate and prepares to continue the war. . . . The Central Committee must openly instruct party organs to strictly follow party decisions and Leninist instructions concerning the conduct of scientific-atheist propaganda. It must say that the use of force and improper administrative methods for eradicating religious superstitions are impermissible. The rights of citizens must be strictly maintained while waging a decisive struggle against violations of the law and strictly observing the constitutional rights of citizens."[4]

On May 30, 1957, Agitprop invited Ivanov and Spiridonov to its office "for conversations concerning matters of interest to them." Agitprop noted in a brief document only that, "Comrades Ivanov and Spiridonov were satisfied with the explanations provided them."[5] The exact explanations given to them are unknown, but the Central Committee reached an obvious conclusion after completing its investigation of disagreements within the Council—supporters of a dramatic change in increasingly complex church-state relations did not exist in the Council's leadership. A speech made by Karpov to a seminar of commissioners in May 1957 supported this conclusion:

> The main purpose for which the Council itself was formed—although unfortunately it is often forgotten, and not merely by local officials—is to maintain stable, normal relations between the state and the church. Also, through communication with the patriarch and other leading bishops in the church . . . it guarantees that the church as a national religious association and its cadres of clergy do not slip and do not return to a position of years long passed, that is, to a position of reactionary politics in relation to the state. And it would be completely impermissible and even criminal if this were to happen as a result of actions by us that were incorrect, thoughtless, hasty, or mistaken in some other way.[6]

Such a view completely disagreed with the Central Committee's opinion that the Council should help contribute to the party line of struggle "for communist education of workers and for extinguishing religion." The Central Committee thought that the Council's leader clearly exaggerated the probability of "the clergy slipping back into reactionary politics." Past service in the secret police prevented him from evaluating the country's situation and prospects for church-state relations in a new way. Successful realization of a new course on religion and the church and implementation of a hard line for limiting church activity depended on changing the composition of staff at the Council for Russian Orthodox Church Affairs. This problem was resolved over the course of 1957. Its resolution was made easier by the fact that members of the Council were already near retirement age.

After G.T. Utkin, member of the Council and head of the Department for Foreign and Publishing Activities of the church retired on May 10, L.A. Shcherbakov was appointed to his position.[7] I.I. Ivanov retired in November.[8] Karpov asked the Central Committee in December 1957 to release Council Vice Chairman Belyshev from his duties "per his request" in connection with his retirement.[9] That same month, Karpov requested confirmation of I.I. Sivenkov and V.I. Vasiliev as members of the Council and P.G. Cheredniak, formerly an instructor for Agitprop, as vice chairman of the Council.[10]

These changes could not slip past attentive church leaders. During a meeting with Karpov at the Barvikh sanatorium in May 1958, Patriarch Aleksii tactfully expressed his concern through a third person. This is evident in Karpov's notes of the conversation:

> The patriarch said, "I repeat once again that I do not have any complaints about the Council, but we eagerly await your return." . . . I told the patriarch that, "I am also trying to get back to work quickly, but I do not think that my absence affected resolution of your issues in any way." The patriarch replied, "Of course, but young people still do not have your experience and, undoubtedly, do not yet have your authority. Our bishops and especially our visitors have noticed this. As one of them said to me, 'But the Council already is not what it once was.'" The patriarch said, "I answered that he was incorrect, since nothing has changed for us. Karpov's assistants have simply retired."

Karpov did not say anything in reply to the patriarch, and the interlocutors moved on to a discussion of other matters.[11]

The chairman of the Council undoubtedly understood that the dismissal of his assistants was not a coincidence. As Odintsov puts it, Karpov found himself "in the sights" of the Central Committee's bureaucracy and "was placed under suspicion for disloyalty to the regime."[12] However, Karpov did not find himself in this position at the end of 1957, as Odintsov writes, but beginning in the second half of 1956. The Party Control Commission of the Central Committee accused Karpov in 1956 of "violating revolutionary legality from 1929 to 1938."[13]

From this time on, as he himself noted, Karpov experienced constant pressure, "bordering on personal insult," "searching for any possibility for compromise and a resulting dismissal."[14] Beginning in 1957, Karpov raised the issue of his removal and retirement three times. Each time, however, the Central Committee decided this was "inexpedient." Karpov was needed by party leaders, certainly not for himself but for his name, his authority, the respect that he enjoyed among Russian Orthodox bishops, and finally for his influence over Patriarch Aleksii. This state of affairs would be useful in no small degree when planning an attack against the church so that at least initial measures for limiting its activity would not lead to conflict with church leaders. Karpov's name would demonstrate continuity between the old core leadership (Ivanov and Utkin worked on the Council from the day of its inception, Belyshev from 1945) and newly arriving people. At the same time, his name would conceal the emergence of a "new line" toward the church—a line that the Council confidently assured representatives of the Moscow Patriarchate did not exist.

Did Karpov understand the role prepared for him? In our day, it is impossible to give either a positive or negative answer to that question. One gets the impression that Karpov was disoriented by the problems confronting him at the time. In addition, frequent heart attacks requiring long treatments in health resorts did not allow him to keep the situation at the Council fully under control.

All the same, Karpov's personal qualities as a strict, demanding leader with fifteen years of experience in political activity, someone who could formulate his own position and views on the course and methods of building church-state relations and on the role and meaning of the agency he headed, all allowed the chairman of the Council for Russian Orthodox Church Affairs to hold off the recurring "cavalry" charge on the church to a certain extent.

An "opinion" on the necessity to limit activity by the Russian Orthodox Church and its influence on the population began forming in the Central Committee, it seems, in the spring of 1957. Data on the status of the church presented by the Council to the Central Committee evoked concern in the nation's ideological headquarters. "Observations on an increase in churches"[15] that were given to the Council also attested to such concern, as did inquiries for more complete information on the status of the church in the USSR and on all aspects of its activity. More evidence of concern came from a previously unseen but clearly emerging interest in "the financial activity of religious organizations." For example, a Council resolution from June 1, 1957, on "Summaries of Instructional Seminars for Commissioners of the Council for Russian Orthodox Church Affairs under the Council of Ministers of the USSR," included a special point that read: "Develop and distribute a letter that orients commissioners to the task of overseeing the church's financial activity."[16] In this connection, attention is drawn to the fact that new members of the Council appointed by the Central Committee (e.g., Sivenkov and Cheredniak) had not merely been educated but also possessed advanced graduate degrees in economics. Development of a hard line in relation to the church was promoted by the situation forming on the political Mt. Olympus. In June 1957, a Central Committee plenum trounced the antiparty group of Molotov, Voroshilov, Malenkov, and Bulganin, plus Shepilov "who sided with them."

In their analysis of church-state relations during the 1950s, certain researchers (in particular, Odintsov) in my opinion clearly exaggerate the theme of a struggle within the Central Committee's bureaucracy over two points of view on the problems of religion and the church. Odintsov makes the following statements in several different works: "Within the party's bureaucracy by the summer of 1954, opposition between two viewpoints on the problems of religion and the church became keener." "There was a clash and struggle of two opposing points of view in the party's bureaucracy." "The victory of supporters within the party's bureaucracy for a hard line in deciding religious matters was finally certain by the fall of 1958."[17]

The religious question could not be found in the struggle for power that unfolded after Stalin's death and was not numbered among those problems over which the interests of various sides clashed.[18] This is particularly evident in the fact that Shepilov, who played a significant role in organizing the antireligious campaign of 1948–49, was included in the camp of "oppositionists" in July 1957.

Undoubtedly, such figures as Molotov and Voroshilov seemed to be potential supporters of a liberal course in treating the church by virtue of the fact that in their time they implemented Stalin's new policy on the church. Another strategy also undoubtedly existed that aimed at limiting the activity of religious organizations, the most consistent exponent of which was Suslov, who headed Agitprop. But attempts to carry out plans "for a broad attack on religion and the church" ended in failure in both 1948–49 and 1954. Advocates of the hard line thus were unsuccessful in gaining either political momentum and strength or political authority for the purpose of changing the nature of church-state relations formed during the war years. "Victory" came of its own accord, when those holding the opposing viewpoint were removed from the political arena.

Defeat of the antiparty group was presented as a blow against opposition to the Twentieth Party Congress and as the "final note" in the struggle with "Stalinists."[19] Evaluation of the opposition as "Stalinists" independently predetermined the next task—to finish off the remaining "manifestations of Stalinism." Supporters of a hard-line religious policy argued that it was finally possible "to make short work of" Stalin's legacy and "to correct" the situation that existed in the religious realm. Some say that Khrushchev, the man then leading the party, distanced himself from church problems right up to the end of the 1950s and that issues of church policy originally did not have any fixed place in his grandiose plans for reconstructing and altering Soviet society. In my view, it was not accidental that problems of religion, faith, and church policy are absent from Khrushchev's own memoirs as well as works by the people closest to him—A.I. Adzhubei and S.N. Khrushchev. This problem is also the subject of research by historians dedicated to learning more about the Khrushchev decade.[20] Still, these authors express the opinion that Suslov, later joined by L.F. Ilichev, controlled official ideology.

Suslov's personality and his role in the country's political life from the 1950s to 1970s are topics that until now have been closed to Russian historiography. We can speak with only a limited degree of certainty about his influence on policy in religious matters. There is no doubt, however, that Suslov supported a hard line in regard to religion and the church. His position was determined by his general worldview as "the nation's chief ideologist," by the orthodoxy of his thought, and by his devotion to the letter and spirit of Marxist-Leninist theory. Suslov clearly played a role in preparing the Central Committee's resolutions of 1949 and July 1954. Under his direct guidance, a typical attack on religion and the church began in 1958. It promised to be successful because objective circumstances seemed favorably aligned. On the one hand, potential opponents who avoided conflict with churchmen had been removed from power. On the other hand, the struggle against religion was essential from the standpoint of achieving the general global mission set by the agenda: construction of a communist society. It was impossible to build a communist future without "altering the people's consciousness" and freeing that consciousness from "religious prejudices and superstitions." In reality, Khrushchev as head of the party and government sincerely believed this; therefore the attack on the church organized by the Central Committee's Agitation and Propaganda Department was guaranteed support at the very highest level. A new "political war" against religion and clergy was predetermined and unavoidable. The Council for Russian Orthodox Church Affairs had to be transformed into an instrument for war against the strongest religious confession in the USSR—the Orthodox Church.

An impulse—a certain stimulus—is essential for the start of any wide-ranging campaign. The impulse that marked the start of a new religious policy in the country came, I believe, in a letter to Suslov, dated April 15, 1958, from a certain V. D. Shaposhnikova, special correspondent for *Literaturnaia gazeta*.

Shaposhnikova shared her personal thoughts with Suslov about the current state of scientific-atheist propaganda. As early as 1953, after a visit to a Baptist prayer meeting, she published a feature story, entitled "Preachers from Kolodna," in her newspaper. In response to its publication, the newspaper received a massive response. Shaposhnikova wrote that this response showed on the one hand "that a great force stands behind a preacher," and on the other hand "that we are very weakly armed against such a force." She also wrote, "In the process of my work, I was persuaded that weakness in our atheistic propaganda lies in the fact that we do not know the place of religion in contemporary life and we cannot even say with certainty the extent of the danger standing before us. I am convinced that the danger is great." The letter's author criticized the activity of organizations charged with atheistic work. "I asked one of the prominent atheists from the Knowledge Society to draft a response to the letters [I had received]. His response was nothing

Suslov

except general phrases and well-known citations from the classics of Marxism-Leninism." "At the Museum of the History of Religion and Atheism in Leningrad, all is *routine and stagnant*."* "Lectures of the Knowledge Society lack atheistic ammunition, [they are full of] dogmatism . . . [and] bitterly disappointing for the listener."[21]

That same day, April 15, Suslov issued instructions after reading the letter, "To Comrades Konstantinov and Moskovskii: I ask you to take notice of this and to report your thoughts."[22]

By April 19, 1958, Agitprop had "informed the Central Committee about the status of scientific-atheist propaganda and measures for strengthening it." However, a "Report by the Agitation and Propaganda Department of the Central Committee of the CPSU for Union Republics" that led to adoption of a Central Committee resolution on October 4, 1958, later appeared. The report resulted from a conference organized by Agitprop on May 8, 1958. This was a conference "of responsible workers in Central Committee CPSU departments for propaganda, science, schools, and institutions for higher education and culture and of the All-Union Society for the Dissemination of Political and Scientific Knowledge, the State Political Publishing Department, newspapers and magazines, the Komsomol Central Committee, and the Councils for Russian Orthodox Church Affairs and Affairs of Religious Cults."[23]

The conference gave birth to a "Report by the Agitation and Propaganda Department of the Central Committee of the CPSU for Union Republics on Shortcomings in Scientific-Atheistic Propaganda."

The report opened with this preamble: "In April of this year, the Central Committee received a letter from special correspondent V.D. Shaposhnikova of *Literaturnaia gazeta* in which she reported on shortcomings in scientific-atheistic propaganda among the population and the strengthening of activity by churchmen." The report later said, "All who spoke [at the conference] . . . noted that the Central Committee Resolution of July 7, 1954, was carried out unsatisfactorily by many party, trade union and Komsomol organizations, institutions, and agencies. Moreover, some party, trade union, soviet, and Komsomol workers assumed that the Central Committee resolution of November 10, 1954, "Mistakes in Conducting Scientific-Atheistic Propaganda" repealed the Central Committee Resolution of July 7 on "Shortcomings in Scientific-Atheist Propaganda and Measures for Strengthening It."[24]

This circumstance is quite remarkable. Certainly, no one had repealed the resolution of July 7, 1954, and the Central Committee formally had the right

---

*The italics are Suslov's.

to demand its execution by communists. The paradox lay in the fact that the requirement to obey the resolution of July 7 was repudiated by the resolution of November 10 that year. Consequently, as Pospielovsky correctly notes, "The basis for state policy in relation to the church became the more severe July resolution, not the milder November one."[25]

The report expressed new criticism for the Councils for Russian Orthodox Church Affairs and for Affairs of Religious Cults. "The Councils . . . and their local representatives carry out their duties poorly. Sometimes they are under the thumb of churchmen and do not inform party and Soviet organs about the activity of church workers and members of sects in a timely manner."[26] Work by the conference helped develop recommendations for energizing scientific-atheistic work.

As early as the summer of 1958, the Council for Russian Orthodox Church Affairs began acting on suggestions given at the conference and worked out a series of measures for limiting the activity of the Orthodox Church. Documents produced by the Council formed the foundation of government resolutions dating from October 16, 1958, on "Monasteries in the USSR" and "Levying Taxes on Income Received by Diocesan Administrative Enterprises and Also on the Income of Monasteries."[27] The Council asked the Central Committee to review its "Proposals on Institutions for Theological Education." These included proposals "that must be recommended to the patriarchate" and that stipulated measures limiting admissions into theological schools and financial guarantees for seminaries and academies.

These documents were discussed and prepared without the participation of the Council's chairman (Karpov at this time was still at a health resort). Council Vice Chairman Cheredniak signed them. Karpov himself was required to prepare the patriarch and "to sound out his possible reaction to the start of an attack on the church."[28] Karpov met with the patriarch in Odessa. The conversation between them was strained and unpleasant for both men.[29] The patriarch was anxious and acknowledged to Karpov, "There has never been a situation where I have spoken with you in this way. . . . They told me that we would have a serious conversation about candle production and monasteries." Karpov, however, did not touch on the matter of candle production in the conversation, though they did discuss the problem of monasteries. In response to examples from Karpov where novices between the ages of twenty and twenty-five had been accepted into monasteries, the patriarch said, "I think it is completely possible to establish a procedure so that monasteries would accept only people who are thirty and older." The issue of the Monastery of the Caves in Kiev provoked a very sharp reaction from the patriarch. And, although Karpov warned that he wanted "only to consult and get opinions and suggestions" on this matter, Patriarch Aleksii understood the truth.

He said, "I see that our conversation is moving again to closing the Monastery of the Caves in Kiev. It is very difficult for me to discuss the proposal you wish to make." In connection with this very matter, the patriarch stated that he intended to "retire . . . I have no interest in remaining patriarch." Despite the fact that Karpov ended practically every issue with a suggestion that they continue its discussion after the patriarch returned to Moscow, it had certainly become clear to the head of the Russian Orthodox Church that decisions had already been made "at the top." Any further discussion at this point would not change anything.

Karpov fulfilled his mission from this standpoint. He informed Agitprop about the conversation that had taken place. But Karpov attached his own report to "Notes of a Conversation with Patriarch Aleksii" and wrote again about the need for review and adoption of decisions on those matters that the patriarch raised when he met with Khrushchev on May 19, 1958. The primary issue was a request, supported by the Council, to open churches in a series of populated areas ("thirteen places in the RSFSR and one in the city of Chervonograd in Ukraine"). Karpov recalled Voroshilov's instructions that, "the Council must conduct its work so that national leaders of the church cannot form the impression that the Soviet government is insincere with them and is playing games." Karpov continued, "If this is still true to some degree even today, then I would request that measures be taken quickly for carrying out your instructions of July 1 and the main point of the Council's letter No. 258/s of June 2, not in the interests of the church (as some in the provinces say in private, thereby hurling undeserved insults) but in the interests of our Soviet government and our policies."[30] Karpov insisted on opening churches by saying that the church should preserve at least "a certain outward appearance" during "a simultaneous and more significant reduction in parish churches."[31]

This was the last letter in which Karpov petitioned the Central Committee to open churches. Resolutions by the Central Committee and the Council of Ministers in the fall of 1958 and criticism of the Council for Russian Orthodox Church Affairs finally forced him to accept that no positive decisions would be made, even "for appearances." In February 1959, Karpov himself already "correctly" explained the problem of opening churches to the patriarch:

In regard to opening churches, I should clarify the matter and express my own opinion on this question. . . . N.S. Khrushchev did not promise to open new churches but said that the state would review the matter after you submitted a letter. . . . Local authorities do not wish to open churches. Generally speaking, is it expedient to do this? The Russian Orthodox Church has over 13,000 churches, and local authorities are called upon to solve

cultural growth

huge tasks in building [communist] culture. Added to all this is the enormous cultural growth of the Soviet people, and [the fact that] believers in our country mainly represent elderly citizens.[32]

On October 4, 1958, the Central Committee adopted a secret resolution, *10/4/58* "Report by the Agitation and Propaganda Department of the Central Committee of the CPSU for Union Republics on Shortcomings in Scientific-Atheistic Propaganda." It formulated anew tasks that were harmonious with the Central Committee's resolution of July 7, 1954, in the area of scientific-atheistic propaganda by using words like "to strengthen . . . to activate," and "to increase its aggressive character." Something new was also present. "The mission set before government organs of power was implementation of a series of administrative measures directed at limiting any rights of the church ——— and religious organizations that ran counter to existing legislation."[33]

The resolution related directly to the Council for Russian Orthodox Church Affairs. It was discussed at party meetings for Council staff members and then at an all-union conference for Council commissioners held in January 1959. At this conference, Council member Svenkov characterized the tasks of the Council as follows:

> Our main task consists of ensuring that the existing ties between church and state do not violate Soviet laws relating to the church. We cannot allow the church to strengthen its position or to increase its influence on the Soviet people. Toward this end, we first will make appropriate recommendations to the Moscow Patriarchate and, when needed, use the route of legislative acts. We will give party and Soviet agencies such information that might be successfully used in the struggle against church influence on the Soviet people.[34]

struggle

Everything that was achieved in church-state relations from the moment of the Council's creation was declared to be "a deformation of ecclesiastical policy of the socialist state" and "an incorrect political and tactical line." This led to the strengthening of religion and the church, plus the creation of favorable conditions for propagandizing "reactionary ideology" and for activity by numerous "open and hidden enemies of Soviet power" among the clergy. Special emphasis was given to the fact that, instead of aiming for the strictest limitation on the activity of religious organizations and actively assisting in shrinking the religious network, the Council made concessions to various "demands," "showing off the church to please foreigners." The whole earlier course in "religious matters" was denounced as "a manifestation of Stalinism."[35] The direct task of limiting the church's activity was laid upon the Council as the government body called upon to implement state policy in the life of the church. At the end of the 1950s this meant party policy. "In obeying instructions" laid out in the Central Committee's resolution, the Council developed specific measures "for eliminating mistakes and short-comings that had entered its work . . . [and] to adopt measures for limiting the church's activity."[36]

Acting on a joint proposal by the Council and the Finance Ministry, the Council of Ministers of the USSR adopted a Resolution on October 16, 1958, concerning "Levying Taxes on Income Received by Diocesan Administra-tive Enterprises and Also on the Income of Monasteries."[37] The heart of this new resolution consisted of a change in procedures for assessing, and there-fore increasing, income taxes on workshops that produced church candles. Moreover, the new taxes took affect on October 1, 1958. This plainly broke the annual budget of the Russian Orthodox Church and, as Patriarch Aleksii wrote to the Council, disorganized church activity. The four members of the Council (Karpov was in the hospital at the time) did not support a request from the patriarch to apply the new tax procedures effective January 1, 1959. The Central Committee backed the Council's decision.[38]

On the recommendation of the Council for Russian Orthodox Church Affairs, the Council of Ministers of the USSR adopted yet another resolution on October 16, 1958, on "Monasteries in the USSR."[39] It ordered the Coun-cils for Russian Orthodox Church Affairs and Affairs of Religious Cults within "a six-month period to study the issue of reducing the number of monaster-ies and hermitages and to bring a corresponding resolution on this matter to the Council of Ministers."[40] After Karpov and Patriarch Aleksii discussed the matter in February and early in April 1959, the patriarch accepted the Council's proposal for eliminating twenty-two Orthodox monasteries and seven hermitages. Patriarch Aleksii sent his written agreement to the Coun-cil on April 4, 1959. He also agreed to Karpov's request to instruct diocesan bishops not to accept persons younger than thirty into monasteries. The pa-triarch eventually concurred with Karpov's demand that "no subsidies of any kind be given to monasteries" without the Council's consent.[41]

As one measure to limit the church, the Council also took on the task of reducing the number of dioceses. At meetings between Karpov and the patri-arch in the winter and spring of 1959, the patriarch consented to "urgent recommendations from the Council" for eliminating dioceses in Sumy (it was united with Chernigov), Drogobych (it was united with the Lvov dio-cese in connection with the elimination of the Drogobych region), Riga (united with Estonia), and Ulyanovsk (united with Kuibyshev). The patriarch with-drew requests for opening independent dioceses in Lugansk, Ternopol, Khabarovsk, and other places.[42] Only one of the measures proposed by the Council to the Central Committee as part of the struggle against prejudices and superstitions was sufficiently painless for both the Council and the Moscow Patriarchate—this was elimination of "holy sites" that were places for mass pilgrimages by believers.[43] Officially, the church at the time thought worship at such sites (mainly springs of water) was paganism. Patriarch Aleksii repeatedly appealed to believers and diocesan bishops on the impermissibility of pilgrimages to so-called "holy sites." He also instructed clergy on explaining the perniciousness of such rites and on refusing to participate in such pilgrimages. On a recommendation from the Council in spring 1959, Patriarch Aleksii again sent a letter to all diocesan administrations in which he required clergy not only "to do educational work among believers on the impermissibility of pilgrimages to so-called 'holy sites' not venerated by the church" but also "to report progress in that work to the patriarchate."[44]

Regarding Orthodox institutions for theological education, the Council sent the following proposals to the Central Committee:

- "The Council does not intend to allow institutions for theological education to admit students into academies and seminaries in the middle of an academic year."
- "Do not accept persons into institutions for theological education who have specialized secondary or advanced education . . ." (Karpov's opinion was that the acceptance of specialists and students from secondary and advanced schools into seminaries "violates plans for educating specialists. Most importantly, it diverts a certain portion of qualified laborers from material production that is basic to the existence of all social construction.")
- "Recommend that the Moscow Patriarchate eliminate the Correspondence Department at Leningrad Theological Seminary . . ." (Karpov justified this decision by saying that the Correspondence Department "without approval from the Council" had been transformed into an independent educational institution in which not only Leningrad regional clergy studied—as agreed upon by the Council—but also clergy from other dioceses.)
- "Merge the smaller seminaries and do not allow financial excess in support of institutions for theological education."[45]

In addition, the Council obtained agreement from the patriarchate for establishing the following rule: Diocesan bishops should verify personal information of all citizens who express a desire to enter an institution for theological education. As Karpov wrote to the Central Committee, "This allows Council commissioners to know beforehand about people who are applying and to take needed steps."[46]

Along with implementing and planning measures to limit church activity throughout the country, the Council "intended to take steps to increase foreign activity of the Moscow Patriarchate by widening and strengthening its ties with other churches abroad and using these ties in the fight for peace and for bans on the testing and use of thermonuclear weapons."[47]

The time came to forget a principle that had guided the Council for over fifteen years. In order for the Moscow Patriarchate to successfully carry out policies in suport of the Soviet government's international agenda, it was essential to create "favorable conditions" for the church domestically.

After review and discussion of suggestions expressed by its commissioners at their conference in January 1959, the Council sent out instructional letter No. 61 on June 6, 1959. All the Council's "interpretations" were in reality consistent with a hard-line course in terms of religious organizations, clergy, and believers.

The Council's attitude toward petitions for opening churches fundamentally changed. One point simply followed from its recommendations. Favorable decisions on opening churches would no longer be given, therefore such applications should no longer made. The letter said,

> In order to reduce and eventually stop petitions for opening churches, commissioners for the Council must do the following: . . . in cases where a petition was instigated by people with mercenary interests, you must tell them that their applications will not be reviewed. . . . When clergy are revealed to be the instigators, you must warn them about the illegality of such acts and, in cases where such efforts continue, revoke their registration. . . . If petitions are submitted by a sizable group of believers, immediately inform local authorities so that they can takes steps to reinforce large-scale political, cultural, and educational work among the population and bring to an end to petitions. . . . When petitions for opening churches are in reality the result of difficulties in completing religious rites, you must suggest that clergy take steps to satisfy requests from believers by performing religious rites; you will localize sources of petitions for opening churches this way.

The Council informed commissioners that it had established a new procedure by which "persons addressing the Council with complaints about decisions by Councils of Ministers of union and autonomous republics or regional executive committees on rejection of petitions for opening churches will be told that their complaints will not be supported by the Council, and commissioners will not forward any type of petition to the Council. Persons who appeal to the Council and bypass local authorities will receive an explanation of where and how to direct a petition to their regional commissioner. Duplicate petitions submitted by the same people will not be reviewed by the Council nor forwarded by commissioners."[48]

This instructional letter set out other positions that gave additional directions to commissioners:

> It is not permissible to have children and adolescents under the age of eighteen serve in the church.
>
> Regarding performance of rites by clergy in homes of believers . . . clergy must be told that the exercise of religious rites in homes of believers can take place only in those circumstances where believers request it and certify that no one in the home or apartment has expressed opposition to performance of religious rituals.*
>
> On parishes in decline: . . . Immediately uncover communities that cannot exist without monetary help from their diocesan administration. . . . Using carefully-thought-out pretexts, you do not need to allow appointment of permanent or temporary priests to these parishes. . . . You must absolutely not conduct this work as a campaign. . . . The Sovnarkom resolution of December 1, 1944, which prohibits closure of churches without agreement from the Council, remains in force.
>
> On charitable activity by clergy: . . . Pay attention to annual reports by diocesan administrations where, in many cases, charitable activity is reflected in line items for revenues.
>
> On work with clergy: . . . Demand that clergy accurately and steadfastly obey Soviet legislation on the church. Do not allow even a single violation to go unpunished through a warning from the diocesan bishop, a request to meet with you, or, when it is necessary, removal from the registry. Moreover, you must use these measures in such a way that all clergy in the diocese know about them and they serve as warnings for others. . . . Systematically develop specific measures for limiting church activity and implement them after getting approval from the Council.[49]

Certain words and phrases once again appeared in Karpov's literary arsenal. These included "churchmen," "mercenary motives of people interested in opening churches," "clergy instigators," "speculative prices for candles," and "individual errors by local authorities." At meetings with the patriarch and Metropolitan Nikolai, especially in the fall and winter of 1959, Karpov spoke certain other phrases as if he had learned them by heart:

---

*On this point, the Council referred to a resolution by the All-Russian Central Executive Committee and Sovnarkom RSFSR of April 8, 1929 that said conducting religious rituals "in public buildings" was forbidden.

Karpov

Scientific-atheistic propaganda is being carried out and will be carried out. . . . However, it does not aim at discrediting the church in the eyes of the people, much less at the church's physical destruction.

It is incorrect to draw the conclusion from individual thoughtless acts by certain commissioners that now they all are following some new policy in regard to the church.

The Council cannot agree with the proposition that closing monasteries would provoke inordinate protests from monks and believers.

There is no evidence to support the proposition that closure of inactive churches is evidence of a new course by the state in relation to the church.

There is no evidence to support the proposition that severely restrictive measures in relation to institutions for theological education have been adopted for the purpose of closing them.

You must not speak about some sort of "campaign"' but rather about specific facts of improper administrative methods—if they exist, of course.

In every specific case, send material to the Council so that it can take measures to correct mistakes through government authorities.[50]

It is impossible not to draw attention to the constant attempts to convince church leaders that there was no "new course" regarding the church or a "new line" in terms of religious organizations. But, as Odintsov remarks, "Even as Aleksii saw all the insincerity behind Karpov's assurances about the absence of 'an attack on the church,' so Karpov understood that the patriarch did not believe him but, at the same time, was aware that Karpov made such claims under duress. They both clearly recognized that 'a new course' existed and had been approved at the highest level."[51] Odintsov suggests that Karpov "internally rejected this 'new course,' which was in essence actually an even older policy, and did not want to be its obedient executor."[52] There is every reason to agree with this claim. Karpov was accustomed to correlating his work with state interests. He could not objectively understand what caused an attack on the church from the standpoint of those interests. Demagogic tricks of a new generation of party functionaries sickened him, since he was accustomed to acting within the boundaries of legislative instructions and resolutions, not party slogans.

Karpov

The hypocrisy of his own position undoubtedly depressed Karpov. Others noted opposition and inconsistency in positions taken by the Council's chairman. Simultaneous with the battle reports to the Central Committee on measures for limiting religious organizations, Karpov sent instructions to commissioners (March 1959) in which he condemned their participation in individual work with believers for the purpose of "exposing children and youth in churches." This provoked the usual "shouting" from the top, and he was forced to recall this document.[53]

Krushev?

In addition to material on illegal activity of churchmen, Karpov asked the Council of Ministers and the Central Committee to review instances of "crude administrative measures" by authorities.[54] While sending a report to the Central Committee in May 1959 about discussions with Patriarch Aleksii and Metropolitan Nikolai, Karpov gave advance warning of its contents in a memorandum in which he expressed his personal opinion, "I think that referring to Metropolitan Nikolai by name in an article entitled 'Religious Legends and Life' in the Kostroma newspaper *Severnaia Pravda* [Northern Truth] on April 29 of this year certainly should not have been permitted. I request that you give instructions to the newspaper's editorial board."[55]

Karpov reacted very negatively to methods for implementing the Council's resolution on closing monasteries in Ukraine, Moldavia, and the Baltic republics. His letter to Konstantin Chernenko* (chief of the Mass Agitation Section of Agitprop) on April 16, 1959, even included the almost forgotten phrase, "The Council categorically objects." Karpov "objected" to the intention of the Central Committee of the Communist Party of the Ukraine to close eighteen monasteries instead of the eight that had been planned and to carry out this act by the end of 1959. Karpov also asked Chernenko to telephone the Ukrainian Central Committee about the monastery closings.[56] In July, Karpov sent the Council of Ministers of the USSR a "Communication on Mistakes Permitted in Implementation of Measures for Closing Monasteries." He cited cases of "mistaken activity" by republic-level soviets and party organizations that violated agreements reached on the number of monasteries to be closed and the timing of their closures. He requested, "In accordance with policy, the Central Committee or the Council of Ministers should warn party and Soviet organs in the republics of the Ukraine, Moldavia, Belorussia, Lithuania, and Latvia on more careful and gradual implementation of measures for reducing the number of monasteries and hermitages, conducting them only in agreement with the Council."[57]

Karpov did not stop his attempts to stress the importance of the Moscow Patriarchate's foreign activities and their significance to the interests of the USSR. He wrote the following in an informational report sent to Khrushchev in January 1960:

> In my opinion, we still are unable to stop the well-known use of church organizations abroad for our state political interests. . . . We must strengthen and improve the foreign work of the church. While we should not over-

---

*K.U. Chernenko (1911–1985) was a protégé of Leonid Brezhnev, who, near the end of his life, briefly served as General Secretary of the Communist Party of the Soviet Union in 1984–85.—Ed.

Khrushchev

value it, we must not undervalue it. . . . With our direction and more active involvement, religious organizations in the USSR could do much that is useful for government interests and, at the same time, is annoying to our enemies.[58]

However, Karpov's position and policy in favor of careful restraint could not change the situation in the religious sphere. Vigorous attacks on religious organizations that had begun in regions around the country were already impossible to stop. Both the head of the Russian Orthodox Church and the chairman of the Council for Russian Orthodox Church Affairs understood this clearly. Patriarch Aleksii expressed this in a remarkable way in a letter to Karpov on November 30, 1959, "My position forces me *to be ill* about everything that disturbs peaceful church life, and now this calm is especially broken—in the attempt (not only by us but also by those in power) to protect the underlying *freedom of the church's internal life.* I have no doubt that you personally understand this *very well.*"[59]*

The only thing that Karpov could do under the circumstances was to inform the highest authorities "about claims made by the Moscow Patriarchate," "about the moods of Patriarch Aleksii," and to pass on requests from church leaders to meet with Khrushchev as head of the Soviet government. Karpov himself also awaited a meeting with Khrushchev. Karpov certainly calculated (this time) that he would receive "directives" and "instructions" from the head of state for the further work of the Council. Thus, together with a report he presented to Khrushchev from Patriarch Aleksii and Metropolitan Nikolai on June 8, 1959, Karpov expressed a request of his own:

> Considering it desirable and necessary, I ask that you meet me so that I might briefly report on the situation in the church and receive directives on principle and fundamental matters relating to the church within the USSR, its foreign activity, and principles for the Council's work. I previously received such directives as president of the Council related to the period from 1943 to 1945 and, later, from 1947 to 1950. Those earlier directives are out of date and, obviously, in many areas have not guided me for a long time. I have not had conversations more recently on the content of our work.[60]

No meeting occurred. Karpov was also unable to hold conversations with Khrushchev's aide, E. A. Furtsev, as Karpov had asked in March 1959.[61]

---

*Emphasis is the patriarch's in the original letter.

Meanwhile, the central party apparatus prepared a new resolution touching on religion. Agitprop asked the Commission for Issues of Ideology, Culture, and External Party Ties to review a memo on "Illegal Activity by Churchmen and Sectarians" and the draft of a resolution on this matter.[62] Agitprop thought that violations of legislation on religious groups "in recent years have become widespread."

What was the basis for this conclusion? It was based primarily on charitable activity by the church, "illegal construction and purchasing of houses for religious uses and acquisition of automotive transportation," and the performance of religious rites in homes. In a word, everything that was permitted by special legislative acts, resolutions, and instructions of the government[63] in the 1940s and early 1950s now was declared a violation of Soviet law. In reality, no one ever abolished legislation—specifically, the 1929 resolution by the All-Russian Central Executive Committee and Sovnarkom RSFSR on "Religious Associations." No changes had even been made to that resolution, despite repeated proposals from the Councils. At the end of the 1950s, the time had come to assess the activity of the church and other religious organizations as a violation of the 1929 legislation. This could not have proven more opportune for the policy being implemented "on the struggle against Stalin's legacy." It was also quite convenient for declaring that the whole system of resolutions and instructions by the government in the 1940s was nothing more than "a manifestation of Stalinism."

The time had come for the Council for Russian Orthodox Church Affairs and the Council for Affairs of Religious Cults "to pay" for the style of building church-state relations that was the foundation of Stalinist religious policy. The memo on "Illegal Activity of Churchmen and Sectarians" plainly stated that the Councils "frequently slipped down the path of serving the church" and that "in recent years control has weakened, especially on the part of the Council for Russian Orthodox Church Affairs. . . . This has resulted in a sharp increase in the number of churches. . . [The number of dioceses is now greater than it was prior to the Revolution."[64] In addition, the memo contained criticism directed against Karpov personally. "Karpov incorrectly understands the mission of the Council and does not wish to take the changes happening in our country into account."[65]

Having familiarized himself with the contents of the memo and with the proposed resolution, Karpov personally sent the Central Committee a response entitled "Explanations to the Memo on 'Illegal Activity by Churchmen and Sectarians.'" This was the last attempt by the chairman of the Council for Russian Orthodox Church Affairs to defend the very cause to which he had devoted sixteen years of his life. Karpov wrote, "I accept criticism of the Council. There have been and continue to be shortcomings in its work. . . . A mistake is a lesson, and recognition of a mistake can only help to correct the matter quickly." At the same time, Karpov expressed his own disagreement in principle with a series of proposals in the memo. Responding to the accusation made against the Council about its "toleration" for the growth in numbers of Orthodox churches, Karpov gave the following arguments, "A sharp increase took place during the war. Prior to 1948, a large increase of 3,001 in the total number of churches took place on account of the reunion of Uniate churches with Orthodoxy. . . . I thought and still think that this was a politically positive factor. But now, they ask why the number of churches increased by 3,000? Because the number of Uniate churches decreased by an even greater number."[66] Karpov pointed out inaccuracies to the Central Committee: "Dioceses are not based on the number of churches. . . . In Russia in 1917, there were 74 provinces and 65 dioceses; now, there are 66 dioceses for 103 provinces in the RSFSR, Ukraine, and Belorussia, plus 12 other union republics." Karpov also opined that, "reducing the number of dioceses, although certainly possible, is not always beneficial for us."[67] In response to a fact presented in the memo that twenty-four out of the sixty-nine bishops in the USSR had been convicted for anti-Soviet activity, Karpov noted, "We are not mainly concerned about those who have been convicted or those who are seventy to eighty-five years old. Instead, we are concerned about those who have become new bishops over the last ten to fifteen years and who, due to age, are more zealous in their religious activity."[68]

Karpov protested against the accusation that the Council had "slipped into service of the church." He wrote, "It was not a process of slipping but one of political expediency and following appropriate decisions that, for example, led the Council to approve applications from the patriarchate for certain restricted supplies—not completely but on the order of 25 to 50 percent—used in its workshops or for building materials, but only for individual architectural landmarks. No one has yet said that we should not do this and obviously no one will, since acquisition of such materials from other sources has an ugly undertone."[69] And finally, Karpov "in a categorical way" rejected the charges leveled against him:

> What is the basis for this? . . . It's possible, if necessary, to ignore everything that was done over the course of sixteen years, but it is impossible and unnecessary to ignore state political interests in the area of the church's foreign activity. I do not want to overrate this work, but it is also unnecessary to undervalue it. . . . The party educated and raised me—a former metalworker in a factory and then a sailor—to leadership of a central institution. To this date, I have occupied my assigned post for seventeen years. Careerism must be ruled out, and no self-interest is involved. I have no

interest in daily contact with an environment that is so alien to us ideologically—an environment in which almost every human vice is widespread. I
am not worried for myself (although injustice does depress me). . . . I am
worried and am very seriously upset over the cause to which I have devoted a quarter of my life. I see serious misunderstandings that, if not corrected, may lead to wrong and undesired consequences; for all of us, the
interests of the whole state are above everything. . . . I cannot understand
why an investigation has taken place for nearly two years now, using every
means to compromise and then dismiss me. And, since there is nothing
else, tendentiousness has set in bordering on personal insult. I have tolerated this for a long time (this is also my liberalism) but no longer have any
strength and want it to end, knowing the Central Committee's current attitude toward cadres.[70]

This letter unquestionably served as the final argument for the Central Committee in making its decision on the need to appoint a "fresh" person to the
position of chairman of the Council for Russian Orthodox Church Affairs. Despite the fact that Karpov presented himself as a leader "who correctly understands the tasks of the Council and accounts for changes taking place in the
country" at meetings with church leaders in December 1959 and January 1960,
his fate was already sealed. Karpov was removed from the position of Council
chairman by a resolution of the Council of Ministers of the USSR on February
6, 1960. This same resolution appointed V.A. Kuroedov to take his place.

The Central Committee adopted a resolution on January 13, 1960, on
"Measures for Eliminating Violations by Clergy of Soviet Legislation on
Cults." Measures for putting it into practice were developed by the Council
now led by its new chairman. Discussion of the Council's tasks in light of
the new resolution took place at an All-Union Conference of Commissioners
held on April 21–23, 1960. The conference was attended by 110 people who
heard Kuroedov's report on "Tasks of the Council and its Commissioners in
Light of the CPSU Central Committee Resolution of January 13, 1960, on
'Measures for Eliminating Violations by Clergy of Soviet Legislation on
Cults.'" Twenty-five people spoke during the debate on this report.[71] Practically every speech contained criticism of the Council's prior work and its
former chairman. For example, Commissioner Biriuchev of Sverdlovsk stated,
"Violations by clergy of legislation on cults became possible first of all as a
result of permissiveness on the Council's part. Moreover, this permissiveness existed from the first years of the Council's creation. . . . I am personally
very pleased with the Central Committee's resolution of January 13, 1960."[72]
Commissioner Koshman of Ulyanovsk expressed the same sentiments related to activity that had been the source of repeated complaints from the

patriarch and Metropolitan Nikolai: "I cannot get it in my head how it is possible to allow so many violations, so much unauthorized behavior, and, crudely speaking, so much permissiveness toward clergy when we make demands. . . . I am for an attack on the church as a remnant of the past that is now becoming obsolete."[73]

Council chairman Kuroedov dedicated a whole section of his report to an analysis of the Council's "mistakes" under its previous leadership:

> The main mistake of the Council for Russian Orthodox Church Affairs consisted in unpredictably carrying out the line of the party and government in relation to the church. The Council conducted a policy of guarding church interests instead of struggling against violations of legislation on cults. . . . The most serious mistake by the Council was that it essentially assisted in strengthening the church's hierarchy. . . . Clear evidence of the Council's permissiveness toward churchmen is found in the lack of any control over the activity of workshops that make candles and other objects used in the religious cult. . . . The Council protected the Moscow Patriarchate from increases in income taxes on candle production. . . . Before 1958, the Finance Ministry raised the issue several times with the Council's leadership about the need to review tax procedures, but every time the Council's leadership found "grounds" for rejecting the proposals. . . . The Council and some of its commissioners reacted liberally to these phenomena, thinking that charity did not bring any great harm. Meanwhile, charity was a powerful, key factor for strengthening the church and expanding its influence. . . . Or, we can take up the issue of methods in the Council's work. Despite the fact that in recent years, especially after the Twentieth and Twenty-first Congresses of the CPSU, the situation in the country has fundamentally changed—new tasks in the emerging construction of a communist society have arisen—the Council continued to work using old methods that had become obsolete. . . . Comrade Karpov, the Council's former chairman, bears great blame for all these mistakes and shortcomings.[74]

These mistakes had to be corrected. As the historian Odintsov notes, "1960 was the first of many years when new leadership in the Council investigated and methodically 'corrected the mistakes' of their predecessors and 'eliminated' violations (for the most part imaginary) by clergy of legislation on cults."[75]

A special period in the history of church-state relations ended with Karpov's dismissal. This was a period when genuine relations existed between the state and the Orthodox Church. It was a period when church policy was established and truly implemented in the interests of the state—undoubtedly, in the interests of both the state in the 1940s and specific leaders in the Soviet government at the time.

A qualitatively new stage in that history started in the 1960s when the character of relations with religious organizations, with the Russian Orthodox Church and believers, was determined exclusively by ideological directives "of the party and state." The renovated Council for Russian Orthodox Church Affairs was assigned the role of a mere tool for realizing and implementing those directives.

The Moscow Patriarchate and the Regime: Preparations for a New Attack

The attack on religion and the church that began in 1958 differed qualitatively in its conduct, methods, and character from the previous one initiated by the Central Committee resolution of July 7, 1954, on "Serious Shortcomings in Scientific-Atheistic Propaganda and Measures for Improving It."

First, party and governmental resolutions from the years 1958–61 were never published in the mass media. They were "adopted as working procedures" and, certainly, local party and Soviet organs tried to follow them. The absence of printed resolutions deprived the Moscow Patriarchate and the international community of the means for proving an official change in church policy in the USSR.

Second, the Soviet government passed a series of legislative acts for the first time, following a hiatus of nearly thirty years, that were directed at undermining the financial base of the Orthodox Church as well as changing its legal status as defined in the postwar period.

Third, a propagandistic attack on religion and the church was accompanied by administrative measures against clergy and laity. The scale and nature of that attack were equivalent to "the campaign against the church" of the 1920s and 1930s.

Even before the Central Committee adopted its resolution of October 4, 1958 ("Report by the Agitation and Propaganda Department of the Central Committee of the CPSU for Union Republics on Shortcomings in Scientific-Atheistic Propaganda"), the Council for Russian Orthodox Church Affairs and Finance Ministry presented proposals to the Central Committee in the summer of 1958 on "Changing Procedures for Levying Income Taxes on Candle Production by Religious Organizations." As previously mentioned, Council Vice Chairman Cheredniak wrote these proposals. He reviewed the issue like a professional economist. The logic behind his argument was as follows.

Activity by churches in the USSR is aided by their high levels of cash income, which steadily increases from one year to the next. . . . Revenues *candles*

from sales of candles to believers provide a large proportion of income received by churches. The Russian Orthodox Church has especially high revenues from candle production. Thus, in the diocese of Moscow, revenues from sales of candles totaled 88 million rubles in 1956, or nearly 70 percent of all income. In the Krasnodar region, it was over 70 percent. In Belorussia, 70 percent. . . . Usually, candle production increases each year. According to statistics from the Finance Ministry, the fifteen candle workshops of the Russian Orthodox Church produced 400,000 kilograms of candles in 1953. In 1957, these same workshops produced 846,000 kilograms. . . . Calculation of taxes is based on the difference between the cost of manufacture and the prices charged to religious communities for candles. The Moscow Patriarchate and its diocesan administrations use this procedure for calculating taxes for their own mercenary ends. This is seen in that fact that for several years they steadily lowered the prices of candles sold to churches. For example, the Moscow candle workshop, which makes candles primarily from raw materials received from state sources at state prices, lowered prices from 27 rubles to 15 rubles per kilogram. The workshop in the diocese of Moldavia lowered prices from 250 to 100 rubles per kilogram. The workshop in Alma-Ata lowered prices from 145 to 80 rubles per kilogram. And so on.

taxes

Such activity by the Moscow Patriarchate and its diocesan administrations has led to their paying less and less income tax from one year to the next. For example, according to Finance Ministry statistics, the Moscow Patriarchate paid over 5.622 million rubles on 400,000 kilograms of candles in 1953. But, in 1957, it paid 4.962 million rubles on 846,000 kilograms of candles.[76]

The Council and the Finance Ministry proposed various alternative ways for calculating taxes in order to increase them. In this regard, the Council suggested that, "an increase in taxation on candle production might give churches grounds to raise retail prices for candles. We would think it expedient to recommend to national church bodies that they not allow an increase in retail prices." In addition, the Council thought it expedient that, "Negotiations with national church bodies on the issue of raising taxes on income from the sale of candles be conducted by the Finance Ministry and not the Council."[77]

On the basis of proposals from the Council and the Finance Ministry, the Council of Ministers on October 16, 1958, adopted Resolution No. 1160 on "Assessing Taxes on the Income of Diocesan Administrations and Also on the Income of Monasteries." The Council of Ministers determined "that the assessment of revenue for income taxes by candle workshops of diocesan administrations should be set on the basis of a sales price of 200 rubles per kilogram of candles minus production expenses." In addition, they established increased rates of taxation on plots of land used by monasteries. The resolution repealed the tax break on rents from buildings and land used by monasteries that had been granted by a Sovnarkom resolution of August 20, 1945.[78]

The Council for Russian Orthodox Church Affairs officially "informed" representatives of the Moscow Patriarchate—Kolchitskii, the patriarchal administrator, Bishop Pimen, the patriarch's assistant, and members of the Administrative Department of the Patriarchate (Patriarch Aleksii was ill and Metropolitan Nikolai was not in Moscow)—about the resolution by the Council of Ministers at meetings on October 28–29, 1958.[79]

Russian Orthodox clergy already knew about the introduction of new procedures for levying taxes and, in the words of Kolchitskii, "experienced panic." Representatives of the Moscow Patriarchate "expressed astonishment" (completely justified, in my view) over "why the Finance Ministry, while preparing a proposal for the government on new procedures for taxing candle workshops, did not consult with staff from the Administrative Department of the patriarchate." But, it is interesting to note that representatives of the Moscow Patriarchate expressed bewilderment, "astonishment," indignation, and even, as Pospielovsky writes, "resorted to the ultimate threat . . . that if the Council did not take measures to limit taxes on candle sales, they would inform foreigners about the situation in the church."[80] Nonetheless, Ostapov as chairman of the Administrative Department of the Moscow Patriarchate and Maliushitskii, a member of the department, concluded discussion of the issue about new tax assessments in this way, "We see that the government seeks tax revenues required for the needs of the state. If it has decided it is necessary that the church should play whatever part it can in the construction [of communism] with its own [financial] means, as it did earlier by subscribing to government loans, then *the Moscow Patriarchate is not opposed to fulfilling the Resolution of the government of October 16* [emphasis added]. However, the Moscow Patriarchate will present a petition to the government through the Council asking that the new tax assessment on candles be introduced on January 1, 1959, because paying taxes from October 1 will break the budget of the church for the fourth quarter of 1958 and provoke panic among clergy. We request that the Council inform the government of our petition."[81]

As stated previously, the petition was signed by Patriarch Aleksii and presented to the Council but did not find support in the Council, in the Central Committee, or in the government.[82]

Also, the words that Patriarch Aleksii spoke during a conversation with Karpov and Cheredniak on February 20, 1959, deserve our attention: "The government's resolution on taxing candle production was correct in principle, for in this matter we had developed procedurally underhanded practices. Urban churches will cope with the new taxes on candles in the end. However, this will be difficult for rural churches."[83]

"The candle issue" was a "sore spot" for the church, as Patriarch Aleksii wrote. Complaints about a significant decline in parish revenues as a result of the new taxes arose both in conversations with leaders of the Council and in letters prepared by the patriarchate for examination by the government and sent personally to Khrushchev. Yet this provided a quicker verification of the fact that increased taxes meant a reduction of church revenues. Taxes on candles increased from 1,500,000 rubles in 1957 to 71,154,038 rubles in 1958.[84] But the church actually learned how "to cope" with the new taxes on candles. Karpov presented an informational report to the Central Committee in May 1959 on "The Process of Realizing the Resolution by the CPSU Central Committee of October 4, 1958, 'On the Memo. . . .'" He noted in particular, "I must say directly that the expected degree of economic weakening of the church has not happened in connection with the government's resolution on increasing taxes on the production of church candles."[85]

Kuroedov, the new Council chairman, wrote about the condition of the Russian Orthodox Church in a report to the CPSU Central Committee in August 1960: "Church revenues in some regions have even increased . . . and this despite the fact that taxes on candle production were raised. . . . Using various schemes, churchmen learned how to transfer [taxes on] candle production to believing citizens and to emerge from the situation in many cases with a profit."[86] From Kuroedov's perspective, it was necessary "to take follow-up steps in coordination with the Finance Ministry of the USSR for limiting church revenues, primarily from candle production as the main source of revenue."[87]

Issues connected with monasteries became more difficult for the Russian Orthodox Church. In connection with the unification of Belorussia, Moldavia, the Baltic republics, and western provinces of Ukraine during the war, sixty-four monasteries came under the Moscow Patriarchate. An additional thirty-seven monasteries were opened on territory occupied by Nazi Germany. Newly opened monasteries, especially in the RSFSR, were economically weak and required constant subsidies, and the Moscow Patriarchate independently decided to close some of them. Thirty-eight monasteries were closed through mergers between 1947 and 1957. A total of fifty-six monasteries and seven hermitages were located in the USSR in 1958.[88] Their financial resources and status varied, but the patriarchate until this time had the financial means to support their activity. The question of additional reductions in the number of monasteries was not discussed. The secular regime initiated this process. The Council of Ministers of the USSR using its resolution of October 16, 1958, "On Monasteries in the USSR,"[89] gave the Councils of

Ministers of the republics working with the Councils for Russian Orthodox Church Affairs and Affairs of Religious Cults "six months to study the issue for the possibility of reducing the number of monasteries and hermitages in the USSR." The resolution envisioned reductions in the amount of land held for use by monasteries, establishment of "monastic norms" for every monastery, and prohibitions on use of hired labor. The situation in many monasteries became desperate due to demands from the Council for Russian Orthodox Church Affairs not to accept citizens younger than thirty into monasteries and to eliminate subsidies given without the Council's consent, combined with the tax increase on buildings. For example, Patriarch Aleksii described the impoverished condition of monasteries in Moldavia connected with the tax increase on buildings in a memo to Khrushchev on November 20, 1959: "Such measures would inevitably require closure of these monasteries. Now, the local Directorate for Communal Management through administrative procedures is seizing all resources of these monasteries and demanding the sale of their property."[90]

Taking these circumstances into account, the patriarch was forced to agree with planned closures of some monasteries—their continued operation became economically impractical. After discussion of specific proposals from the Council for eliminating twenty-two monasteries and seven hermitages over the course of two years, the patriarch sent Karpov a letter on behalf of himself, Metropolitan Nikolai, and Kolchitskii:

> Under conditions created when it became necessary to continue reductions in the number of monasteries, as was done before 1958, we are finding that the plan for reductions projected by the Council is the most painless solution of this matter that generally and undoubtedly affects the situation of many monks, depriving them of their accustomed place in their familiar nests—the monasteries.
>
> The painlessness of the plan mainly comes from its proposals to close few currently functioning monasteries, to transfer people from the closed communities to other monasteries and, primarily, to close the affected monasteries gradually over several years and not all at once. Through the plan, this reduction will not be perceived as quite so harsh either by the monks themselves or by believers in general.[91]

Karpov presented the agreed-upon plan for a reduction of monasteries to the Soviet government on April 7, 1959, as a draft resolution for the Council of Ministers. In a letter attached to the draft resolution, Karpov directed the government's attention to these points: The reduction must be conducted by means of mergers with other monasteries and the transfer of monks; and the reduction must not take place immediately but over the course of

1959–60. (On the latter point, he indicated a disagreement he had with the Council of Ministers of Ukraine. "The Ukrainian Council of Ministers raised the possibility of closing the monasteries this summer. The Council cannot agree to this, since the nearly simultaneous closure of eighteen monasteries in the Ukraine will spark unneeded incorrect interpretations abroad and an uproar within the church. The Council thinks it best to close the monasteries gradually.") Karpov also insisted, "If the church in a monastery is a parish—meaning that its parishioners are not only monks but also residents of nearby regions—such a church should not be closed."[92]

The resolution, however, was not adopted. F. Kozlov, deputy chairmen of the Council of Ministers of the USSR, moved, "The Councils of Ministers of Ukraine, Belorussia, Lithuania, Latvia, and Moldavia are to resolve this matter in agreement with the Council for Russian Orthodox Church Affairs under the Council of Ministers of the USSR."[93]

That decision by the center led to republic-level Council of Ministers establishing their own timetables and ignoring the opinion of the Council for Russian Orthodox Church Affairs. For example, the Council of Ministers of Moldavia decided in a resolution on June 5, 1958 to eradicate three monasteries as of July 1, two others as of August 1, and the remaining three in the first quarter of 1960.[94] The Council of Ministers of Ukraine adopted a resolution on June 17 to eradicate eight of the forty monasteries in the republic in 1959, but a timetable for elimination of these monasteries was not set.[95]

As a result, initiative for closing monasteries passed to regional authorities who, as Karpov wrote to the government of the USSR, "made haste to implement measures for liquidating monasteries . . . and are trying to eradicate those monasteries in two or three days without advance preparations or educational work."[96]

This "hasty eradication" (any understanding of "reduction through merger" was simply missing in information from the provinces), and its methods vividly recalled the campaign of the 1920s for closing monasteries. Instead of transferring monks to other functioning monasteries, representatives of the regime in many cases "suggested that monks who were evicted from a monastery go wherever it was convenient—to a home for invalids, to relatives, and so forth."[97] The authorities certainly knew that most people residing in monasteries were elderly, and that the majority of them were bedridden.[98] For example, the eradication of the Ovruch convent in the Zhitomir region lasted only twenty-six hours and, according to information from the Council, was conducted in this way,

> On June 24 at 11:00 A.M., the Ovruch district executive committee summoned the entire governing body of the Ovruch convent. The district executive committee's vice chairman, Comrade Udovitskii, read the committee's

decision on closing the convent to them. By 4:00 P.M. on June 25, the eviction of nuns from the convent was completed. Ten trucks, students from the mechanization school, and policemen in official uniforms were assigned to the evacuation. As a result, all sixty-two nuns were dispersed by category to places selected for them to live, and their requests to be transferred to other convents were ignored. On the morning of June 26, the Ovruch interdistrict children's hospital opened in the buildings of the former convent.[99]

Local authorities closed all churches attached to monasteries, even parish churches, publicly removed bells and crosses, and smashed iconstases.[100]

A "serious incident" took place between government representatives and believers in a convent church during "liquidation" of the Rechul convent in Moldavia. As a consequence of the decision by officials to close the church ("crudely and clearly in haste") despite requests from believers to preserve it as a parish church, "many residents from surrounding villages went to the convent and organized an around-the-clock guard near the convent's church that consisted of fifty people armed with pitchforks, sticks, and stones." In his report to the Central Committee, Karpov wrote, "Every time local representatives from the government and society appeared and attempted to close the church, (the guards) rang the bell. People gathered from the fields and would not allow anyone near the church. This began on June 23. In the first two to three days, organizers successfully gathered some 200–250 collective farmworkers, including some people with dubious pasts, and widely spread rumors alleging all monks would be forced out of their homes and sent to the North." The "incident" turned into direct conflict. A group of twenty to twenty-five people "savagely beat up the collective farm's agronomist . . . and inflicted injury on certain other persons." Karpov further informed them, "Police Lieutenant Dolgan was seriously injured with a pitchfork by a drunkard and loafer named Davyd who helped organize the assault and battery; the lieutenant shot that bandit in self-defense. Eleven people who organized excesses and hooliganism were arrested, and an investigation has begun."[101]

A stream of protests poured into the patriarch, who was in Odessa at the time, the patriarchate, and the Council for Russian Orthodox Church Affairs. Worried, the patriarch wrote to Karpov, "Here, cries from monasteries tire me out—written ones and even nuns who come to visit, complaining that they are forcibly evicted 'into the world,' without any consideration of either their age or local church conditions. This causes not only unrest among them but also disturbances among the people. Obviously, those in the provinces are not following the principle promoted in the center—do not evict monks from monasteries but transfer them to different cloisters."[102]

The Council reported to the government "on complications encountered" during closures of monasteries. As already mentioned, Karpov appealed to both the Central Committee and government to exert influence on republic-level party and Soviet organs. However, no answer came from the Central Committee, and Vice Chairman F. Kozlov of the Council of Ministers of the USSR proposed the usual resolution in response to Karpov's letter: "To the Councils of Ministers of Ukraine, Belorussia, Lithuania, Latvia, and Moldavia. I request that you review the memo and take measures to eliminate the problem. July 14, 1959."[103] It was a circular process. Such events had already become a tragedy.

Fourteen monasteries and hermitages were closed in the summer of 1959, and as Cheredniak reported to the Central Committee and the Council of Ministers of the USSR in October 1959, "The reduction proceeded in an organized way and without any major conflicts or complications."[104]

In a tone similar to that of his deputy, Karpov assessed the situation developing around the closure of monasteries during a meeting at the Council with Patriarch Aleksii, Metropolitan Nikolai, and Protopresbyter Kolchitskii in December 1959:

> The Council also does not agree that closures of monasteries provoked strong protests from monks and believers. True, disturbances took place among monks at the Kremenets and Ovruch monasteries. But, you know that these disturbances were caused by provocative activity by Archbishop Palladii of Lvov.[105]

Fourteen monasteries and five hermitages were closed in 1959. By August 1, 1960, eleven of the fifteen monasteries marked for liquidation that year had been closed.[106] Thus, negotiations and agreements with the patriarchate on the number of monasteries to be closed and the length of time over which closures would occur existed only on paper and were ignored by civilian authorities.

In the process of fulfilling the party resolution on a "Report by the Agitation and Propaganda Department of the Central Committee of the CPSU for Union Republics on Shortcomings in Scientific-Atheistic Propaganda," the Council for Russian Orthodox Church Affairs worked to close churches as one means of limiting church activity. It targeted churches "where no services ha[d] been held for a long time and an insignificant number of believers remain[ed] in the community." The Council also raised the issue with the patriarchate about stopping subsidies to diocesan administrations and parish churches. The patriarchate agreed to these demands. The complex economic situation in which the church found itself in the fall of 1958 without a doubt forced it to make that decision.[107]

One must note, however, that the Council did not set a goal for the reduction in the number of churches around the country; this was not an end in itself for Council leaders in 1958–59. Even in the summer of 1958, Karpov supported the patriarch's request to open churches in ten populated areas of the USSR.[108] The Council was made aware in the fall of that year that no discussion of any kind was possible in connection with opening churches and that it had to carry out the opposite policy of eliminating churches and chapels. The Council framed that task very carefully by setting certain conditions. Commissioners were instructed not to conduct mass or unjustified church closures but to close so-called "dying parishes" and attached churches. Moreover, Karpov stated in his instructions to commissioners on June 6, 1959, "You must not conduct this work as a campaign using administrative pressure. It can be done only in those cases where an insignificant number of believers actually remains in the parish community."[109]

Even during a situation of personal crisis in January 1960, Council chairman Karpov continued giving his views on the matter through an informational report addressed to Khrushchev:

> It is possible first to close churches where services are held only once or twice a year (there are 1,512 such churches), where parishes have small numbers of people, or that are attached churches. But I cannot agree with actions taken as in the following examples:
>
> a) In the Yakutsk ASSR, there are only two chapels located 612 kilometers apart. Nonetheless, the Council of Ministers of the Yakutsk ASSR raised the possibility of closing one of them this year, specifically the chapel in the town of Olekminsk.
>
> b) The Council of Ministers of the Mordovian [Mordvinian] ASSR raised the possibility of closing the church in the town of Insar (where there are no other churches) and gave the community of believers a former slaughterhouse and this provoked complaints. . . .
>
> We must warn against such administrative activity as occurred, for example, in the Poltava region. They recently used crude methods and caused mass protest while closing a church in the town of Lokhvitsa by unsealing doors and removing crosses with a blowtorch and throwing out the church's furnishings.[110]

A total of 305 churches and chapels were removed from the registry in 1959.[111] But, the many complaints that flowed into the Council and the patriarchate in 1958–59 were caused not so much by closures of church buildings (incidents of crude administrative closures of churches were very few in this period) as by the campaign against believers and clergy—a campaign that

agitprop

openly resembled the years of "militant atheism" in form and methods. Once again, material on scientific atheism filled the pages of newspapers and magazines. Despite the attempt to impart a scholarly character to their contents, the majority of authors fell into old patterns. They presented clergy basically as caricatures by directing readers to the amoral behavior of a few clergymen. They ridiculed religious rites and sacraments and on the whole insulted the religious sentiments of believers. Attacks that insulted clergy and believers, in the words of Metropolitan Nikolai, "overshadowed all that were known before the Central Committee decree of November 1954 in number and degree of expression."[112] In a letter to Khrushchev on May 31, 1959, Patriarch Aleksii and Metropolitan Nikolai cited a series of excerpts with such attacks from newspapers, magazines, and brochures:

The newspaper *Pivdenna Pravda* [Pivdenna Truth] (in the town of Nikolaev) on November 28, 1958, depicted the priests Zelnitskii, Lubianoi, Vdodovich, and Shniaruk as drunkards. But, according to our investigation, this is completely uncorroborated.

The newspaper *Rabochii Krai* [Worker's Region] (in the town of Ivanovo) defamed clergymen Andrei Sergeenko, Lozinskii, and others by name. The editor refused to print a retraction, despite having received vindicating material.

The newspaper *Ferganskaia Pravda* [Fergana Truth] slandered Archbishop Hermogen of Tashkent in issue No. 60, on March 22, 1959, by saying that he takes bribes. The archbishop sent vindicating documents and demands to the Procurator of the Uzbek SSR in order to bring the newspaper editor to court for slander. The procurator presented a resolution that essentially referred the matter to the regional Party committee in Fergana and refused to investigate.

The newspaper *Severnaia Pravda* on April 29, 1959, called sermons by Metropolitan Nikolai "clear examples of contemporary religious obscurantism." The newspaper quoted citations from his printed sermons in mocking tones. Moreover, it misrepresented the thoughts expressed in his sermons by taking the citations out of context. Metropolitan Nikolai is a public figure and well known internationally.

An article entitled "The Life of Father Terentii" from the newspaper *Pravda* on April 10, 1959, slandered Archbishop Antonii of Stavropol by saying that he ordered exhumation of a grave and seized the cross from the body of a dead priest. An investigation did not corroborate this.[113]

During a meeting at the Council in December 1959, church leaders once again presented cases where the press insulted believers. Patriarch Aleksii said, "Attacks on clergy and believers under the banner of antireligious propaganda continue with distortions and presentations of unverified facts, with conclusions that insult the religious sentiments of the believer, and with general discrediting of clergy in the eyes of the people for the purpose of defaming the whole church and its servants." The patriarch continued, "In addition, we face an obstacle in that not a single editor meets with clergymen or wishes to print a retraction for uncorroborated facts."[114]

Responding to these charges, leaders of the Council said only, "Yes, in the provinces it sometimes happens that certain newspapers and magazines allow clergy and believers to be insulted. The state and government have corrected and will continue to correct such press organs." In December, as in previous meetings, Karpov asked the patriarch and the metropolitan to send material to the Council on every specific instance so that he could take steps to correct mistakes through state agencies. Karpov also said that the Council would instruct its commissioners that they should undertake an examination of requests by clergy about false material appearing in the press.[115]

But despite instructions to editors that actually prohibited insulting attacks, material of that nature steadily and extensively entered into the propagandistic arsenal of the press. Its publication was initiated by Central Committee resolutions, decisions of Communist Party plenums and congresses, and also by vigorous leadership from Agitprop, the Knowledge Society, and the magazine *Nauka i religiia* [Science and Religion], which began to be published in September 1959.

Public lectures became a new form of atheistic propaganda. These were evenings of questions and answers at which "miracles were exposed" through chemical experiments.

It must be said that presentations having a certain "scientific" bent were quite effective. Clergy even said this was true. For example, a priest from the village of Kholoev in the Radekhov district of the Lvov region said, "Previously, almost no one went to atheistic lectures. Now, one of our teachers attracts so much interest from people by his discussions that not only the youth but also people middle-aged and older come to hear him." A priest from the village of Svirn in that same region complained to a commissioner, "They often give lectures on atheism and science at our club. A significant portion of the village attends these lectures. They show documentary films and conduct chemical experiments, and these arouse great interest. As a result, believers now pose questions to me that previously they dared not ask for fear of sinning. And many schoolchildren have stopped greeting me when we meet. Those that greet me do not remove their caps."[116]

But these are isolated facts from the archive of the Council for Russian Orthodox Church Affairs for this period.

Tactful and intelligent propagandistic work undeniably produced notice-

a generation of romantics

youth

able results. The social atmosphere at the end of the 1950s and at the beginning of the 1960s also assisted in the exodus of people, mostly youth, from the church. During this same period, a generation of romantics was born. Most representatives of the "sixties" generation were characterized by "purposefulness, lively activism, optimism, and sustained everyday effort toward the communist ideal."[117] Unfortunately, this period gave birth to other phenomena, namely intolerance toward people who held a different, "idealistic" worldview and an attitude that believers were people "of bygone days," a part of society that must be opposed by the segment of society that was active, energetic, and striving for "a brighter tomorrow." These very attitudes justified both insulting the religious feelings of believers and clergy and supporting the policies of administrative pressure against the church and other religious organizations.

Once again believers and their relatives were called into offices and heard threats and demands from authorities to leave parish "twenties." Once again, films were shown and dance music played near churches during services. And in some places hooligans again broke church windows and insulted priests.[118]

A large amount of attention was directed toward "alienating youth from the church." Authorities forbade and strictly controlled attempts to attract anyone younger than eighteen years of age to serve in churches and "to conduct training of youth in churches and monasteries for entrance into institutions for theological education."[119] Thanks to work by "discussion leaders"* and the chicanery of bureaucrats from various agencies, only two of the eight Orthodox seminaries were able to enroll a class of first-year students in the 1959–60 academic year.[120] Seminary applicants were often suddenly drafted into the military while they were taking their entrance exams. Those already admitted were sometimes denied residence permits for the seminary in which they planned to study. In a conversation with Karpov on November 6, 1959, the patriarch mentioned the fact that, according to information received from Kiev, seminarians "are summoned to appear somewhere and come back worn out and weakened."[121]

In a letter to Karpov on November 30, 1959, Patriarch Aleksii said that "stories surrounding admissions" to theological seminaries and academies were "unprecedented." The patriarch wrote, "In places, there were *all sorts* of impediments, even summoning** people who expressed intentions to ap-

---

*The Central Committee resolution of October 4, 1958, that was issued in response to the Agitprop report used this phrase to describe people who were responsible for doing work with individual believers.

**The implication is that the applicants were summoned into the local offices of the police or KGB for questioning and intimidation.—Ed.

ply to seminary and taking their passports from them. There were cases where the authorities, without any explanation of their reasons, demanded the *dismissal* of people who were graduating from seminary and planned to continue at an academy."[122]* At his meeting with church leaders in December 1959, however, Karpov claimed that the Council knew of only two cases— in Moscow and Ryazan—"of crude administrative methods being used against those persons who expressed a desire to enter an institution for theological education."[123]

A policy was set by the end of 1958 for reducing the number of clergy in *clergy* the Orthodox Church. Placed in difficult economic straits as a consequence of strict tax policies, many clergy were forced "to lay the parish bare" by retiring or taking secular employment. In addition, focused efforts tried to convince clergy to voluntarily defrock themselves, although often the authorities simply demanded this from priests. Thus, local representatives of the regime summoned Fr. Ustinov from the village of Petrovskoe in the Stavropol district and "demanded that he renounce his ordination." These officials also presented the same demand to Fr. Moroz of Stavropol, only they did it indirectly through the people closest to him—his wife and a friend.[124] Commissioner Koshman from Ulyanovsk advised young priests to break with the church and promised to find them jobs and other support.[125]

Such efforts yielded some results. According to information from Karpov, nine men renounced their clerical orders between October 1958 and May 1959 alone. The majority of these did so publicly. For example, former priest N.S. Petukhov from the Novgorod region made his public renunciation and then systematically gave lectures on the radio from an auditorium that was made available by the Knowledge Society.[126] It was not only rank-and-file clergy who became renegades. Pospielovsky notes that two betrayals especially damaged the church: Professor Alexander Osipov of the Leningrad Theological Academy and a young theologian named Evgraf Duluman from the Saratov seminary.[127]

By a Patriarchal Order dated December 30, 1959, "Former Archpriest . . . Osipov, former Archpriest N. Spasskii, former Priest P. Darmanskii, and other clerics who have publicly rejected the Lord's name are henceforth deprived of any relations with the church. . . . Evgraf Duluman and all other former lay members of the Orthodox Church who have publicly rejected the Lord's name are excommunicated from the church."[128]

Cases frequently began to appear where a priest was removed from the registry for "a violation of Soviet laws relating to the church." Between Oc-

---

*Emphasis appeared in the original letter.

tober 1958 and May 1959, commissioners removed twenty-seven men from the registry for this reason. During the first half of 1960, that number grew to sixty men.[129]

Generally speaking, the activity of many regional commissioners became an issue that Patriarch Aleksii constantly raised with the Council in 1958–59. According to information presented by the patriarch, many commissioners grossly interfered in the church's internal affairs and issued orders on appointments of clergy and members of the "twenty" and auditing commissions. Thus, in the town of Rostov-on-the-Don, the commissioner demanded that churches discontinue ringing their bells. In the cities of Kalinin, Riga, and Simferopol, among others, commissioners removed priests from the registry without notifying their bishops in advance. The commissioner in Kalinin also announced that payments for the needs of the patriarchate were "involuntary." He forbade the bishop from demanding an end to drunkenness or debauchery by individual priests and did not allow the bishop to complete a trip to towns in his diocese. Commissioners in a host of dioceses (in Perm, Sumy, and others) "hindered" the conduct of church services or prohibited believers from lingering on church grounds after services were finished.[130]

The patriarch especially noted that some commissioners' pronouncements "cannot help but cause concern and provoke unnecessary proposals and conclusions." For example, the commissioner from Rostov told his archbishop, "Whatever was the case a month ago or earlier, or even yesterday, might not be so today." The commissioner from Kalinin explained measures he had implemented in the province for limiting church activity by saying, "The well-known document 'Regulations for Administration of the Russian Orthodox Church' adopted in January 1945 with the consent of the Council for Russian Orthodox Church Affairs violates the 1929 law on religious organizations."[131] Commissioner Usanov from Rostov told his bishop that a new policy would now be followed in terms of the church. Commissioner Khevronov from Kalinin informed his bishop that the cause of the church was hopeless.[132] As a result, in the words of Metropolitan Nikolai, "persistent rumors are spreading [among clergy] that the highest authorities have issued orders to pressure the church over the next seven years as was done before the war."[133]

The patriarch showed the Council numerous dispatches from bishops "in which some deem themselves unable to work in contact with their commissioners."[134] Karpov promised to investigate statements by the Moscow Patriarchate on this matter. Every "investigation" as a rule ended with a decision either to force the diocesan bishop into retirement or to transfer him to another diocese. For example, the Council determined that Bishop Ioann of Ulyanovsk in "discussions with his commissioner acts irritably, speaks with a haughty tone and pays insufficient attention to the commissioner's proposals." Karpov told the patriarch, "You know that Ioann was removed from governing the Ufa diocese for similar conduct. The Council recommends that the patriarchate merge the Ulyanovsk diocese with its total of seventeen churches and the Kuibyshev diocese and send Ioann into retirement."[135] Commissioner Koshman from Ulyanovsk got his way. Later, he explained his position on Ioann in this way, "I engaged in single combat with him. . . . Either I would be dismissed for mistakes, or Ioann would not be in Ulyanovsk, the birthplace of Lenin."[136] A conflict between the commissioner of the Perm region and Bishop Paul of Perm ended with the bishop's transfer to another diocese. At a meeting between Karpov, Cheredniak, and Patriarch Aleksii on May 19, 1958, the Council leaders stated, "We have carefully investigated this matter and ascertained that the commissioner acted properly and developed a relationship. For his part, Bishop Paul acted improperly." The transcript of the conversation later notes, "Comrade Cheredniak gave a detailed account of Bishop Paul's improper conduct to the patriarch and Metropolitan Nikolai. Comrades Cheredniak and Karpov then presented the patriarch with the necessity of transferring Paul to another episcopal see. The patriarch consented to this."[137]

Confrontation between the commissioner of the Uzbek SSR and Archbishop Hermogen Golubov also ended with the archbishop's removal.[138]

The Council next planned the removal of Archbishop Luke,[139] for whom "disagreements existed" with a series of commissioners for the Council. As a result of the patriarch's position (he always delayed making a decision), the matter was never resolved before the archbishop's death in June 1961.

The leadership of the Moscow Patriarchate, after assessing developments in the sphere of church-state relations, reached the totally correct conclusion on the start of a new line and a new policy in the USSR toward the church and believers. However, not even the many concrete cases and examples that manifested the new course—the same cases and examples that Patriarch Aleksii and Metropolitan Nikolai presented to the Council and raised during personal meetings—clarified the situation. Church leaders heard only these responses: "No, there is no new course. People are deserting religion and the church on their own in response to scientific-atheistic propaganda." "Yes, individuals are making mistakes in some places that must be rectified."

Metropolitan Nikolai tried to affect the situation by constantly raising possible negative reactions by the international community over what was happening in the religious arena in the USSR.[140]

This did not yield results. Paradoxically, the Russian Orthodox Church at precisely this time activated its international work on the government's recommendation. Its contacts with foreign churches intensified.[141]

Foreign
policy *↗*

By following all "recommendations" of the government and the Council in the area of international policy (per the tradition of previous years), the patriarchate possibly figured on a mollification of the church's domestic position and a return to a normal pattern in its relations with the state. But this did not happen.

Patriarch Aleksii and Metropolitan Nikolai presented Karpov with a request in the spring of 1959 to give a memo personally to Khrushchev.[142] Their memo, dated May 31, 1959, was delivered to Khrushchev according to the Council's records. Russian Orthodox Church leaders included numerous instances in the memo "of insults to religious sentiments of believers and also individual clergy who had done nothing to discredit themselves" in the press and by certain commissioners for the Council for Russian Orthodox Church Affairs. The point of appealing to Khrushchev was inferred by their request "to somehow affirm the efficacy of the party's resolution of November 10, 1954."[143]

The patriarch had to wait until autumn for an answer. According to testimony from Karpov, the patriarch suffered from "an unhealthy disposition" and "had a flawed understanding of measures being implemented." Karpov cited excerpts from letters sent by the patriarch from Odessa, where he was resting, to Kolchitskii in Moscow:

> I am nervous about the general course of church affairs. I am nervous — everything is more troublesome than conciliatory. . . . Some commissioners have assumed overbearing rights for themselves and even gone so far as to give commands like gendarmes—this appears to be the grossest violation of the principle of freedom for the church and noninterference in the church's internal affairs.[144]

The patriarch became ill in September, so the Council delivered the reply to his appeal to Khrushchev to Metropolitan Nikolai on September 17, 1959. Karpov informed the metropolitan that the appeal had been reviewed. "But," Karpov said, "practically nothing blameworthy on the part of the regime has come to light in relation to religious communities except for isolated cases. The press will be instructed not to allow either insulting attacks on the patriarch and Metropolitan Nikolai or insults of believers' sentiments."[145]

Such an answer definitely could not satisfy church leaders. While at a reception in the Kremlin on November 7, 1959, the patriarch personally approached Khrushchev with a request to meet with him.[146] Karpov was not warned in advance about this request and demanded an explanation, which Metropolitan Nikolai provided at a meeting with the Council on November 24, 1959. Karpov in turn informed the Central Committee:

> Metropolitan Nikolai said on November 24 that—based on the content of published speeches, provincial administrative activity, and actions by re-

gional commissioners for the Council—they [church leaders] concluded: "the physical destruction of the church and religion was taking place"; "all this was now established more broadly and deeply than even in the 1920s"; and the patriarch did not want to be the one who liquidated the church, so he intends to go into retirement. Metropolitan Nikolai told us that they intend first to ask Khrushchev to clarify relations of the Soviet government and state toward the church and religion after the Twenty-first Party Congress and then to tell clergy and believers about this. According to Metropolitan Nikolai's statements, "a period of 'Cold War' ensued in relation to the church" after the Congress.[147]

In response to Metropolitan Nikolai, church leaders proposed to send "information about those matters" that the patriarch wished to raise in his conversation with Khrushchev. So, a letter was prepared. In the letter, the patriarch indicated a series of such matters: closure of churches and distortions in antireligious propaganda, pressure on clergy and believers and the ban on charitable activity, limitations on admissions to institutions for theological education, the closing of a string of dioceses, etc. Concluding the letter, Aleksii noted, "By raising these matters, we are by no means complaining about anyone in particular. We are only setting down facts related to all these phenomena that cause the gravest concern in church circles. These phenomena are relatively new in comparison with the recent past. They provide grounds, not only here among ourselves but even abroad, to speak about nothing less than persecution of the church or in any case about a change in the attitude of the regime toward the church."[148]

The Council's leadership expressed its own opinion of this letter when it received Patriarch Aleksii, Metropolitan Nikolai, and Protopresbyter Kolchitskii on December 10, 1959. Karpov's conclusions relating to each specific issue raised by the patriarch have already been mentioned. The meeting resulted in the following statement by the chairman of the Council for Russian Orthodox Church Affairs: "Thus, summing up our discussions, we once again say that from our perspective there is nothing that needs to be raised with the government on these matters."[149]

Despite the Council's position, the patriarch continued to insist on a meeting with Khrushchev. On December 26, 1959, he requested in a letter sent through the Council that the head of state receive him and Metropolitan Nikolai "for a report on church affairs . . . if possible before New Year's Day or in the first days of the new year up to Orthodox Christmas."[150] *Feb. 1960*

The meeting never took place. At the beginning of February 1960, Patriarch Aleksii made up his mind on a key step. "He used his speech [at a conference in the Kremlin for Soviet civil society on the topic of disarmament] to announce the tragic situation of the church to the court of public

Courage

opinion."[151] The patriarch began his speech with these words, "The Russian Orthodox Church, uniting millions of Orthodox Christians—citizens of our nation—speaks to you through my voice." He then told of the role and significance of the church in the history of the Russian state and its contributions to the country's culture. He referred to its prominent patriotic activity during World War II and its work in promoting world peace following the war. He concluded with these words, "Despite all this, the Church of Christ . . . is experiencing insults and attacks on its people. Nonetheless, it does not give up its responsibility for calling humanity to live in peace and to love one another. The church finds comfort in its current situation in . . . the words of Christ about the invincibility of the church when He said, 'The gates of hell will not prevail against the church.'"[152] The audience in the hall responded to the patriarch's speech with angry cries.

Somewhat later, in July 1960, Metropolitan Nikolai described to Archbishop Vasilii Krivoshein the atmosphere in the hall after the patriarch's speech. "And do you know what happened next? When the patriarch finished reading the speech, two or three weak claps were heard. After this, one after another representatives of 'civil society' stood up and began to threaten the patriarch, 'You want us to believe that all Russian culture was created by the church, that we owe everything to it. But, this is not true.' And so on. A great scandal took place." Archbishop Vasilii (who came to Moscow in July 1959 as the representative of the French Exarchate at the invitation of the Moscow Patriarchate) said that the West knew the patriarch's speech had made a sensation. Metropolitan Nikolai responded, "I wrote that speech, the patriarch only read it."[153]

The new leadership at the Council for Russian Orthodox Church Affairs let the patriarch know "that his speech at the Moscow conference of Soviet civil society on the topic of disarmament, held in Moscow in February of this year, was mistaken and politically harmful." Kuroedov told the conference of commissioners in April 1960 that "this speech was essentially an attack against scientific-atheistic propaganda, . . . that such views are hostile."[154]

Commissioners also expressed opinions on the patriarch's speech. Against the background of unanimous condemnation of the speech, the words of Commissioner Koshman from Ulyanovsk stand out most sharply, "I would advise you, Comrade Kuroedov, that Patriarch Aleksii snuck around behind us while Metropolitan Nikolai created a diversion. It turns out that we do not know what Aleksii will say when he makes a speech. This is a violation of order."[155]

As a matter of fact, matters related to the leadership of the Moscow Patriarchate followed the same procedure that Koshman instituted in his region. Those "at the top" had long sought to replace Metropolitan Nikolai as leader of the patriarchate's Department for External Church Relations. The issue was settled in the summer of 1960 when the Central Committee adopted a motion "On Strengthening the Department for External Church Relations of the Moscow Patriarchate." Kuroedov reported to the Central Committee in September 1960: "Fulfilling the Central Committee's decision of July 25, 1960, the Council carried out its work. . . . In August of this year, Metropolitan Nikolai was relieved (per his request) from leadership of external affairs for the patriarchate. Bishop Nikodim Rotov was appointed to replace him."[156] Metropolitan Nikolai remained for a brief time in the post of metropolitan of Krutitskii and Kolomenskoe and administrator of the Moscow diocese—in essence the second-highest-ranking person in the church's hierarchy. Nikolai himself was confident that secular government officials could not remove him from the position of metropolitan of Krutitskii. "This is not in their power. No, the Synod will never go for it."[157] It seemed only a matter of time, however. We do not know the extent to which Kuroedov, as new chairman of the Council for Russian Orthodox Church Affairs, was informed about Patriarch Aleksii's personal qualities. But Kuroedov undoubtedly kept Karpov's opinion in mind. Karpov constantly highlighted the patriarch's sincerity, directness, and trustfulness. Kuroedov obviously played upon these qualities when resolving the question of Metropolitan Nikolai's dismissal. Thus, Kuroedov informed the Central Committee that, "the matter of the improper, provocative conduct of Metropolitan Nikolai* was the topic of our repeated discussions with the patriarch."[158] Finally, Patriarch Aleksii expressed the idea that "he would think about placing the metropolitan in other work, for example, transferring him to the position of heading the diocese of Leningrad or Lvov."[159]

Soon afterward, Nikolai met with Kuroedov and said that the patriarchate was discussing the possibility of transferring him to Leningrad. Nikolai reacted negatively to this possibility. Kuroedov replied that this was a good, honorable proposal and suggested that Nikolai might want to think about it seriously before rushing to any conclusions.[160]

Understanding that a decision on his fate did not depend on the Council or on the Holy Synod of the Russian Orthodox Church but rather on opinion in the very highest echelons of the government, Metropolitan Nikolai wrote *9/9/60* a letter to Khrushchev on September 9, 1960. This letter—from a man who until recently was "all but the most influential and strongest bishop of the

---

*In Kuroedov's opinion, Nikolai explained his departure from leadership in the Department for External Church Relations as the result of conflict with the Council and not due to illness. Kuroedov also believed that Nikolai spread other rumors, including one identifying himself as a victim of the new persecution against the church.

Moscow Patriarchate" (according to Archbishop Vasilii Krivoshein), a man whose name was widely known internationally and who enjoyed well-deserved authority abroad—can only evoke pity and resentment. Nikolai's humiliation in this situation was also based on his extremely low and very vocal opinions about Khrushchev and his policies.[161] Here are some excerpts from the letter:

> Like all Soviet citizens, I am well aware of your deep intellect and your fair and open heart. I admire these things. You know about my work over many years for the good of the Motherland. . . . I have not spared either strength or health or life in the name of world peace. . . . This gives me the courage to appeal to you with a fervent request. The Council for Russian Orthodox Church Affairs has now proposed to transfer me to a position in Leningrad. It is extraordinarily difficult for me to abandon national church administration and the work that emanates from here in defense of peace and to accept this undeserved demotion. . .
>
> I fervently ask you, dear Nikita Sergeevich, to allow me to remain at work in Moscow in my current rank of metropolitan of Krutitskii. . . . I have sufficient strength and many years of experience for patriotic work in social organizations and for domestic church work in the cause of world peace. . . . Have mercy on me for the sake of my dedicated work over many years for our great Motherland. . . .
>
> I believe deeply in your wise justice, dear Nikita Sergeevich.
>
> Nikolai, metropolitan of Krutitskii and Kolomenskoe[162]

Nikolai never received an answer. It is not known whether the letter even reached its addressee.

Fr. Gordun cites a transcript of a conversation that took place between Kuroedov and Patriarch Aleksii on September 15, 1960. This document attests, "The patriarch was disposed to defer making a decision at that moment on Nikolai's dismissal and to grant him a six-month vacation and then return to this matter."[163] This reversal did not suit the chairman of the Council. He knew how to change the patriarch's disposition by familiarizing him with a transcript of a conversation with Metropolitan Nikolai in which, according to Kuroedov, "He [Nikolai] attempted to accuse the patriarch, by his reactionary activities, of supposedly trying to oppose the interests of the church against the interest of the state."[164]

Gordun did not find a transcript of the conversation with Nikolai in the Council's archives. A similar document is, however, in the archival collections of both the Council and the Central Committee. I offer excerpts from a conversation between Kuroedov and Nikolai that took place on September 13, 1960, and was arranged by the Council chairman:

Nikolai is out!

On September 13, Metropolitan Nikolai visited the Council and in a conversation with me opined that he viewed the proposal to go to work in Leningrad as hurting his position since he would not still then be the highest official after the patriarch. . . .

The metropolitan spoke at length about his contributions and in the process belittled the patriarch's role, slandered him, and depicted him as a reactionary church figure. He hypocritically stated that he, the metropolitan, restrained the patriarch from many wrong steps and directed him toward progressive issues. In particular, Nikolai unceremoniously trampled upon the truth and stated that for a long time he dissuaded the patriarch from attempting to meet with Khrushchev with complaints about supposed new oppression of the church and with requests to repeal unfavorable developments in church laws (the repeal of taxes on candles, a change in income taxes for clergy, maintaining existing monasteries, etc.). In conclusion, Nikolai said that his transfer to Leningrad and his resulting dismissal from responsibilities as patriarchal *locum tenens* would inflict obvious damage on the church and provoke unfavorable cries from abroad.[165]

In accord with Kuroedov's information, "Aleksii was most indignant over the double-dealing conduct of Nikolai. He repeatedly exclaimed, 'What a liar, what an insolent person!' The patriarch said, 'It never happened that the metropolitan urged me to refrain from presenting certain church issues before the government. On the contrary, he himself always built up these issues and pressed me to resolve them.'"[166]

The matter was settled. That evening, the patriarch signed an order dismissing Metropolitan Nikolai from administrative responsibility for the diocese of Moscow.[167]

Metropolitan Nikolai's removal was symbolic, as was Karpov's retirement. With their departure, an entire era in the history of church-state relations faded into the past. New people came on the scene, and their arrival changed both the nature and content of those relations. *Change*

On the one hand, for the secular regime, party functionaries arrived for whom leadership and action meant party orders and upholding communist positions. On the other hand, within the church, representatives of a new generation arrived whose mentality differed qualitatively from that of the previous generation. Pospielovsky quotes the Moscow priest V. Shpiller (a re-émigré educated in Bulgaria) who described the new generation of priests and bishops in the USSR. Shpiller wrote at the end of the 1960s, "This generation does not perceive the church as a social institution. . . . As a consequence of this in the future there will be total subordination to civilian authorities—to their demands, laws and procedures—not simply out of fear *New gen. of clerics* but from the conviction that there can be only one power and one law in the government."[168] The following must be added to his completely justified conclusion. First, in Soviet society as a whole the boundaries had "dissolved" between laws, resolutions, orders, and instructions. Second, clergy were unfamiliar with the contents of documents in these various categories, because the documents in the majority of cases were marked as being "for official use only." As long as both of these facts were true, clergy regarded and obeyed demands from state representatives expressed as either written instructions or verbal directions. For Church leaders, the law took the form of "recommendations" from the Council for Russian Orthodox Church Affairs. For clergy in the provinces, the law was directives from a commissioner (even if his request to close an urban church was motivated by the idea that the town was Lenin's birthplace or had "a glorious revolutionary tradition"). Everything that happened in the sphere of church-state relations in the first half of the 1960s testified to this.

On January 13, 1960, the Central Committee adopted a resolution that related directly to the legislative arena—"Measures for Eliminating Violations of Soviet Legislation on Cults." Violations of the law were defined as construction and purchase of parish houses, attracting "new segments of the population" to the bosom of the church, charitable activity (which also included help for parishes and monasteries), "undemocratic" principles for the administration of church communities, and speeches by certain clergy who "in their sermons advise believers on the need to educate children in a religious spirit and train them to pray to God."[169]

Church leaders agreed that these were violations of the law. The patriarch promised to give appropriate instructions to the dioceses.[170] But this was not enough for the Soviet regime.

A certain boundary in the history of church-state relations was crossed in 1961. Everything that developed in the course of 1959–60 and was approved in terms of religious organizations received its own juridical formulation.

On March 16, 1961, the Council of Ministers of the USSR adopted a resolution "On Strengthening Control over Obeying Legislation on Cults." That same day, the Council for Russian Orthodox Church Affairs along with the Council for Affairs of Religious Cults approved "Instructions Concerning the Application of Legislation on Cults."[171]

These documents were adopted and implemented under the slogan of a return "to Leninist socialist legality." They essentially returned the church to its situation at the end of the 1930s. Religious organizations were prohibited from any type of charitable activity. Without the Council's permission, they were prohibited not only from opening institutions for theological education and publishing religious literature but also from organizing religious congresses and conferences. All clergy, not only those in parishes, were assessed income taxes according to Article 19 of the Decree of the Supreme Soviet of the USSR of April 30, 1943, "On Assessing Taxes on the Population." These decrees even envisaged limiting bell-ringing ("if this is necessary and is supported by local residents").[172]

Through a special article in the resolution of March 16, 1961, the Council of Ministers pointed out "the need to restore rights to executive organs of church communities in the area of financial management, in accordance with legislation on cults."[173] Guided by governmental instructions, the Council for Russian Orthodox Church Affairs "recommended" that Patriarch Aleksii review individual sections of the 1945 Regulation for Administering the Russian Orthodox Church. In particular, he was to adopt amendments for pushing clergy out of financial management in their communities and transfer this task to the authority of the parish council.[174]

The state's demand to carry out reforms in the church was obeyed. The matter of changing the Regulation for Administering the Russian Orthodox Church was a primary concern for the Council of Bishops that met in July 1961. They adopted a new version of the regulation, which said, "The senior priest of a church is responsible for spiritual leadership of parishioners, for overseeing the grandeur and conduct of the liturgy, and for satisfying the religious needs of parishioners in a timely and conscientious manner."[175] In other words, the regulation made the priest a "hired hand" for the community of believers.

Government resolutions and instructions from the Council essentially oriented commissioners toward fulfilling the functions of supervision and control over the activity of religious organizations. Commissioners were to see their basic task as "limiting the influence of the church on the population." I must add that many commissioners did not need to change their methods for working. For example, the Council commissioner from Kalinin had already taken a similar position. Speaking at a conference for the Council in 1960, he insisted on expanding the rights of commissioners so that they could better carry out this task: "The role of commissioner must be acknowledged in the business of reducing the number of functioning churches, restraining church activity, and ending violations of Soviet legislation. His rights are expanded significantly. No other public servant in this sector can do as much as the commissioner will do. And, because of this, we must get to work."[176]

As a result, the administrative onslaught against church, believers, and clergy acquired the character of a political war. Between 1960 and 1964, the number of churches and chapels decreased by 5,457 (on January 1, 1960, there were 13,008; on January 1, 1965–7,873).[177] Eight theological seminaries were open on January 1, 1960; five of them had been closed by 1964—in Kiev, Saratov, Stavropol, Minsk, and Volyna (Lutsk).[178] By the mid-1960s, the Russian Orthodox Church had only 18 functioning monasteries in the USSR (on January 1, 1959, that number stood at 63; on January 1, 1960, it was 44). Those closed included the Monastery of the Caves in Kiev, the most ancient of sacred places in the Russian Orthodox Church.[179]

In the pursuit of decreasing qualitative indices (local party and Soviet functionaries thought that functioning churches in territory under their authority attested to their personal qualities as leaders), representatives of the regime resorted to deception, insults against believers and adoption of unfounded administrative solutions. Frequently one encounters instances of direct vandalism against closed churches. Icons, crosses, and other religious items were trampled on and torn down. Churches were blown up or razed to the ground by bulldozers. This policy was blessed, directed, and justified by ideological directives from the Communist Party. In this regard, the decisions of the Twenty-second Congress of the CPSU were especially significant in the establishment of a new program and charter for the party.

Among the basic tasks presented to the party, the Twenty-second Congress established a mission of communist education for the Soviet people. Khrushchev said in his report to the congress that, "Communist education intends to free consciousness from religious prejudices and superstitions that continue to prevent individual Soviet citizens from fully realizing their creative potential."[180]

The new charter for the CPSU that was adopted at the Congress required every party member "to conduct a decisive struggle against religious prejudices."[181]

In accepting the mission to build a communist society by 1980, the program for the CPSU revealed the prospects for the Orthodox Church and other religious organizations in the USSR; the church should cease to exist within twenty to thirty years, since all Soviet citizens would be atheists by that time. Thus, a goal established on the basis of libertarianism [the principle of total, unrestricted freedom in thought and action—Ed.] also brought about a libertarian resolution of the religious question in our country.

The Unspoken Conditions

Conclusion

World War II opened a new chapter in the history of relations between the Soviet government and the Russian Orthodox Church. For the first time since the creation of the socialist state, the regime attempted to abandon policies aimed at destroying the Russian Orthodox Church as a social institution and moved toward constructive dialog with the church.

The fundamental change in Stalin's position on religious matters was caused by a set of circumstances, the most important of which was foreign policy. International problems during the final phase of World War II and the new geopolitical situation in Europe after the war's end forced the Stalinist leadership to use all means possible for establishing and strengthening its influence in the international arena. The Russian Orthodox Church was assigned a significant role in this strategy. The Kremlin regarded essential Russian Orthodox activity as including establishment of active contacts by the Moscow Patriarchate with other Orthodox churches, primarily in Eastern Europe, and with non-Slavic confessions around the world. Foreign policy agencies within the Soviet government saw the possibility of influencing the international situation through ecclesiastical channels. Stalin's government was ready to create "favorable conditions" for the Orthodox Church within the country so that the Moscow Patriarchate's activity in foreign policy could be effective and successful from the perspective of state interests.

Such were the unspoken conditions of the agreement that was "presented" to the leaders of the Russian Orthodox Church on September 4, 1943. There was never any doubt that they would accept the conditions. For the Orthodox hierarchy, this was not simply a chance for revival of the ravaged and oppressed Russian Church; it was also Divine Providence. They responded with satisfaction and gratitude to the new course taken by the Stalinist leadership. As a result, the Russian Orthodox Church during and immediately after World War II was able to improve its financial situation significantly, to replenish the ranks of clergy, and to increase its authority and influence domestically and abroad.

A majority of the Soviet people responded positively to the state's new policy on the church. Signs of the times included overflowing churches on Orthodox holidays, the possibility of conducting religious rites in homes, ringing bells to call believers to services, and festive religious processions with large crowds of people.

The changed situation for religion during and immediately after the war outwardly "operated" on the basis of strengthening the existing regime and increasing Stalin's personal authority. In conditions where ideas of statehood and Soviet (in reality, Russian) patriotism were being actively and firmly established, a restoration and strengthening of the Orthodox Church as the traditional repository of these ideas served as an additional source of legitimacy for Stalin's power.

Thus, it was logical that Soviet leaders gave the Orthodox Church priority over all other religious confessions.

The clearest demonstration of this special attitude toward the Russian Orthodox Church was the formation of an agency in charge of matters solely related to it, namely the Council for Russian Orthodox Church Affairs under the Council of Ministers of the USSR. The official status of the Council for Russian Orthodox Church Affairs, as spelled out in the "Regulations on the Council" of October 7, 1943, was only as an intermediary between the Soviet government and the patriarch of Moscow and All Russia. The real activity of the Council, however, immediately crossed this official boundary. This change was caused by expansion of international contacts with the Moscow Patriarchate and sustained activity of the Russian Orthodox Church within the country—its revival actually proceeded "at bolshevik speed" (at a rapid clip). From the moment it was formed, the Council in fact turned into a political organ responsible for the implementation of the state's new ecclesiastical policy. Such responsibility could not help but aid the transformation of the Council into an organ for controlling not merely the activity of Russian Orthodox organizations but more broadly the whole sphere of church-state relations in the country.

In this sense, the Council for Russian Orthodox Church Affairs in essence became hostage to the contradictory and inconsistent approach taken by the nation's highest leaders toward formulating church policy.

The principles of any policy are reflected and stated in officially adopted legislative documents. A peculiarity of Stalin's new course regarding the church lay in the absence of such documents; there was a new policy but no law that formulated it. A resolution of the All-Russian Central Executive

Committee and Sovnarkom RSFSR from April 8, 1929, "On Religious Associations" officially had the force of law in the country. In fact, the new religious policy after 1943 was implemented through resolutions and instructions by the government and various agencies that were adopted "for official use only" and related to specific aspects and trends in the activity of the Russian Orthodox Church.

According to many government decisions—particularly the Sovnarkom resolution "On Procedures for Opening Churches"—the Council for Russian Orthodox Church Affairs could only play the role of statistician. The Council was a department for transmitting information between regional executive committees and the Soviet government. It did not have any real leverage for influencing local situations as they developed.

Also complicating the Council's work in implementing the new religious policy was its inability to choose regional commissioners. The right to appoint people to these positions belonged to regional party organizations, as spelled out in the "Regulations for the Council." Nonetheless, despite inconsistencies and contradictions in the state's policy on the church, the Council's work and its persistence in implementing legislative acts that were adopted helped establish a legal basis—if only a limited one—for church-state relations. As a whole, the Council made the relations between the Soviet government and the Russian Orthodox Church sufficiently civilized. Credit for this achievement undeniably belonged to Georgii Karpov, chairman of the Council for Russian Orthodox Church Affairs.

Attitudes in the center and regions appear in a completely different light when seen through the prism of church-state relations in the 1940s. If the regions as a rule played the role of dutiful executors of Moscow's will in decisions on production and economics, "the provinces" responded differently to the question of religion. Regional party-state bureaucrats did not simply accept the government's new policy on religious organizations. At best, the majority of local authorities tolerated that policy only as temporary and necessary due to the extreme situation of World War II. In some regions of the country, opinions on how to solve problems in the religious arena often contradicted instructions and orders from Moscow. This inconsistency found particular expression in the fact that not all regions fulfilled government resolutions on appointing commissioners and organizing their work. Some regional executive committees secretly disobeyed Sovnarkom orders (including ones signed personally by Stalin) on opening institutions for theological education. The process of opening new Orthodox churches and chapels was impeded almost everywhere.

After the war ended, a sentiment "for doing away with the policy of flirting with the church and priests" predominated among low-level party-state activists. This sentiment was supported and encouraged in higher units of the party. The Agitation and Propaganda Department of the CPSU Central Committee took concrete steps in this direction in the years 1948–49. Despite the fact it was never completed, Agitprop's campaign for discrediting the Council for Russian Orthodox Church Affairs and changing state policy toward the church marked the end of normalization in church-state relations.

Not a single proposal related to fundamental issues regarding the Russian Orthodox Church was adopted in the USSR between 1948 and 1954. This "standardization" of church-state relations testified that religion was steadily excluded from the list of state priorities. The Council for Russian Orthodox Church Affairs also no longer had the lofty status that it earlier enjoyed among Soviet leaders. As a result, by the end of the 1940s the work of this governmental body increasingly moved toward influencing ideological structures within the Party Central Committee.

Thus, a process began to subordinate strictly governmental policy on religious organizations to party politics. Along with this, a process began to change the nature of relations with the church—from toleration and peaceful coexistence to political struggle under slogans for the atheistic education of the population.

An attempt at a new attack on religion and the church, started by the Central Committee in July 1954, also ended in defeat. But, it allowed ideological bodies to define fundamental mistakes and blunders and thus to designate the future direction of their work.

The attack on the church that began in 1958 was carefully thought out and took into account all circumstances, both subjective and objective:

- Liquidation of the "antiparty group" eliminated possible opponents in the highest echelons of power.
- The propaganda campaign for atheism adopted a certain scientific form and, consequently, effectiveness.
- The ideological attack was supported by governmental legislative acts, the implementation of which undermined the church's financial base.
- The secret nature of adopted documents (both by the government and party) deprived public opinion, including international public opinion, of any possibility for quick and convincing reaction against the new attack on the church.
- A change in leadership within the Council for Russian Orthodox Church Affairs and a change in the "burdensome" traditions of building relations with the church on the basis of constitutional law helped party functionaries transform the Council into an obedient executor of the party's new course.

"The state is the general category"

- Measures that were phased in between 1958 and 1960 and the incremental character of demands presented to the patriarchate disoriented church leaders, steadily forcing them to concede.

public opinion

The ideological bureaucracy also took into account emerging public opinion in the country—the establishment in the social consciousness of the popular majority (primarily of young people) of a new idea—the idea of construction of a new communist society. This was helpful because society became more and more indifferent to problems of religion and the church.

A wave of totally unrestrained administrative pressure began in 1961 against this background. It was a wave of lawlessness in terms of the church, clergy and believers, often taking on features of a political war.

In the history of Soviet society, relations between the state and the Russian Orthodox Church have their own special place. This history has its own ebb and flow, crises and resolutions, moments of tragedy and periods of calm. Finding any kind of conformity to law in this process would be a vain task. The history of church-state relations correlates to the generally accepted periodization of the Soviet era for the most part.

Undoubtedly, the single highest priority in church-state relations was the position of the regime. State ecclesiastical policy determined the nature and content of relations with the church in this and any other period of society's development. This was natural, since the state is the general category and the church is a more specific one. The peculiarity of the Soviet state was that its ecclesiastical policy was founded on the Marxist-Leninist concept that socialism and religion were incompatible. In this sense, the church in the USSR was doomed because it carried a religious worldview. Realization of the Soviet state's basic task—the construction of a socialist and then a communist society—did not leave viable space for the existence of a different religious ideal.*

No space for religion

On certain occasions, however, domestic and international circumstances forced the Soviet regime to use flexible tactics. Concerns of the political moment brought about the possibility for agreements, compromises, and concessions on the part of the state. For pragmatic reasons, the church was used as an instrument for achieving specific goals and tasks. Interests changed and goals were attained, so the tactical line of the state also changed along with the nature of church-state relations.   *tactics*

---

*It is not surprising therefore that a national law on religious cults was not adopted in the USSR until the mid-1970s. When it became clear that the outlook for construction of communism was put off until some indeterminable time in the future, this meant that the existence of the church would be prolonged. The question arose about the need legislatively to shape relations between the state and religious organizations.

progressive elimination

freedom of conscience — does it exist?

The principle of freedom of conscience did not exist and could not exist in the ideologically based Soviet socialistic state. Lenin's decree proclaiming that principle thus remained merely a declaration.

ROC's position

While it is established that the Soviet regime undoubtedly influenced the nature of church-state relations, it is impossible not to take into account the position of the other side—the position of the Russian Orthodox Church. This position also had its own roots in history and dogma.

Identification of church with the state characterizes the dogmatic tradition of ecumenical Orthodoxy. Russian Orthodoxy was shaped by historical circumstances in such a way that the very institution of the church in Russia was established only thanks to the initiative and support of princely (governmental) power. Movement toward a doctrine that identified the church with the state, through the steady strengthening of the latter, led to the church's loss of independence in the final analysis. From the beginning of the eighteenth century, the church simply became part of the state apparatus in Russia. With the fall of the monarchy and establishment of Soviet power, the doctrines of the Orthodox Church did not change, but the historical experiment was transformed into a tragedy. *Coopted → state power*

Historical circumstances also provided the foundation for the Soviet government's ecclesiastical policy as it existed in the USSR. These same circumstances also established the position of the church's leadership in new, Soviet historical conditions. Starting with the idea that all authority is from God, they organized an active church within the confines of state policies and did everything for the survival of the Russian Orthodox Church during any possible metamorphosis of this policy.

survival

History was written, and the church's position proved to be viable. But the question still remains: how do we deal with these traditions?

⊛ loss of independence

Notes

Archival abbreviations using the Russian system:

f.   *fond* (collection)
op.   *opis'* (inventory)
d.   *delo* (file)
l., ll.   *list, listy* (leaf, leaves)
ob.   *oborot* (verso)

Notes to Introduction

1. See Vladimir Tsypin, *Istoriia Russkoi pravoslavnoi tserkvi, 1917–1990* (Moscow, 1994), 95, 104, 106; N.S. Godienko, *Sovremennoe russkoe pravoslavie* (Leningrad, 1987), 67.

2. See Tsypin, *Istoriia Russkoi pravoslavnoi tserkvi*, 107; M.I. Odintsov, "Khozhdenie po mukam," *Nauka i religiia*, 1990, no. 8: 19. The number of churches increased to 3,021 after the annexation of western regions of Ukraine and Belorussia, Bessarabia, and the Baltic states; at the same time, the Moscow Patriarchate acquired sixty-four monasteries. See S. Gordun, "Russkaia pravoslavnaia tserkov' pri sviateishikh patriarkhakh Sergii i Aleksii," *Vestnik russkogo khristianskogo dvizheniia* (Paris), 1990, no. 158: 105; GARF, f. 6991s, op. 1s, d. 153, l. 2.

3. *Russkaia pravoslavnaia tserkov' i Velikaia Otechestvennaia voina. Sbornik tserkovnykh dokumentov* (Moscow, 1943), 4–5.

4. Archpriest A. Medvedskii recalled appearances by Metropolitan Nikolai (Iarushevich) during his travels to the front lines: "At large gatherings of officers, Metropolitan Nikolai spoke about faith, religion, and the meaning of life. The officers listened to him with deep attention and interest and with much sympathy. He made quite an impression on them, and very interesting conversations then took place." Quoted in Krivoshein, "Metropolit Nikolai (Iarushevich): Vospominaniia Vladyki Vasiliia Krivosheina," *Tserkovno-obshchestvennyi vestnik*, no. 17 (Appendix to *Russkaia mysl'*, June 5, 1997: 11).

5. Tsypin, *Istoriia Russkoi pravoslavnoi tserkvi*, 118–19. "'Opredelenie' Sobora

arkhiereev ot 28 marta 1942 g." in *Russkaia pravoslavaia tserkov' i Velikaia Otechestvennaia voina* (Moscow, 1943), 22–23. The reason for this sudden meeting was a statement released by Bishop Polikarp Sikorskii of Lutsk that renounced obedience to the Moscow Patriarchate and announced the organization of an autocephalous Ukrainian church. GARF, f. 6991, op. 1, d. 5, l. 19. See V.A. Alekseev, *Illiuzii i dogmy* (Moscow, 1991), 340–41.

6. *Zhurnal Moskovskoi Patriarkhii* (hereafter *ZhMP*) 1945, no. 4: 54.

7. GARF, f. 6991, op. 2, d. 50, l. 3.

8. *Russkaia pravoslavaia tserkov' i Velikaia Otechestvennaia voina*, 94–95.

9. E.I. Lisavtsev asserts that Stalin's first meeting with Metropolitan Sergii actually took place in July 1941 (see his article, "Istoricheskii put' pravoslaviia v Rossii posle 1917 g." in *Konferentsiia S.-Peterburgskogo otdela obshchestva "Memorial"* (St. Petersburg, 1993). That assertion is not supported, however, by the archives of the Council for Russian Orthodox Church Affairs. If such a meeting had actually taken place, G.G. Karpov would certainly have mentioned it in his informational report to the government of G.M. Malenkov, informing the country's new leaders about Stalin's meetings with bishops in September 1943 and April 1945.

10. V.A. Alekseev, "Neozhidannyi dialog," *Agitator*, 1989, no. 6: 41–44; M.I. Odintsov, "Drugogo raza ne bylo," *Ateistitcheskie chteniia*, 1989, issue 19. For the full text of Karpov's notes see M.I. Odintsov, *Russkie patriarkhi XX veka: Sud' by Otechestva i Tserkvi na stranitsakh arkhivnykh dokumentov* (Moscow, 1999), 283–91.

11. G. Yakunin, "V sluzhenii kul'tu" in *Na puti k svobode sovesti* (Moscow, 1989), 172–206. The official view of reasons for the change in the government's religious policy (as due to the display of religiosity by the population during the war years and the active patriotic stance of the Russian Orthodox Church) excluded other interpretations of this problem for Soviet historians. In foreign historiography, the issue was clearly debated. For example, see: Rar Gleb (A. Vetrov), *Plenennaia Tserkov': Ocherk razvitiia vzaimootnoshenii mezhdu Tserkov'iu i vlast'iu v SSSR* (Frankfurt, 1954); A.A. Bogolepov, *Tserkov' pod vlast'iu kommunizma* (Munich, 1958); D. Konstantinov, *Gonimaia Tserkov' (Russkaia Pravoslavnaia Tserkov' v SSSR)* (New York, 1967).

12. Alekseev, *Illiuzii*, 336–37.

13. D.V. Pospielovskii, *Russkaia pravoslavnaia tserkov' v XX veke* (Moscow, 1995), 192–93.

14. M.V. Shkarovskii, "Russkaia pravoslavnaia tserkov' v 1943–1957 godakh," *Voprosy istorii*, 1995, no. 8: 36–41.

15. See M.I. Odintsov, *Gosudarstvo i tserkov' v Rossii: XX vek* (Moscow: Luch, 1994); "Khozhdenie po mukam," *Nauka i religiia*, 1990, no. 5–8, and 1991, no. 7; idem, "Gosudarstvenno-tserkovnye otnoshenii nakanune i v gody Velikoi Otechestvennoi voiny" in *Religioznye organizatsii v SSSR v gody Velikoi Otechestvennoi voiny, 1941–1945 gg.* (Moscow, 1995); idem, "Uniaty i sovetskaia vlast'," *Otechestvennye arkhivy*, 1994, no. 3: 56; idem, "Krestnyi put' patriarkha Sergiia," *Otechestvennye arkhivy*, 1994, no. 2: 44–51; idem, "Pis'ma i dialogi vremen 'khrushchevskoi ottepeli' (Desiat' let iz zhizni patriarkha Aleksiia)," *Otechestvennye arkhivy*, 1994, no. 5, 25–33; idem, "Russkaia pravoslavnaia tserkov' stala na pravil'nyi put'," *Istoricheskii arkhiv*, 1994, no. 3, 139–40; idem, *Russkie patriarkhi*, 194–203.

16. Odintsov, "Pis'ma i dialogi," 27–31.

17. Gordun, "Russkaia pravoslavnaia tserkov'," 92–142, 158. Pospielovskii, *Russkaia pravoslavnaia tserkov' v XX veke*, chapters 7, 10.

18. For example, Gordun, "Russkaia pravoslavnaia tserkov'"; Pospielovskii, *Russkaia pravoslavnaia tserkov' v XX veke*; Tsypin, *Istoriia Russkoi pravoslavnoi tserkvi.*

19. Iu. M. Degtiarev, "Kak Stalin priznal Tserkov,'" *Religiia v SSSR. Biulleten' APN* (Moscow), 1991, no. 12: 41–52.

20. See V.A. Alekseev, *Shturm nebes otmeniaetsia? Kriticheskie ocherki po istorii bor' by s religii v SSSR* (Moscow, 1992).

21. O. Iu. Vasil'eva, "Vatikan v gornile voiny," *Nauka i religiia*, 1995, no. 6: 15.

22. Odintsov, "Uniaty," 44–51.

23. For example, see V. Tsypin, "Patrioticheskoe sluzhenie Russkoi pravoslavnoi tserkvi v Velikuiu Otechestvennuiu voinu," *Novaia i noveishaia istoriia*, 1995, no. 2: 41–47; G. Iakunin, "Russkaia Pravoslavnaia Tserkov' v gody Velikoi Otechestvennoi voiny," *Moskovskii zhurnal*, 1995, no. 1: 14–21, no. 2: 15–20, no. 7: 41–46, no. 9: 31–39, and no. 11: 24–28; M.V. Shkarovskii, *Peterburgskaia eparkhiia v gody gonenii i utrat 1917–1945* (St. Petersburg, 1995).

24. M.V. Shkarovskii, *Russkaia pravoslavnaia tserkov' pri Staline i Khrushcheve (Gosudarstvenno-tserkovnye otnosheniia v SSSR v 1939–1964 gg.)*, (Moscow, 1999); idem, "Russkaia pravoslavnaia tserkov' v 1943–1957 godakh," *Voprosy istorii*, 1995, no. 8: 36–56.

25. Shkarovskii, *Russkaia pravoslavnaia tserkov' pri Staline i Khrushcheve*, 204.

26. Pospielovskii, *Russkaia pravoslavnaia tserkov' v XX veke.*

27. D. Pospielovskii, "'Osen' sviatoi Rusi.' Stalin i Tserkov': 'konkordat' 1943 g. i zhizn' Tserkvi," *Tserkovno-istoricheskii vestnik*, 2000, no. 6–7: 215, 227.

28. G. Shtrikker, ed., *Russkaia pravoslavnaia tserkov' v sovetskoe vremia (1917–1991). Materialy i dokumenty po istorii otnoshenii mezhdu gosudarstvom i Tserkov'iu*, 2 vols. (Moscow, 1995).

29. Archbishop Vasilii (Krivoshein), "Poslednie vstrechi s mitropolitom Nikolaem (Iarushevichem)," *Vestnik russkogo khristianskogo dvizheniia*, 1976, no. 117: 209–19. Idem, "Mitropolit Nikolai (Iarushevich)," *Tserkovno-obshchestvennyi vestnik* (Appendix to *Russkaia mysl'*), 1997, no. 16, 17. Archibishop Luka (Voino-Iasenetskii), *Ia poliubil stradanie. Avtobiografiia* (Moscow, 1996). Metropolitan Ioann (Snychev), *Mitropolit Manuil (Lemeshevskii)* (St. Petersburg, 1993). Metropolitan Evlogii (Georgievskii), *Put' moei zhizni*, (Moscow, 1994).

Notes to Chapter 1: Church and State from World War II until 1948

1. Georgii Grigor'evich Karpov was born in 1898 and became a member of the Bolshevik Party in 1920. He became head of operations for the Second Department of the Chief Directorate of State Security in the People's Commissariat for Internal Affairs (GUGB NKVD USSR) in 1922. Until 1936, he was a captain in the state security apparatus and served as deputy chief for the Karelia ASSR under the NKVD Administration for the Leningrad Region. On July 21, 1936, he was released from those duties and was appointed deputy chief of the Fourth Department of the Directorate for State Security under the NKVD Administration in the Leningrad Region. He became chief of the Fourth Department a year later (July 29, 1937). On January 10, 1938, he was awarded the Order of the Red Star "for fulfilling the most important assignments from the government" (by order of the NKVD USSR dated January 10, 1938, per a decision by the Central Executive Committee USSR of December 19,

1937). Until February 27, 1941, Karpov was a section chief in the Second Department of the Main Directorate for State Security in the NKVD USSR; after that date, he became the deputy chief of the Third Department of the Third Directorate (USP) in the NKGB USSR with the rank of major of state security. On December 24 that year, he was appointed chief of the Fourth Department of the NKVD's Third Directorate. He received the special rank of colonel of state security on February 14, 1943. He was awarded the Order of Lenin on February 2, 1945 (letter from L. Beria to Stalin; decree of the Presidium of the Supreme Soviet of the USSR, February 2, 1945). On July 9, 1945, he was promoted to the rank of major general per a motion by Sovnarkom. On July 27, 1945, he became chief of the Fifth Department of the Second Directorate in the NKGB USSR; he was a commissar of state security until August 25, 1947. In 1947, he became chief of Department "0" of the MGB USSR. In 1954, he was in the active reserve of the KGB under Sovnarkom. On March 2, 1955, he was released by the KGB USSR (order No. 159). Source: Main Archival Administration, FSB RF.

2. GARF, f. 6991, op. 1, d. 1, ll. 1–10.

3. GARF, f. 6991, op. 1, d. 2, l. 18.

4. GARF, f. 6991, op. 1, d. 2, l. 16.

5. GARF, f. 6991, op. 1, d. 2, l. 2. By comparison, the average monthly salary for a worker at the time was 700 rubles (see V. F. Zima, "Golod v Rossii," *Otechestvennaia istoriia*, 1993, no. 1: 49).

6. GARF, f. 6991, op. 2, d. 1, l. 11.

7. GARF, f. 6991, op. 1, d. 2, l. 18.

8. GARF, f. 6991, op. 2, d. 7, ll. 1–3.

9. GARF, f. 6991, op. 2, d. 31, ll. 1, 4–8.

10. GARF, f. 6991, op. 2, d. 46, l. 2.

11. GARF, f. 6991, op. 1, d. 606, l. 128.

12. GARF, f. 6991, op. 2, d. 31, ll. 1–11, 13.

13. GARF, f. 6991, op. 1, d. 80, l. 15.

14. GARF, f. 6991, op. 1, d. 80, ll. 15, 83.

15. GARF, f. 6991, op. 1, d. 1, l. 18.

16. GARF, f. 6991, op. 1, d. 2, l. 9.

17. GARF, f. 6991, op. 2, d. 1, l. 31.

18. GARF, f. 6991, op. 2, d. 2, l. 45.

19. GARF, f. 6991, op. 1, d. 1, l. 47. Thereafter, the number of Council commissioners gradually declined: in January 1947 it was 106 men (GARF, f. 6991, op. 1, d. 149, l. 24); in January 1948, 104 men (GARF, d. 6991, op. 1, d. 153, l. 26).

20. GARF, f. 6991, op. 1, d. 30, l. 61.

21. GARF, f. 6991, op. 1, d. 30, l. 61.

22. GARF, f. 6991, op. 1, d. 290, l. 176.

23. GARF, f. 6991, op. 1, d. 29, l. 77.

24. GARF, f. 6991, op. 1, d. 30, l. 61.

25. GARF, f. 6991, op. 1, d. 153, l. 26.

26. GARF, f. 6991, op. 1, d. 81, l. 61.

27. GARF, f. 6991, op. 1, d. 149, l. 24.

28. GARF, f. 6991, op. 1, d. 290, l. 176.

29. GARF, f. 6991, op. 1, d. 29, l. 146.

30. GARF, f. 6991, op. 2, d. 2, l. 38.

31. GARF, f. 6991, op. 1, d. 149, l. 24.

32. GARF, f. 6991, op. 1, d. 1, l. 47.
33. GARF, f. 6991, op. 2, d. 31, l. 10.
34. GARF, f. 6991, op. 2, d. 12, ll. 7, 11, 38, 54.
35. GARF, f. 6991, op. 2, d. 2, l. 51.
36. GARF, f. 6991, op. 2, d. 30, l. 8.
37. GARF, f. 6991, op. 2, d. 30, l. 28.
38. GARF, f. 6991, op. 2, d. 35, ll. 38, 39.
39. GARF, f. 6991, op. 2, d. 60, l. 47.
40. GARF, f. 6991, op. 2, d. 2, l. 26.
41. GARF, f. 6991, op. 1, d. 7, ll. 12–14.
42. GARF, f. 6991, op. 2, d. 31, l. 1.
43. GARF, f. 6991, op. 1, d. 7, l. 42.
44. GARF, f. 6991, op. 2, d. 12, l. 147.
45. GARF, f. 6991, op. 2, d. 18, l. 14.
46. GARF, f. 6991, op. 2, d. 8, ll. 7, 8.
47. GARF, f. 6991, op. 1, d. 7, l. 38; op. 2, d. 13, l. 23; op. 2, d. 30, l. 10; op. 2, d. 52, l. 12.
48. GARF, f. 6991, op. 1, d. 7, l. 47.
49. GARF, f. 6991, op. 1, d. 3, l. 28.
50. GARF, f. 6991, op. 2, d. 8, l. 9.
51. GARF, f. 6991, op. 1, d. 7, l. 28.
52. GARF, f. 6991, op. 1, d. 7, l. 40.
53. GARF, f. 6991, op. 1, d. 7, l. 91.
54. GARF, f. 6991, op. 1, d. 7, l. 36.
55. GARF, f. 6991, op. 1, d. 7, l. 60.
56. GARF, f. 6991, op. 1, d. 148, l. 12.
57. GARF, f. 6991, op. 1, d. 7, l. 94.
58. GARF, f. 6991, op. 1, d. 148, l. 13.
59. GARF, f. 6991, op. 1, d. 7, l. 97.
60. GARF, f. 6991, op. 1, d. 7, l. 98.
61. GARF, f. 6991, op. 1, d. 7, l. 35.
62. GARF, f. 6991, op. 2, d. 60, ll. 42, 43.
63. GARF, f. 6991, op. 1, d. 7, l. 47; d. 148, l. 27.
64. GARF, f. 6991, op. 1, d. 7, ll. 66, 114.
65. GARF, f. 6991, op. 1, d. 149, l. 91.
66. GARF, f. 6991, op. 2, d. 8, l. 29.
67. GARF, f. 6991, op. 2, d. 30, l. 64.
68. Ibid.
69. GARF, f. 6991, op. 1, d. 149, l. 24.
70. Ibid.
71. GARF, f. 6991, op. 2, d. 29, l. 36.
72. Odintsov, "Russkaia pravoslavnaia tserkov'," 144–45. GARF, f. 6991, op. 1, d. 3, l. 7.
73. GARF, f. 6991, op. 1, d. 4, l. 9.
74. GARF, f. 6991, op. 2, d. 2a, l. 58.
75. GARF, f. 6991, op. 1, d. 3, l. 6; d. 4, ll. 19, 22.
76. GARF, f. 6991, op. 1, d. 4, l. 19.
77. GARF, f. 6991, op. 1, d. 3, l. 137.
78. GARF, f. 6991, op. 1, d. 4, l. 22.

79. GARF, f. 6991, op. 2, d. 2a, 1. 79.

80. GARF, f. 6991, op. 1, d. 3, ll. 138–39.

81. GARF, f. 6991, op. 1, d. 3, l. 137.

82. GARF, f. 6991, op. 1, d. 3, l. 139.

83. Shkarovskii, "Russkaia pravoslavnaia tserkov' v 1943–1957," 39–40. [All three schisms formed in the 1920s as a result of disagreements among Orthodox groups over issues connected to patriarchal succession and accommodation with the Soviet government.—Ed.]

84. Tsypin, *Istoriia Russkoi pravoslavnoi tserkvi*, 135.

85. GARF, f. 6991, op. 1, d. 3, l. 173.

86. Archbishop Luke Voino-Iasenetskii reminded participants of the council that, in accordance with the decision of the National Church Council of 1917–18, delegates to the council should make nominations for patriarchal candidates and should vote by secret ballot. Archbishop Luke stated that he would vote against Metropolitan Aleksii, since his nomination as the sole candidate for the patriarchate violated that decision. As a result, Archbishop Luke became the only bishop not invited to the National Church Council of 1945. Archbishop Luka (Voino-Iasenetskii), *Ia poliubil*, 169.

87. Tsypin, *Istoriia Russkoi pravoslavnoi tserkvi*, 138.

88. GARF, f. 6991, op. 2, d. 2a, ll. 10–13.

89. Tsypin, *Istoriia Russkoi pravoslavnoi tserkvi*, 136.

90. Pospielovsky expresses a supposition that "apparently, Sergii and Aleksii hoped that the Church thus organized might better withstand new ordeals and persecution from the state." (Pospielovskii, *Russkaia pravoslavnaia tserkov'*, 199). I would add that it would hardly have been possible even to discuss introducing any democratic principles within the church in the 1940s under the control of a governmental system that itself was a rigidly centralized structure.

91. GARF, f. 6991, op. 1, d. 29, ll. 16–18.

92. "Materialy po Pomestnomy Soboru RPTs 31 ianvaria 1944–10 fevralia 1945 g." (GARF, f. 6991, op. 2, d. 32).

93. *ZhMP*, 1945, no. 2: 8–10.

94. Letter from L. Beria to Stalin, February 2, 1945, and Order of the Presidium of the Supreme Soviet of the USSR of February 21, 1945 (in the Archive of the Central Administration FSB RF). The majority of clergy who participated in the council's work, however, gave a different evaluation of "all the forms of attention" from the government. Bishop Mikhail of Kherson expressed the majority opinion in a conversation with a Council commissioner, "The vast majority of clergy and laity—in the recent past politically repressed almost to a man—related to all this very critically, with great caution, with many doubts, and even with total disbelief. They think that all this was implemented by some still obscure factors of political necessity." Odintsov, "Gosudarstvo i tserkov' v gody voiny," *Otechestvennye arkhivy*, 1995, no. 2, 123.

95. *ZhMP*, 1945, no. 3: 3, 25–27.

96. Tsypin, *Istoriia Russkoi pravoslavnoi tserkvi*, 141–43.

97. The Soviet leadership in 1944–1945 made attempts to reach a compromise and normalize relations with the Vatican. See Odintsov, "Uniaty," 56–71. When the patriarchate prepared to print an article by S.I. Plotnitsyn entitled "Battle for Faith in Galician Russia" in the *Journal of the Moscow Patriarchate* in May 1944, the Central Committee forbade its publication. The reason was, "At present it is forbidden to frame the issue that way. Comrade Stalin has just had a conversation with Orlemansky

(an American Catholic priest) in which Comrade Stalin spoke about the possibility of cooperating with the Roman pope against violence and persecution of the Catholic church. He stated that a policy of persecuting Catholicism was intolerable and ruled out. . . . In light of these pronouncements, an anti-Catholic article, even if it appears in a religious journal, is tactless at the very least" (GARF, f. 6991, op. 1, d. 3, l. 77).

98. GARF, f. 6991, op. 1, d. 29, l. 82.

99. GARF, f. 6991, op. 1, d. 29, ll. 65–68.

100. GARF, f. 6991, op. 1, d. 29, l. 110.

101. GARF, f. 6991, op. 1, d. 29, l. 112.

102. GARF, f. 6991, op. 1, d. 29, ll. 181–83.

103. Tsypin, *Istoriia Russkoi pravoslavnoi tserkvi*, 143–44.

104. GARF, f. 6991, op. 1, d. 80, l. 96.

105. GARF, f. 6991, op. 2, d. 52, l. 61.

106. GARF, f. 6991, op. 1, d. 83, ll. 27, 46; op. 2, d. 45, l. 155; op. 2, d. 52, l. 61.

107. GARF, f. 6991, op. 1, d. 153, ll. 6–7.

108. GARF, f. 6991, op. 1, d. 153, l. 7.

109. GARF, f. 6991, op. 1, d. 150, l. 182.

110. GARF, f. 6991, op. 1, d. 453, l. 350. In October 1953, Karpov reported that all Greco-Catholic monasteries had been shut down (GARF, f. 6991, op. 1, d. 1009, l. 93).

111. GARF, f. 6991, op. 1, d. 1, l. 22.

112. GARF, f. 6991, op. 1, d. 1, l. 20.

113. GARF, f. 6991, op. 1, d. 1, l. 28.

114. *ZhMP*, 1945, no. 3: 57.

115. GARF, f. 6991, op. 2, d. 34a, l. 3.

116. GARF, f. 6991, op. 1, d. 29, l. 144.

117. GARF, f. 6991, op. 1, d. 4, l. 32.

118. Pospielovskii, *Russkaia pravoslavnaia tserkov'*, 250–54.

119. GARF, f. 6991, op. 1, d. 153, ll. 7–8.

120. The Council had a card file for ordinary church leaders who lived abroad and dossiers on the heads of Orthodox churches and on exarchs working abroad. GARF, f. 6991, op. 1, d. 452, l. 73.

121. GARF, f. 6991, op. 2, d. 35, l. 62.

122. GARF, f. 6991, op. 2, d. 60, l. 47.

123. In his autobiography, Archbishop Luke cites a telling episode. During the presentation of a medal "For Valorous Service in the Great Patriotic War, 1941–1945" to the archbishop, the chairman of the regional executive committee expressed his desire that "the professor will in the future share his great experience with doctors in the city." Luke answered: "I have returned life and health to hundreds and maybe thousands of wounded. I certainly would have helped even more if you had not detained me for one reason or another and had not locked me behind bars or sent me into exile for eleven years." Officials who were present reacted to these words with shock and confusion. Archbishop Luka (Voino-Iasenetskii), *Ia poliubil*, 168–69.

124. Odintsov, "Krestnyi put'," 76.

125. GARF, f. 6991, op. 1, d. 81, ll. 50–51; d. 453, l. 186.

126. GARF, f. 6991, op. 2, d. 12, l. 57; op. 2, d. 34a, ll. 67–68; op. 2, d. 59a, ll. 46, 54, 70.

127. GARF, f. 6991, op. 2, d. 59a, ll. 43–45.

128. GARF, f. 6991, op. 2, d. 59a, l. 22.

129. GARF, f. 6991, op. 1, d. 153, l. 7.

130. GARF, f. 6991, op. 2, d. 73a, l. 27.

131. GARF, f. 6991, op. 2, d. 34, l. 77.

132. GARF, f. 6991, op. 1, d. 149, l. 82; d. 453, l. 186.

133. GARF, f. 6991, op. 1, d. 122, l. 12.

134. GARF, f. 6991, op. 1, d. 149, l. 90; d. 289, l. 182.

135. GARF, f. 6991, op. 1, d. 149, l. 90.

136. GARF, f. 6991, op. 1, d. 291, l. 51.

137. GARF, f. 6991, op. 1, d. 871, l. 56.

138. GARF, f. 6991, op. 1, d. 1, l. 27.

139. GARF, f. 6991, op. 1, d. 29, l. 194.

140. GARF, f. 6991, op. 1, d. 30, l. 84.

141. GARF, f. 6991, op. 1, d. 80, l. 193.

142. ZhMP, 1946, no. 9: 19.

143. GARF, f. 6991, op. 2, d. 34, ll. 67–68.

144. GARF, f. 6991, op. 1, d. 451, l. 139. It is worth noting that the patriarch brought a copy of this letter to the Council for Karpov's information.

145. GARF, f. 6991, op. 1, d. 1, l. 17.

146. GARF, f. 6991, op. 1, d. 4, l. 17.

147. GARF, f. 6991, op. 2, d. 32, ll. 28–30.

148. During the years of perestroika and glasnost, this line of the Moscow Patriarchate became the subject of stormy debate and discussion on its justification, appropriateness, degree of necessity, etc. In my view, a contemporary and direct participant in these events—Archbishop Luke Voino-Iasenetskii—formed an objective and realistic position on events in "the highest sphere" of church politics. He wrote, "We must not condemn the patriarch but pity him." Archbishop Luka (Voino-Iasenetskii), *Ia poliubil.*

149. GARF, f. 6991, op. 2, d. 33, l. 118. Alekseev believes that a second meeting between Stalin and Patriarch Aleksii was planned for September 1947 in Sochi, and the meeting's cancellation (officially due to the patriarch's illness) supports the fact that Stalin had lost interest in church problems by that time. See Alekseev, *Shturm,* 193–94. However, no documentary evidence exists to indicate that such a meeting was actually planned. A visit by Poskrebyshev to Aleksii for the purpose of communicating Stalin's interest in the state of the patriarch's health was, in my view, nothing more than a gesture and an act of formal courtesy from Stalin's perspective. The patriarch's reaction to this visit was another matter. Undoubtedly, such a happy coincidence of place and time for a vacation by Stalin in Sochi could not help but give the patriarch reason to think that it did not happen by chance and to wish and hope for a meeting with Stalin. He wrote about this to Karpov with complete openness on September 15, 1947. In the letter, Aleksii noted that he made up his mind not to raise the issue of a meeting because "I have not fully recovered from generally infectious tonsillitis." Quoted in Alekseev, *Shturm,* 194.

150. GARF, f. 6991, op. 1, d. 29, l. 68. See also Shkarovskii, "Russkaia pravoslavnaia tserkov'," 44.

151. GARF, f. 6991, op. 1, d. 150, ll. 1–2.

152. On that conference, see Tsypin, *Istoriia Russkoi pravoslavnoi tserkvi,* 146–47.

153. GARF, f. 6991, op. 1, d. 451, l. 302.

154. "Deianiia Sobora preosviashchennykh arkhiereev RPTs 8 sentiabria 1943 goda," *ZhMP,* 1943, no. 1: 17–19.

155. GARF, f. 6991, op. 1, d. 4, l. 15; op. 1, d. 83, ll. 6, 21; op. 2, d. 2a, l. 29.

156. GARF, f. 6991, op. 2, d. 4, l. 2.

157. *ZhMP*, 1943, no. 1: 17. Gordun, "Russkaia pravoslavnaia tserkov'," 93.

158. The level of religiosity was high even prior to the war. The 4th Plenum of the Central Council of the League of the Militant Godless in 1938 spoke about this (see Alekseev, *Illiuzii*, 330–31). Data from the 1937 census also testified to this, when 31 out of over 68 million people questioned stated that they believed in God, and 24.4 million of those were Orthodox (see V. Zhiromskaia, "'Pravoslavnyi khristianin' i 'grazhdanin Rossiiskoi derzhavy,'" *Nauka i religiia*, 1993, no. 9: 14–16).

159. GARF, f. 6991, op. 2, d. 1, ll. 25–26.

160. GARF, f. 6991, op. 1, d. 1, l. 3.

161. GARF, f. 6991, op. 1, d. 1, ll. 29, 65.

162. GARF, f. 6991, op. 1, d. 3, l. 65. On February 5, 1944, the Council for Russian Orthodox Church Affairs passed its first motion to approve decisions by regional executive committees to open sixteen churches (GARF, f. 6991, op. 2, d. 1, l. 11).

163. GARF, f. 6991, op. 1, d. 1, l. 31.

164. GARF, f. 6991, op. 2, d. 8, ll. 7–9, 11, 12.

165. GARF, f. 6991, op. 1, d. 3, l. 121.

166. GARF, f. 6991, op. 1, d. 3, l. 217. Active churches, particularly in regions that had been occupied by the nazis, were distributed unevenly. For example, seventy-seven churches were opened during the war in twenty-two regions that had been occupied in the Voronezh region (which had a total of eighty-four districts); in thirty other regions, there was not a single active church (GARF, f. 6991, op. 1, d. 81, l. 27).

167. GARF, f. 6991, op. 1, d. 452, l. 85.

168. GARF, f. 6991, op. 1, d. 290, l. 146.

169. GARF, f. 6991, op. 1, d. 5, l. 34; d. 291, l. 243.

170. GARF, f. 6991, op. 1, d. 4, ll. 11, 34.

171. GARF, f. 6991, op. 2, d. 13, ll. 56, 59.

172. GARF, f. 6991, op. 1, d. 60, l. 41.

173. GARF, f. 6991, op. 2, d. 35, l. 83.

174. GARF, f. 6991, op. 1, d. 81, l. 98.

175. GARF, f. 6991, op. 2, d. 52, l. 12.

176. For example, see Odintsov, "Gosudarstvo i tserkov' v gody voiny," 125.

177. GARF, f. 6991, op. 2, d. 8, l. 28 ob.

178. GARF, f. 6991, op. 1, d. 7, l. 22.

179. GARF, f. 6991, op. 1, d. 7, l. 22.

180. GARF, f. 6991, op. 1, d. 289, l. 176.

181. GARF, f. 6991, op. 1, d. 30, l. 75.

182. GARF, f. 6991, op. 1, d. 7, l. 39.

183. GARF, f. 6991, op. 1, d. 148, l. 44.

184. GARF, f. 6991, op. 1, d. 149, l. 55.

185. GARF, f. 6991, op. 2, d. 8, l. 28 ob.

186. GARF, f. 6991, op. 1, d. 82, l. 54.

187. GARF, f. 6991, op. 1, d. 148, l. 3.

188. GARF, f. 6991, op. 1, d. 81, l. 102; op. 2, d. 13, l. 39.

189. GARF, f. 6991, op. 1, d. 153, l. 18.

190. GARF, f. 6991, op. 1, d. 30, l. 108; op. 2, d. 8, l. 29; op. 2, d. 12, l. 56; op. 2, d. 13, l. 153.

191. GARF, f. 6991, op. 1, d. 290, l. 159.

192. GARF, f. 6991, op. 1, d. 291, l. 244; d. 149, l. 85.

193. GARF, f. 6991, op. 1, d. 149, l. 87.

194. GARF, f. 6991, op. 1, d. 287, l. 37.

195. GARF, f. 6991, op. 1, d. 153, l. 21.

196. Ibid.

197. GARF, f. 6991, op. 1, d. 289, l. 51.

198. GARF, f. 6991, op. 2, d. 8, l. 27 ob.

199. GARF, f. 6991, op. 2, d. 12, l. 94.

200. Ibid.

201. GARF, f. 6991, op. 2, d. 2, l. 24.

202. GARF, f. 6991, op. 2, d. 52, ll. 39–40.

203. GARF, f. 6991, op. 1, d. 1013, l. 43.

204. GARF, f. 6991, op. 1, d. 451, l. 74.

205. GARF, f. 6991, op. 1, d. 290, l. 146.

206. GARF, f. 6991, op. 1, d. 30, l. 158; d. 81, l. 41; d. 49, l. 81; d. 153, l. 2.

207. GARF, f. 6991, op. 1, d. 149, l. 83.

208. GARF, f. 6991, op. 2, d. 2a, l. 26.

209. GARF, f. 6991, op. 2, d. 34a, l. 4.

210. GARF, f. 6991, op. 2, d. 59a, l. 66.

211. GARF, f. 6991, op. 1, d. 2, l. 15.

212. GARF, f. 6991, op. 1, d. 80, l. 66; d. 149, l. 82; d. 153, l. 8. As is evident from the data presented, the number of clergy was significantly less than the number of open churches. Therefore, diocesan bishops also assigned some priests to conduct services in nearby churches—such churches were called "attached" (pripisnyi).

213. GARF, f. 6991, op. 2, d. 12, l. 51; op. 1, d. 5, l. 29; op. 1, d. 7, l. 6.

214. GARF, f. 6991, op. 1, d. 81, l. 52; d. 153, ll. 8–9. Statistics for 1947 are not available.

215. GARF, f. 6991, op. 2, d. 2a, ll. 1, 99; d. 34a, ll. 53, 57; d. 59a, l. 63.

216. GARF, f. 6991, op. 2, d. 8, l. 27; op. 2, d. 52, l. 27; op. 1, d. 153, l. 5. See also Metropolitan Ioann (Snychev), *Mitropolit Manuil (Lemeshevskii)*, (St. Petersburg, 1993), 197–203.

217. GARF, f. 6991, op. 1, d. 153, l. 10; op. 1, d. 81, ll. 50, 54; op. 2, d. 53, l. 31; op. 2, d. 2a, l. 68.

218. GARF, f. 6991, op. 1, d. 153, l. 12.

219. GARF, f. 6991, op. 2, d. 2, l. 64.

220. GARF, f. 6991, op. 2, d. 34a, l. 57.

221. GARF, f. 6991, op. 1, d. 7, l. 33.

222. Ibid.

223. GARF, f. 6991, op. 2, d. 34a, l. 54.

224. GARF, f. 6991, op. 1, d. 7, l. 79.

225. GARF, f. 6991, op. 2, d. 2a, l. 51.

226. GARF, f. 6991, op. 1, d. 2, l. 18.

227. GARF, f. 6991, op. 1, d. 122, l. 12.

228. GARF, f. 6991, op. 2, d. 1, l. 37.

229. GARF, f. 6991, op. 1, d. 2, l. 123. The decision to organize the majority of institutions for theological education in western regions of the country arose out of the necessity to strengthen the position of the Russian Orthodox Church in those regions and was connected with the campaign then just under way for reuniting the Uniate Church with the Moscow Patriarchate.

230. GARF, f. 6991, op. 1, d. 123, l. 332.

231. GARF, f. 6991, op. 2, d. 37, l. 3.

232. GARF, f. 6991, op. 1, d. 80, l. 153.

233. GARF, f. 6991, op. 1, d. 122, l. 53.

234. GARF, f. 6991, op. 2, d. 52, l. 24.

235. GARF, f. 6991, op. 1, d. 122, l. 191.

236. GARF, f. 6991, op. 2, d. 37, l. 89.

237. GARF, f. 6991, op. 1, d. 122, l. 160.

238. Quoted in Pospielovskii, *Russkaia pravoslavnaia tserkov' v XX veke*, 268.

239. GARF, f. 6991, op. 1, d. 122, l. 165.

240. GARF, f. 6991, op. 1, d. 122, ll. 14, 95, 165.

241. GARF, f. 6991, op. 1, d. 122, ll. 2–21.

242. GARF, f. 6991, op. 1, d. 7, l. 80.

243. GARF, f. 6991, op. 1, d. 122, ll. 62, 198.

244. GARF, f. 6991, op. 1, d. 122, l. 69.

245. GARF, f. 6991, op. 1, d. 122, l. 197.

246. GARF, f. 6991, op. 1, d. 122, ll. 198, 200.

247. GARF, f. 6991, op. 1, d. 122, l. 200. Directions to commissioners on their personal participation in leading [observances of] Soviet holidays in church schools were countermanded in December 1947. The instructional letter sent to them on December 3 said, "The Council, guided by instructions from the Central Committee, announces that a commissioner should not present reports at institutions for theological education and that either the regional or city committee of the Communist Party will be responsible for assigning lecturers. A commissioner should not accept invitations to participate in celebratory gatherings." GARF, f. 6991, op. 1, d. 148, l. 27.

248. GARF, f. 6991, op. 2, d. 37, ll. 29, 34, 40, 41; op. 1, d. 83, l. 22.

249. GARF, f. 6991, op. 2, d. 37, ll. 42, 54, 47.

250. GARF, f. 6991, op. 1, d. 150, ll. 87, 125.

251. The Vilnius seminary was opened by an order from the Education Committee of the Moscow Patriarchate, an order about which the Council for Russian Orthodox Church Affairs was apparently not notified. Having received information from Commissioner Linev from Lithuania, Karpov sent him the following instructions in January 1947: "The Council requests that you quickly inform it of the basis for such decisions and by whom it was opened, since the Council did not make such a decision. . . . Gedvilas, chairman of the Council of Ministers of the Lithuanian SSR, expressed opposition to permission for opening an Orthodox theological seminary. . . . You personally will report to him that the seminary is functioning, that you gave permission, and that the Council for its part thinks it expedient to have an Orthodox theological seminary in Vilnius since the archbishop raised this matter and a Catholic seminary functions in Kaunas" (GARF, f. 6991, op. 1, d. 122, l. 146). A resolution to open a seminary in Vilnius was drawn up in August 1946. However, in August 1947 the government of Lithuania stopped the seminary's work. In response to this, Karpov sent to Gedvilas and Snechkus (the Lithuanian secretary of the Central Committee of the Communist Party) a letter with requests to clarify "motives for the prohibition" and to review the question of the seminary anew, noting that there were only twenty students at the Orthodox seminary but 150 at the Catholic seminary (GARF, f. 6991, op. 1, d. 122, l. 239).

252. GARF, f. 6991, op. 2, d. 37, ll. 47, 57.

253. GARF, f. 6991, op. 1, d. 153, l. 15; op. 2, d. 37, l. 142.

254. GARF, f. 6991, op. 2, d. 2, l. 9.
255. GARF, f. 6991, op. 2, d. 45, l. 95.
256. GARF, f. 6991, op. 2, d. 46, l. 73.
257. GARF, f. 6991, op. 1, d. 4, l. 37.
258. GARF, f. 6991, op. 1, d. 81, l. 174.
259. GARF, f. 6991, op. 1, d. 150, ll. 60, 63.
260. GARF, f. 6991, op. 2, d. 1, l. 48.
261. GARF, f. 6991, op. 2, d. 1, l. 55.
262. GARF, f. 6991, op. 2, d. 34a, l. 24.
263. GARF, f. 6991, op. 2, d. 46, l. 4.
264. GARF, f. 6991, op. 1, d. 5, l. 68.
265. GARF, f. 6991, op. 1, d. 4, l. 37.
266. GARF, f. 6991, op. 1, d. 4, l. 38.
267. GARF, f. 6991, op. 2, d. 29, l. 38.
268. GARF, f. 6991, op. 2, d. 8, l. 90.
269. GARF, f. 6991, op. 1, d. 4, l. 37; op. 2, d. 8, ll. 72, 46.
270. GARF, f. 6991, op. 2, d. 8, l. 69.
271. GARF, f. 6991, op. 2, d. 8, ll. 118–19. The Council for Russian Orthodox Church Affairs prepared this document as a Sovnarkom resolution to be signed by Stalin. The Council's draft was dated December 3, 1946 (GARF, f. 6991, op. 2, d. 44, ll. 18–20). It was issued, however, as a Circular Letter of the Ministry of Finance with the signature of Deputy Finance Minister Uriupin.
272. GARF, f. 6991, op. 1, d. 147, ll. 14, 19, 23, 26.
273. Pospielovskii shows that as early as 1954, Russian Orthodox bishops were taxed in accordance with Article 5, at the same rate as Soviet employees. See Pospielovskii, *Russkaia pravoslavnaia tserkov'*, 276.
274. GARF, f. 6991, op. 2, d. 34a, l. 24.
275. GARF, f. 6991, op. 1, d. 7, l. 33.
276. GARF, f. 6991, op. 1, d. 7, l. 62.
277. Ibid.
278. GARF, f. 6991, op. 1, d. 1, l. 58.
279. GARF, f. 6991, op. 1, d. 149, l. 280.
280. GARF, f. 6991, op. 1, d. 150, l. 228.
281. GARF, f. 6991, op. 1, d. 147, ll. 49, 57.
282. GARF, f. 6991, op. 1, d. 153, l. 6.
283. RGASPI, f. 17, op. 132, d. 286, l. 3.
284. GARF, f. 6991, op. 2, d. 13, l. 16.
285. Pospielovskii, *Russkaia pravoslavnaia tserkov'*, 256.
286. See *KPSS v rezoliutsiiakh i resheniiakh s"ezdov, konferentsii i plenumov TsK* (Moscow, 1985), 521–22.
287. Alekseev, *Shturm*, 196–97.
288. Quoted in Tsypin, *Istoriia Russkoi pravoslavnoi tserkvi*, 134.
289. GARF, f. 6991, op. 1, d. 2, l. 56.
290. GARF, f. 6991, op. 1, d. 81, l. 47.
291. GARF, f. 6991, op. 1, d. 149, l. 81.
292. GARF, f. 6991, op. 1, d. 149, l. 91.
293. GARF, f. 6991, op. 2, d. 2, l. 3.
294. Odintsov, *Gosudarstvo i tserkov' v Rossii, XX vek*, 108.

Notes to Chapter 2: Church-State Relations Between 1948 and 1957

1. This step was considered premature, however, since there were no staff members for the Institute and the Museum of the History of Religion and Atheism in Leningrad was not itself functioning. Its director, V.D. Bonch-Bruevich, tried to find a location for the museum in Leningrad (made necessary because "some film organization took over the building by fraud") or to relocate the Museum to Moscow, where the question of a building was also sharply debated. GARF, f. 6991, op. 2, d. 48, l. 1; RGASPI, f. 17, op. 125, d. 407, l. 51.

2. RGASPI, f. 17, op. 125, d. 407, l. 88.

3. RGASPI, f. 17, op. 125, d. 407, ll. 88–89.

4. RGASPI, f. 17, op. 125, d. 407, l. 89.

5. The Council's report for 1946 referred to loyalty to the Soviet regime by Russian Orthodox Church bishops, and not by all clergy as Aleksandrov thought.

6. RGASPI, f. 17, op. 117, d. 946, ll. 57–59, 78–80, 153.

7. RGASPI, f. 17, op. 117, d. 946, l. 153.

8. RGASPI, f. 17, op. 117, d. 946, l. 53.

9. GARF, f. 6991, op. 1, d. 150, ll. 113–17.

10. GARF, f. 6991, op. 1, d. 286, l. 1.

11. GARF, f. 6991, op. 1, d. 286, l. 8.

12. GARF, f. 6991, op. 1, d. 286, l. 1.

13. GARF, f. 6991, op. 1, d. 286, l. 8.

14. GARF, f. 6991, op. 1, d. 289, l. 8.

15. GARF, f. 6991, op. 1, d. 289, l. 33.

16. GARF, f. 6991, op. 1, d. 289, l. 58.

17. GARF, f. 6991, op. 1, d. 289, ll. 207, 209.

18. GARF, f. 6991, op. 1, d. 291, l. 12.

19. GARF, f. 6991, op. 1, d. 286, ll. 2, 10; d. 153, l. 21; d. 606, l. 195. RGASPI, f. 17, op. 132, d. 285, ll. 123–25, 194.

20. GARF, f. 6991, op. 1, d. 287, l. 14; d. 290, ll. 186, 189; d. 291, l. 24.

21. GARF, f. 6991, op. 1, d. 291, ll. 243–49.

22. RGASPI, f. 17, op. 132, d. 10, ll. 19–20.

23. RGASPI, f. 17, op. 132, d. 10, ll. 21–23.

24. RGASPI, f. 17, op. 132, d. 10, l. 24.

25. GARF, f. 6991, op. 1, d. 451, ll. 162–67.

26. RGASPI, f. 17, op. 132, d. 110, ll. 32–33.

27. GARF, f. 6991, op. 1, d. 451, ll. 162–68.

28. *Pravda*, February 19, 1949.

29. RGASPI, f. 17, op. 132, d. 110, l. 29. GARF, f. 6991, op. 1, d. 451, l. 162.

30. GARF, f. 6991, op. 2, d. 73a, l. 14.

31. GARF, f. 6991, op. 2, d. 451, l. 235.

32. RGASPI, f. 17, op. 132, d. 110, ll. 28–29.

33. RGASPI, f. 17, op. 132, d. 110, ll. 6–57; d. 10, ll. 25–26.

34. RGASPI, f. 17, op. 132, d. 10, ll. 25–26.

35. GARF, f. 6991, op. 1, d. 451, l. 211.

36. GARF, f. 6991, op. 1, d. 451, l. 227.

37. GARF, f. 6991, op. 1, d. 451, l. 257; d. 452, l. 71; d. 453, l. 281.

38. RGASPI, f. 17, op. 132, d. 10, l. 26.
39. Alekseev, *Illiuzii*, 352.
40. GARF, f. 6991, op. 1, d. 451, l. 257.
41. GARF, f. 6991, op. 1, d. 602, ll. 5–6.
42. GARF, f. 6991, op. 1, d. 602, ll. 6–7; d. 604, l. 96; d. 606, l. 130.
43. GARF, f. 6991, op. 1, d. 602, ll. 7–112.
44. GARF, f. 6991, op. 1, d. 746, ll. 1–8; d. 747, ll. 24–25.
45. GARF, f. 6991, op. 1, d. 748, l. 1.
46. GARF, f. 6991, op. 1, d. 1224, l. 183.
47. GARF, f. 6991, op. 1, d. 190, l. 156.
48. GARF, f. 6991, op. 1, d. 190, l. 155.
49. GARF, f. 6991, op. 1, d. 190, l. 156.
50. GARF, f. 6991, op. 1, d. 284, l. 37.
51. GARF, f. 6991, op. 1, d. 286, l. 18.
52. GARF, f. 6991, op. 1, d. 286, ll. 19–20.
53. GARF, f. 6991, op. 1, d. 291, l. 139; d. 1114, l. 170. By that time, all twenty-eight church buildings listed in the March order had been transferred to religious communities. The communities had undertaken repairs and put the buildings in order. Senior priests in twenty of the newly opened churches had already been appointed by bishops and registered by commissioners. The fall order of the government on closing parishes that had just begun their activity provoked protests from clergy and laity. The archbishops of Arkhangelsk and Irkutsk traveled to the patriarch in Moscow about this matter. Even the head of the regional Department of Architecture in Irkutsk asked the Council for Russian Orthodox Church Affairs not to prevent the religious community from finishing the church. The church was an architectural monument, the community expended significant resources for capital repairs, and the regional department was unable to complete the work using its own resources.
54. GARF, f. 6991, op. 1, d. 291, l. 199; d. 1114, l. 171.
55. GARF, f. 6991, op. 1, d. 1114, l. 171.
56. GARF, f. 6991, op. 1, d. 1114, l. 173.
57. Ibid.
58. GARF, f. 6991, op. 1, d. 872, l. 74; op. 2, d. 87, l. 13.
59. GARF, f. 6991, op. 1, d. 872, l. 74.
60. GARF, f. 6991, op. 1, d. 872, l. 78.
61. GARF, f. 6991, op. 1, d. 1013, l. 17.
62. GARF, f. 6991, op. 1, d. 452, l. 68.
63. Gordun, "Russkaia pravoslavnaia tserkov'," 101.
64. GARF, f. 6991, op. 1, d. 451, l. 303.
65. GARF, f. 6991, op. 1, d. 452, l. 46.
66. GARF, f. 6991, op. 1, d. 606, l. 196.
67. GARF, f. 6991, op. 1, d. 1013, l. 44.
68. GARF, f. 6991, op. 1, d. 1013, l. 44.
69. GARF, f. 6991, op. 1, d. 454, l. 6.
70. GARF, f. 6991, op. 1, d. 454, l. 31.
71. GARF, f. 6991, op. 1, d. 454, l. 108.
72. GARF, f. 6991, op. 1, d. 288, l. 27.
73. GARF, f. 6991, op. 1, d. 1013, l. 45.
74. GARF, f. 6991, op. 1, d. 604, l. 108; d. 744, l. 47; d. 870, l. 57; d. 1013, l. 15; d. 1224, l. 105; d. 872, l. 199.

75. GARF, f. 6991, op. 1, d. 871, l. 130.

76. GARF, f. 6991, op. 1, d. 1224, l. 105.

77. Council Commissioner Popov gave permission to presidents of all the district executive committees to use these churches. As a result of checking the multitude of complaints from the region, the facts were confirmed and measures were taken. By July 1, 1952, almost all buildings were vacated. Commissioner Popov, whose candidacy the Council had opposed and who worked in that position without confirmation, was fired from his post. GARF, f. 6991, op. 1, d. 872, l. 199.

78. GARF, f. 6991, op. 1, d. 606, ll. 196–200.

79. GARF, f. 6991, op. 1, d. 291, l. 243.

80. GARF, f. 6991, op. 1, d. 748, l. 106.

81. GARF, f. 6991, op. 1, d. 604, l. 170.

82. RGASPI, f. 17, op. 132, d. 285, ll. 138–40.

83. GARF, f. 6991, op. 1, d. 1012, l. 119.

84. GARF, f. 6991, op. 1, d. 744, l. 41.

85. GARF, f. 6991, op. 1, d. 606, l. 195.

86. GARF, f. 6991, op. 1, d. 288, l. 27.

87. GARF, f. 6991, op. 1, d. 288, l. 34; d. 605, l. 290; d. 747, l. 63; d. 751, l. 95; d. 1012, ll. 12, 127.

88. GARF, f. 6991, op. 1, d. 288, ll. 39–40.

89. GARF, f. 6991, op. 1, d. 454, l. 31; d. 604, l. 15; d. 748, l. 106; d. 749, l. 60.

90. GARF, f. 6991, op. 2, d. 87, l. 13; d. 103, l. 10; d. 130, l. 13; d. 156, l. 11.

91. GARF, f. 6991, op. 2, d. 71, l. 26; d. 75, ll. 31–34; d. 81, ll. 1–2; d. 87, l. 1; d. 96, l. 1.

92. See A.N. Sakharov, ed., *Istoriia Rossii. XX vek* (Moscow: AST, 1996), 514.

93. GAChO, f. 274, op. 3, d. 4479a, l. 20.

94. GARF, f. 6991, op. 1, d. 871, l. 132.

95. GARF, f. 6991, op. 2, d. 66a, l. 44.

96. GARF, f. 6991, op. 1, d. 290, l. 224.

97. GARF, f. 6991, op. 1, d. 288, l. 19.

98. GARF, f. 6991, op. 2, d. 73a, l. 2.

99. GARF, f. 6991, op. 1, d. 288, ll. 33.

100. GARF, f. 6991, op. 1, d. 453, l. 6.

101. GARF, f. 6991, op. 1, d. 457, l. 20.

102. GARF, f. 6991, op. 2, d. 73a, ll. 27–28.

103. GARF, f. 6991, op. 1, d. 454, l. 197.

104. GARF, f. 6991, op. 1, d. 288, l. 19; d. 452, l. 288.

105. GARF, f. 6991, op. 1, d. 453, l. 206.

106. GARF, f. 6991, op. 1, d. 454, l. 85; d. 452, l. 10.

107. GARF, f. 6991, op. 1, d. 148, l. 42.

108. GARF, f. 6991, op. 1, d. 605, l. 262.

109. GARF, f. 6991, op. 1, d. 451, ll. 109–13.

110. GARF, f. 6991, op. 1, d. 150, l. 210; d. 289, l. 191.

111. GARF, f. 6991, op. 1, d. 287, l. 71.

112. GARF, f. 6991, op. 1, d. 451, l. 58.

113. GARF, f. 6991, op. 1, d. 287, l. 61.

114. GARF, f. 6991, op. 1, d. 411, l. 143.

115. At a meeting with Karpov in June 1949, Patriarch Aleksii expressed the opin-

ion that Metropolitan Ioann (exarch of Ukraine) apparently did not want to open an academy in Kiev. GARF, f. 6991, op. 1, d. 457, l. 95.

116. GARF, f. 6991, op. 2, d. 73a, l. 35.

117. GARF, f. 6991, op. 1, d. 449, l. 14.

118. GARF, f. 6991, op. 1, d. 457, l. 95. Relative stabilization of church-state relations at the start of the 1950s meant no reduction in the number of educational institutions of the Russian Orthodox Church.

119. GARF, f. 6991, op. 1, d. 293, l. 52; op. 2, d. 37, l. 130.

120. GARF, f. 6991, op. 2, d. 37, l. 143.

121. GARF, f. 6991, op. 1, d. 569, l. 1.

122. GARF, f. 6991, op. 1, d. 604, l. 112.

123. GARF, f. 6991, op. 1, d. 606, l. 42. However, a decree by the Council of Ministers of the USSR on April 15, 1954, annulled the granting of deferments. GARF, f. 6991, op. 1, d. 1116, l. 49.

124. GARF, f. 6991, op. 1, d. 457, ll. 17–18. Archimandrite Veniamin, Inspector at the Moscow Theological Academy, was arrested in 1948 on the charge of anti-Soviet propaganda and furthermore, according to Karpov, said, "Communists have ties with the Moscow Theological Academy because the Council for Russian Orthodox Church Affairs participates in the recruitment of students." V.A. Sretenskii was an instructor in English language at the Moscow Theological Academy.

125. GARF, f. 6991, op. 1, d. 751, l. 66.

126. GARF, f. 6991, op. 1, d. 457, l. 21.

127. GARF, f. 6991, op. 1, d. 872, l. 184.

128. GARF, f. 6991, op. 1, d. 872, l. 178.

129. GARF, f. 6991, op. 1, d. 1225, l. 79.

130. GARF, f. 6991, op. 1, d. 872, l. 178.

131. GARF, f. 6991, op. 1, d. 872, l. 178.

132. GARF, f. 6991, op. 1, d. 451, l. 59.

133. GARF, f. 6991, op. 1, d. 451, l. 62.

134. GARF, f. 6991, op. 1, d. 451, l. 250.

135. GARF, f. 6991, op. 1, d. 452, l. 19.

136. GARF, f. 6991, op. 1, d. 871, l. 55; d. 1013, l. 174.

137. GARF, f. 6991, op. 1, d. 871, l. 53.

138. GARF, f. 6991, op. 1, d. 871, ll. 54–55.

139. GARF, f. 6991, op. 1, d. 291, ll. 47–48; d. 451, l. 24.

140. GARF, f. 6991, op. 1, d. 457, l. 27.

141. GARF, f. 6991, op. 1, d. 454, l. 28.

142. GARF, f. 6991, op. 1, d. 451, l. 178. In a memorandum to Stalin in May 1949, D.T. Shepilov indicated, however, that Karpov "acquired a television costing 4,000 rubles for the patriarch" in February 1949 (RGASPI, f. 17, op. 132, d. 110, l. 27). If Karpov did indeed give this to the patriarch under those circumstances, his action can surely be seen only as personal kindness.

143. GARF, f. 6991, op. 1, d. 450, l. 166; d. 457, ll. 25–27, 70, 102; d. 608, l. 47; d. 751, l. 181; d. 875, l. 29.

144. GARF, f. 6991, op. 1, d. 871, ll. 51–53; d. 1013, ll. 172–73.

145. GARF, f. 6991, op. 1, d. 1225, l. 81.

146. GARF, f. 6991, op. 1, d. 872, l. 182.

147. GARF, f. 6991, op. 1, d. 873, l. 182.

148. GARF, f. 6991, op. 1, d. 875, l. 246.

149. GARF, f. 6991, op. 1, d. 871, ll. 107–8.

150. GARF, f. 6991, op. 2, d. 44, l. 30.

151. GARF, f. 6991, op. 1, d. 872, l. 178; d. 1225, l. 79.

152. See Shkarovskii, "Russkaia pravoslavnaia tserkov' v 1943–1957 godakh," 48–49.

153. GARF, f. 6991, op. 1, d. 1114, ll. 35–36.

154. GARF, f. 6991, op. 1, d. 872, l. 86.

155. GARF, f. 6991, op. 1, d. 1114, l. 45.

156. GARF, f. 6991, op. 1, d. 748, ll. 19–20.

157. See *Deviatnadtsatyi s"ezd KPSS. 5–14 oktiabria 1952 g. Biulleteni zasedanii.*

158. See *KPSS v rezoliutsiiakh. . .* (Moscow, 1985), 8: 279–300.

159. GARF, f. 6991, op. 1, d. 1012, l. 68.

160. GARF, f. 6991, op. 1, d. 748, l. 108.

161. GARF, f. 6991, op. 1, d. 873, l. 173; d. 749, l. 274; d. 606, l. 38. RGASPI, f. 17, op. 132, d. 285, l. 142.

162. GARF, f. 6991, op. 1, d. 870, l. 61; d. 872, l. 71.

163. GARF, f. 6991, op. 1, d. 1012, l. 127.

164. See, for example, material on the results of a verification of political-propagandistic work in the provinces that was done in 1949 by commissioners for the Central Committee. Data from this verification showed that many party agitators and propagandists—not only from the rank-and-file but also leaders of related sections of district party committees—did not have any idea about decisions made at the top or about events around the country and the world. Sakharov, *Istoriia Rossii*, 499.

165. GARF, f. 6991, op. 2, d. 46, l. 63.

166. GARF, f. 6991, op. 1, d. 605, l. 84.

167. RGASPI, f. 17, op. 132, l. 109, ll. 121–24.

168. RGASPI, f. 17, op. 132, l. 109, ll. 91–98.

169. RGASPI, f. 17, op. 132, l. 109, ll. 46–50, 52.

170. RGASPI, f. 17, op. 132, l. 109, ll. 55–58.

171. RGASPI, f. 17, op. 132, l. 109, ll. 60–76.

172. GARF, f. 6991, op. 1, d. 604, l. 224.

173. GARF, f. 6991, op. 1, d. 872, ll. 120–21.

174. GARF, f. 6991, op. 1, d. 605, ll. 84–88; d. 1115, l. 15.

175. Odintsov, "Pis'ma," 26.

176. GARF, f. 6991, op. 1, d. 1012, l. 102.

177. GARF, f. 6991, op. 1, d. 1009, ll. 146–53; d. 1012, l. 109; d. 1114, ll. 77–79, 167–68, 187–88.

178. GARF, f. 6991, op. 1, d. 1012, l. 109; d. 1114, l. 168; d. 1115, ll. 36–38; d. 1224, l. 125.

179. GARF, f. 6991, op. 1, d. 1114, l. 187.

180. A reorganization of ministries conducted by Malenkov affected the Councils in only one way—in May 1953, the Council of Ministers of the USSR adopted a resolution on ending payments of "monetary bonuses" to commissioners for the Councils who worked on the territory of the RSFSR (GARF, f. 6991, op. 1, d. 1013, l. 96). Continuous petitions by presidents of the Councils on restoring payments ended in December 1955, when they were informed by the Central Committee in a telephone call that, "Requests from the Councils are not supported because it is an inopportune time to raise the matter" (GARF, f. 6991, op. 1, d. 1226, l. 41).

181. GARF, f. 6991, op. 1, d. 1114, ll. 77–79.

182. GARF, f. 6991, op. 1, d. 1114, l. 79.

183. GARF, f. 6991, op. 2, d. 103, l. 10; d. 130, l. 13.

184. GARF, f. 6991, op. 1, d. 1114, l. 36.

185. GARF, f. 6991, op. 1, d. 1013, ll. 145–46.

186. GARF, f. 6991, op. 1, d. 1013, l. 142; d. 1224, l. 12.

187. GARF, f. 6991, op. 1, d. 1113, l. 144; d. 1224, l. 122; d. 1226, l. 58.

188. GARF, f. 6991, op. 1, d. 1111, ll. 101–13; d. 1114, ll. 3–40; d. 1224, l. 12.

189. GARF, f. 6991, op. 1, d. 1114, l. 181.

190. The Council for Russian Orthodox Church Affairs repeatedly raised this issue with the government. In a memorandum to Malenkov in the fall of 1953, the Council brought it up again and proposed to instruct the Finance Ministry to develop a draft for changing procedures for levying taxes. GARF, f. 6991, op. 1, d. 1009, l. 149.

191. In September 1953, the Council asked the government to ratify its decision to open eleven churches and chapels for which local authorities had given approval. GARF, f. 6991, op. 1, d. 1008, ll. 184–86.

192. GARF, f. 6991, op. 1, d. 1008, l. 178.

193. GARF, f. 6991, op. 1, d. 1114, l. 181.

194. *KPSS v rezoliutsiiakh*, 8: 428.

195. *KPSS v rezoliutsiiakh*, 8: 430.

196. *KPSS v rezoliutsiiakh*, 8: 431–32.

197. GARF, f. 6991, op. 1, d. 1118, l. 153.

198. GARF, f. 6991, op. 1, d. 1115, ll. 87–112.

199. GARF, f. 6991, op. 1, d. 1115, l. 88.

200. GARF, f. 6991, op. 1, d. 1115, l. 112.

201. GARF, f. 6991, op. 1, d. 1115, l. 113.

202. GARF, f. 6991, op. 1, d. 1111, l. 181.

203. Metropolitan Grigorii of Leningrad said at the August 1954 session of the Synod, "There are now three basic lines of struggle—the struggle against alcoholism, the struggle against us churchmen, and a third struggle against hooliganism. This means that we find ourselves connected with these issues." GARF, f. 6991, op. 1, d. 1115, l. 129.

204. GARF, f. 6991, op. 1, d. 1116, ll. 33, 38.

205. GARF, f. 6991, op. 1, d. 1115, l. 127.

206. GARF, f. 6991, op. 1, d. 1116, ll. 28–39, 90, 153, 173.

207. GARF, f. 6991, op. 1, d. 1115, l. 192; d. 1224, l. 209; d. 1226, l. 31. "Militant" conduct by youth resulted from the political line that the Central Committee of the Komsomol introduced into its local organizations at the end of the 1940s and that, in turn, was directed by the CPSU Central Committee through Agitprop. For material on this problem, see Alekseev, *Shturm*, 201–21.

208. GARF, f. 6991, op. 1, d. 1116, l. 11.

209. GARF, f. 6991, op. 1, d. 1115, ll. 170, 172.

210. GARF, f. 6991, op. 1, d. 1115, ll. 129–30.

211. Metropolitan Nikolai made a special request of the Moscow City Reference Bureau to have all press clippings on antireligious topics in newspapers given to him.

212. GARF, f. 6991, op. 1, d. 1115, ll. 131, 157, 159, 195.

213. GARF, f. 6991, op. 1, d. 1116, l. 35.

214. GARF, f. 6991, op. 1, d. 1115, l. 180.

215. GARF, f. 6991, op. 1, d. 1116, l. 10.

216. GARF, f. 6991, op. 1, d. 1116, l. 34.

217. GARF, f. 6991, op. 1, d. 1115, l. 159.

218. GARF, f. 6991, op. 1, d. 1115, l. 171.

219. GARF, f. 6991, op. 1, d. 1115, ll. 164, 168. The opinion of the patriarch, as passed on to the Council by Archpriest Medvedskii, is interesting in this connection. "They attack us every day and at the same time demand that we receive delegations and show foreigners the grandeur of the Russian Orthodox Church." GARF, f. 6991, op. 1, d. 1115, l. 147.

220. T. Arinina, "Bol'she nastupatel'nosti v antireligioznoi propagande," *Stalinskaia smena*, October 20, 1954. GARF, f. 6991, op. 1, d. 1116, l. 43.

221. V. Vladko and A. Galitskii, "Za stenami Lavry," *Literaturnaia gazeta*, October 28, 1954.

222. GARF, f. 6991, op. 1, d. 1116, l. 175.

223. GARF, f. 6991, op. 1, d. 1116, l. 7.

224. GARF, f. 6991, op. 1, d. 1116, ll. 3–7.

225. GARF, f. 6991, op. 1, d. 1116, l. 36.

226. Odintsov, "Khozhdenie," no. 7: 2.

227. *KPSS v rezoliutsiiakh*, 8: 448–49.

228. GARF, f. 6991, op. 1, d. 1116, l. 54. Only Metropolitans Grigorii and Nikolai withheld their opinions both during discussion of the patriarch's resolution by the Synod and at the Council's reception. Kolchitskii explained the restraint by Metropolitans Nikolai and Grigorii this way: "They thought that the patriarch would insist on being received by Malenkov and would decide at that meeting matters related to the transfer of buildings [at Novodevichy Convent], opening of churches, taxation, and the like. The resolution upset their plans." GARF, f. 6991, op. 1, d. 1116, l. 48.

229. GARF, f. 6991, op. 1, d. 1116, ll. 53–56.

230. GARF, f. 6991, op. 1, d. 1116, ll. 57–59.

231. GARF, f. 6991, op. 1, d. 1116, l. 53.

232. GARF, f. 6991, op. 1, d. 1118, l. 96. *Pravda*, December 12, 1954.

233. The conversation primarily concerned the foreign policy of the Russian Orthodox Church—"so that the voice of the Russian Church in pursuit of peace would be more sonorous." The patriarch spoke very warmly about this meeting and Malenkov. "He showed concern for me and had already telephoned a doctor." Learning about the upcoming ten-year anniversary of Aleksii's patriarchate, Malenkov, in the patriarch's words, "indicated that this event must be observed by meetings with people from abroad, so that it would be useful for both the church and the state." (GARF, f. 6991, op. 1, d. 1116, l. 222.) Metropolitan Nikolai was extremely dissatisfied that the meeting was held without him (he returned from Prague on December 14) and said, "I would have raised additional issues." (GARF, f. 6991, op. 1, d. 1116, l. 223.)

234. GARF, f. 6991, op. 1, d. 1116, ll. 118–19, 121.

235. GARF, f. 6991, op. 1, d. 1116, l. 107.

236. GARF, f. 6991, op. 1, d. 1116, l. 110.

237. See E. Iu. Zubkova, *Obshchestvo i reformy, 1945–1964* (Moscow, 1993), 149–50.

238. GARF, f. 6991, op. 2, d. 44, l. 92.

239. GARF, f. 6991, op. 1, d. 1543, l. 74.

240. GARF, f. 6991, op. 1, d. 1222, l. 153.

241. Odintsov, "Khozhdenie," No. 7: 2.

242. In the context of Pospielovsky's characterization, the following fact related

by Karpov to the Central Committee in February 1956 appears startling: "Grebinskii, senior priest of Znamenskii Cathedral in the city of Irkutsk, freed from prison, wrote his first sermon clearly and in a patriotic spirit, ending with the words: 'Praise to our nation's Communist Party!'

"Bishop Palladii Sherstennikov corrected Gredinskii's written sermon and recommended that he replace the ending of the sermon with the words, 'Praise to our nation's government, praise to our Motherland.' The bishop explained that such praise for the party is awkward when expressed in church, since the ideologies of party and church are alien to one another. Bishop Palladii himself saturates his sermons with patriotic content, and priests talk about this saying, 'If you close your eyes and listen to Palladii's sermon, it is as if a good political orator is speaking rather than a bishop." GARF, f. 6991, op. 1, d. 1331, l. 49.

243. GARF, f. 6991, op. 1, d. 1439, ll. 82–84. See also Pospielovskii, *Russkaia pravoslavnaia tserkov'*, 298–99.

244. GARF, f. 6991, op. 1, d. 1224, ll. 37–39.

245. GARF, f. 6991, op. 1, d. 1224, l. 39 ob.

246. GARF, f. 6991, op. 1, d. 1332, l. 14. The patriarchate asked permission for a press run of 100,000 copies, but the Council for Russian Orthodox Church Affairs thought, "It is expedient to support the request of the patriarchate, but extend the press run to only 25,000 copies. 1,000 copies of these should be finely bound."

247. GARF, f. 6991, op. 1, d. 1332, l. 87; d. 1543, l. 74. Groups of believers in the RSFSR were especially active. In 1955, they submitted 935 applications to open 472 churches; in 1956, 1,673 applications for 669 churches; and in 1957, 1,529 applications for 629 churches.

248. GARF, f. 6991, op. 1, d. 1225, l. 86; d. 1331, l. 189; d. 1332, ll. 55–56. The Trinity Cathedral in Leningrad was given to the Russian Orthodox Church, and institutions in buildings at the Holy Trinity Monastery of St. Sergius were transferred.

249. GARF, f. 6991, op. 1, d. 1332, l. 55.

250. GARF, f. 6991, op. 1, d. 1332, l. 55. The standard draft proposal of the Council for Russian Orthodox Church Affairs, worked out jointly with the Council for Affairs of Religious Cults, was not approved by the Council of Ministers for the USSR.

251. GARF, f. 6991, op. 1, d. 1439, l. 87.

252. Ibid.

253. See Shkarovskii, "Russkaia pravoslavnaia tserkov' v 1943–1957 godakh," 54.

254. GARF, f. 6991, op. 1, d. 1332, l. 57.

255. GARF, f. 6991, op. 1, d. 1118, l. 117; d. 1224, l. 46.

256. GARF, f. 6991, op. 1, d. 1438, ll. 94–95.

Notes to Chapter 3: The Soviet State and the Russian Orthodox Church, 1958–61

1. RGANI, f. 5, op. 33, d. 53, ll. 34–40.

2. This is the interpretation presented in Shkarovskii, "Russkaia pravoslavnaia tserkov' v 1943–1957 gg.," 55.

3. RGANI, f. 5, op. 33, d. 53, ll. 34–37.

4. RGANI, f. 5, op. 33, d. 53, ll. 39–40.

5. RGANI, f. 5, op. 33, d. 53, l. 44.

6. Quoted in Odintsov, *Gosudarstvo i tserkov' v Rossii*, 117–18.

7. GARF, f. 6991, op. 1, d. 1438, l. 99.

8. GARF, f. 6991, op. 1, d. 1439, l. 56.

9. GARF, f. 6991, op. 1, d. 1439, l. 145. Belyshev requested retirement after a conflict with Karpov. The reason for the conflict is unknown, but it caused people who had worked side-by-side for nearly fifteen years to part under circumstances that were unpleasant for both of them. Karpov reminisced about this in a letter in 1959, "Belyshev . . . was insulted and ranted in connection with my dismissal of him in 1957 at the suggestion of the Central Committee." GARF, f. 6991, op. 1, d. 1649, l. 159.

10. GARF, f. 6991, op. 1, d. 1439, ll. 144–45.

11. *Otechestvennye arkhivy*, 1994, no. 5: 42. Publication compiled by M.I. Odinstov.

12. See Odintsov, "Pis'ma," 27.

13. Shkarovskii lists the charges leveled against Karpov. "He conducted mass arrests of innocent citizens, used distorted methods in the conduct of investigations, and also falsified the examination records of those arrested." Shkarovskii further states, "They took up the question of expelling Karpov from the CPSU but, taking into account 'his positive work in recent years,' the Party Control Commission limited its announcement to a strict reprimand that was noted in his permanent file." M.V. Shkarovskii, *Russkaia pravoslavnaia tserkov' i sovetskoe gosudarstvo v 1943–1964 gg.: ot peremiriia k novoi voine* (St. Petersburg, DEAN-ADIA-M, 1995), 196. Unfortunately, he does not provide a footnote for the cited document. But, indirect confirmation that such an accusation was made against Karpov is found in the archives of the Council for Russian Orthodox Church Affairs. For example, Karpov included a personal admission in his letter to the Central Committee in 1959, "I have already been deservedly and severely punished for violations of revolutionary legality in the past." GARF, f. 6991, op. 1, d. 1649, l. 159.

14. GARF, f. 6991, op. 1, d. 1649, l. 160.

15. RGANI, f. 5, op. 33, d. 53, l. 32.

16. RGANI, f. 5, op. 33, d. 53, l. 51.

17. Odintsov, "Pis'ma," 26–27, and *Gosudarstvo i tserkov'*, 115–16.

18. See, for example, P.G. Pikhoia, "O vnutripartiinoi bor'be v sovetskom rukovodstve. 1945–1958," *Novaia i noveishaia istoriia*, 1995, no. 6: 3–15.

19. See Sakharov, *Istoriia Rossii*, 540–41; Pikhoia, "O vnutripartiinoi bor'be," 10–12.

20. See A.I. Adzhubei, *Te desiat' let* (Moscow, 1989); S.N. Khrushchev, *Pensioner soiuznogo znacheniia* (Moscow, 1991); R.A. Medvedev, *N.S. Khrushchev. Politicheskaia biografiia* (Moscow, 1990); E.Iu. Zubkova, *Obshchestvo i reformy. 1945–1964 gg.* (Moscow, 1993) and "O 'detskoi' literature i drugikh problemakh nashei istoricheskoi pamiati," *Istoricheskie issledovaniia v Rossii. Tendentsii poslednikh let (pod red. Bordiugova G.A.)* (Moscow, 1996), 155–75; R.A. Medvedev and D. Ermakov, *"Seryi kardinal": M.A. Suslov. Politicheskii portret* (Moscow, 1992).

21. RGANI, f. 5, op. 33, d. 91, ll. 23–29.

22. RGANI, f. 5, op. 33, d. 91, l. 23.

23. RGANI, f. 5, op. 33, d. 91, l. 30.

24. Ibid.

25. Pospielovskii, *Russkaia pravoslavnaia tserkov'*, 281.

26. RGANI, f. 5, op. 33, d. 91, ll. 30–31.

27. GARF, f. 6991, op. 1, d. 1543, ll. 152–60, 164–69.

28. Quotation from Odintsov, "Pis'ma," 27.
29. Odintsov, "Pis'ma," 44–48.
30. GARF, f. 6991, op. 1, d. 1544, ll. 21–22. The Central Committee passed a resolution on a joint decision by the Council of Ministers of the RSFSR, the Ministry of Culture of the USSR, and the Council for Russian Orthodox Church Affairs "concerning timely printing of publications of the Moscow Patriarchate" and "on measures for speeding up construction of apartments in the town of Zagorsk," as well as a resolution addressed to the Councils of Ministers of the RSFSR, Ukraine, and Belorussia "on reviewing and fulfilling" a proposal by the Council for Russian Orthodox Church Affairs to open churches. GARF, f. 6991, op. 1, d. 1543, l. 76.
31. GARF, f. 6991, op. 1, d. 1543, l. 22.
32. Odintsov, "Pis'ma," 49–50.
33. Quotation from Alekseev, *Shturm*, 222.
34. Quotation from Odintsov, *Gosudarstvo i tserkov' v Rossii*, 119.
35. Ibid.
36. GARF, f. 6991, op. 1, d. 1649, l. 29.
37. See Gordun, "Russkaia pravoslavnaia tserkov'," 111.
38. GARF, f. 6991, op. 1, d. 1544, ll. 74–75.
39. Gordun, "Russkaia pravoslavnaia tserkov'," 110.
40. Ibid.
41. GARF, f. 6991, op. 1, d. 1648, ll. 44–47, 121–25, 134–35.
42. GARF, f. 6991, op. 1, d. 1649, ll. 42–43; Odintsov, "Pis'ma," 50.
43. On November 28, 1958, the Presidium of the CPSU Central Committee adopted a resolution "On Measures for Stopping Pilgrimages to So-Called 'Holy Sites.'"
44. GARF, f. 6991, op. 1, d. 1649, l. 83.
45. GARF, f. 6991, op. 1, d. 1541, ll. 108–9; d. 1544, ll. 78–79.
46. GARF, f. 6991, op. 1, d. 1649, l. 30.
47. GARF, f. 6991, op. 1, d. 1649, l. 80.
48. GARF, f. 6991, op. 1, d. 1649, ll. 74–75.
49. GARF, f. 6991, op. 1, d. 1649, ll. 75–79.
50. Odintsov, "Pis'ma," 28, 49, 54–57.
51. Odintsov, "Pis'ma," 29.
52. Ibid.
53. GARF, f. 6991, op. 1, d. 1745, l. 203.
54. GARF, f. 6991, op. 1, d. 1649, ll. 39–40, 228–29; d. 1747, ll. 14–15.
55. GARF, f. 6991, op. 1, d. 1747, l. 41.
56. GARF, f. 6991, op. 1, d. 1648, ll. 138–138 ob.
57. GARF, f. 6991, op. 1, d. 1649, ll. 115–18.
58. GARF, f. 6991, op. 1, d. 1747, ll. 19–20.
59. GARF, f. 6991, op. 1, d. 1649, l. 230.
60. GARF, f. 6991, op. 1, d. 1649, l. 62.
61. GARF, f. 6991, op. 1, d. 1648, ll. 62–63.
62. GARF, f. 6991, op. 1, d. 1649, l. 157.
63. It is true that there were differences of opinion in understanding the question about conferring rights of a juridical person on the church by the Council. I. Ivanov, a member of the Council, wrote to the Central Committee about this in 1956: The Council for Affairs of Religious Cults thought that buildings purchased by religious organizations were national property and, per agreement, were given to them for free and permanent use. But, the Council for Russian Orthodox Church Affairs, according to

its resolution, "gave communities the right to use such buildings under laws for private property." RGANI, f. 5, op. 33, d. 53, l. 38.

64. GARF, f. 6991, op. 1, d. 1649, ll. 158, 161, 162.
65. GARF, f. 6991, op. 1, d. 1649, l. 158.
66. GARF, f. 6991, op. 1, d. 1649, l. 161.
67. GARF, f. 6991, op. 1, d. 1649, l. 162.
68. GARF, f. 6991, op. 1, d. 1649, l. 163.
69. GARF, f. 6991, op. 1, d. 1649, l. 158.
70. GARF, f. 6991, op. 1, d. 1649, ll. 159–60.
71. GARF, f. 6991, op. 1, d. 1747, ll. 14–228.
72. GARF, f. 6991, op. 1, d. 1747, ll. 14, 65.
73. GARF, f. 6991, op. 1, d. 1747, l. 131.
74. GARF, f. 6991, op. 1, d. 1747, ll. 203–5.
75. Odintsov, "Pis'ma," 30.
76. GARF, f. 6991, op. 1, d. 1543, ll. 164–68.
77. GARF, f. 6991, op. 1, d. 1543, ll. 168–69.
78. Gordun, "Russkaia pravoslavnaia tserkov'," 111.
79. GARF, f. 6991, op. 1, d. 1544, ll. 62–65.
80. Pospielovskii, *Russkaia pravoslavnaia tserkov'*, 286. According to Cheredniak's report to the Central Committee, however, the context of the application was this: "Kolchitskii and Maliushitskii in response to the introduction of new tax assessments said that now, it seems, they would be required to inform foreign delegations in the USSR differently about the situation of the Russian Orthodox Church." GARF, f. 6991, op. 1, d. 1544, l. 62.
81. GARF, f. 6991, op. 1, d. 1544, l. 65.
82. GARF, f. 6991, op. 1, d. 1544, ll. 74–75.
83. Odintsov, "Pis'ma," 49.
84. GARF, f. 6991, op. 1, d. 1649, l. 233; d. 1747, l. 19.
85. GARF, f. 6991, op. 1, d. 1649, l. 34.
86. GARF, f. 6991, op. 1, d. 1747, l. 178.
87. GARF, f. 6991, op. 1, d. 1747, l. 180.
88. GARF, f. 6991, op. 1, d. 1648, ll. 127–28.
89. See Gordun, "Russkaia pravoslavnaia tserkov'," 110.
90. Odintsov, "Pis'ma," 52.
91. GARF, f. 6991, op. 1, d. 1648, l. 134.
92. GARF, f. 6991, op. 1, d. 1648, ll. 127–30.
93. GARF, f. 6991, op. 1, d. 1648, l. 127.
94. GARF, f. 6991, op. 1, d. 1649, l. 115.
95. GARF, f. 6991, op. 1, d. 1649, l. 117.
96. Ibid.
97. GARF, f. 6991, op. 1, d. 1649, l. 118.
98. GARF, f. 6991, op. 1, d. 1747, l. 15.
99. GARF, f. 6991, op. 1, d. 1649, l. 116.
100. GARF, f. 6991, op. 1, d. 1649, ll. 115, 117–19.
101. GARF, f. 6991, op. 1, d. 1649, ll. 116–17.
102. GARF, f. 6991, op. 1, d. 1649, l. 118.
103. GARF, f. 6991, op. 1, d. 1649, l. 115.
104. GARF, f. 6991, op. 1, d. 1649, l. 185.
105. Odintsov, "Pis'ma," 55.

106. GARF, f. 6991, op. 1, d. 1747, ll. 15, 180.

107. GARF, f. 6991, op. 1, d. 1541, l. 153. Pospielovskii, *Russkaia pravoslavnaia tserkov'*, 287.

108. GARF, f. 6991, op. 1, d. 1543, l. 75.

109. GARF, f. 6991, op. 1, d. 1649, l. 77.

110. GARF, f. 6991, op. 1, d. 1747, ll. 14–15.

111. GARF, f. 6991, op. 1, d. 1747, l. 14.

112. GARF, f. 6991, op. 1, d. 1648, l. 49.

113. GARF, f. 6991, op. 1, d. 1649, ll. 64–65.

114. Odintsov, "Pis'ma," 51, 53.

115. Odintsov, "Pis'ma," 55.

116. GARF, f. 6991, op. 1, d. 1649, ll. 33–34.

117. Quoted in E.Iu. Zubkova, *Obshchestvo i reformy* (Moscow, 1993), 167.

118. GARF, f. 6991, op. 1, d. 1649, ll. 64–65. Odintsov, "Pis'ma," 51, 59. Gordun, "Russkaia pravoslavnaia tserkov'," 119.

119. GARF, f. 6991, op. 1, d. 1747, l. 18.

120. GARF, f. 6991, op. 1, d. 1649, l. 228.

121. Gordun, "Russkaia pravoslavnaia tserkov'," 128.

122. GARF, f. 6991, op. 1, d. 1649, l. 232.

123. GARF, f. 6991, op. 1, d. 1649, l. 228.

124. GARF, f. 6991, op. 1, d. 1649, l. 65.

125. Odintsov, "Pis'ma," 51.

126. GARF, f. 6991, op. 1, d. 1649, l. 32.

127. Pospielovskii, *Russkaia pravoslavnaia tserkov'*, 281. For a certain group of people, Osipov's "betrayal" was not unexpected and, with full certainty, was a considered and well-planned act. Archpriest Osipov was a secret informant in the Leningrad Academy. His report from June 1951 to Commissioner Kushnarev of the Leningrad region ("On Conditions in the Moscow Patriarchate") is published in Shkarovskii, *Russkaia pravoslavnaia tserkov' i sovetskoe gosudarstvo v 1943–1964 gg.*, 140–62.

128. Quoted in Pospielovskii, *Russkaia pravoslavnaia tserkov'*, 281–82.

129. GARF, f. 6991, op. 1, d. 1649, l. 39; d. 1747, l. 181.

130. GARF, f. 6991, op. 1, d. 1649, ll. 44, 46, 63–64. Odintsov, "Pis'ma," 51–53.

131. GARF, f. 6991, op. 1, d. 1649, l. 65.

132. Odintsov, "Pis'ma," 53–54.

133. GARF, f. 6991, op. 1, d. 1649, l. 49.

134. GARF, f. 6991, op. 1, d. 1649, l. 65.

135. Quoted in Gordun, "Russkaia pravoslavnaia tserkov'," 117.

136. GARF, f. 6991, op. 1, d. 1745, l. 131.

137. GARF, f. 6991, op. 1, d. 1649, l. 44.

138. Gordun, "Russkaia pravoslavnaia tserkov'," 117–18.

139. GARF, f. 6991, op. 1, d. 1649, l. 166.

140. GARF, f. 6991, op. 1, d. 1648, ll. 48–49; d. 1649, ll. 45, 65–225.

141. Tsypin, *Istoriia Russkoi pravoslavnoi Tserkvi*, 162–64. Pospielovskii, *Russkaia pravoslavnaia tserkov'*, 311–13.

142. GARF, f. 6991, op. 1, d. 1649, ll. 63–67.

143. GARF, f. 6991, op. 1, d. 1649, l. 63.

144. GARF, f. 6991, op. 1, d. 1649, ll. 165–66.

145. Quoted in Odintsov, "Pis'ma," 29.

146. GARF, f. 6991, op. 1, d. 1649, l. 225.

147. GARF, f. 6991, op. 1, d. 1649, l. 225.

148. Quoted in Odintsov, "Pis'ma," 29.

149. Ibid.

150. GARF, f. 6991, op. 1, d. 1649, l. 240.

151. Pospielovskii, *Russkaia pravoslavnaia tserkov'*, 289.

152. Ibid., 289–90.

153. Archbishop Vasilii (Krivoshein), "Poslednie vstrechi s mitropolitom Nikolaem (Iarushevichem)," *Vestnik russkogo khristianskogo dvizheniia* (Paris), 1976, no. 117: 210–11.

154. Odintsov, "Pis'ma," 62.

155. GARF, f. 6991, op. 1, d. 1745, l. 131.

156. RGANI, f. 5, op. 33, d. 162, l. 175.

157. Archbishop Vasilii (Krivoshein), "Poslednie vstrechi," 210.

158. RGANI, f. 5, op. 33, d. 162, l. 176.

159. Ibid.

160. Ibid.

161. See Alekseev, *Illiuzii*, 372.

162. RGANI, f. 5, op. 33, d. 162, ll. 180–81.

163. Gordun, "Russkaia pravoslavnaia tserkov'," 118.

164. Quoted in Gordun, "Russkaia pravoslavnaia tserkov'," 118–19.

165. RGANI, f. 5, op. 33, d. 162, ll. 176–77.

166. RGANI, f. 5, op. 33, d. 162, ll. 177–78.

167. RGANI, f. 5, op. 33, d. 162, l. 178.

168. Quoted in Pospielovskii, *Russkaia pravoslavnaia tserkov'*, 293.

169. Odintsov, "Pis'ma," 60.

170. Odintsov, "Pis'ma," 58–61.

171. Gordun, "Russkaia pravoslavnaia tserkov'," 122–23.

172. Ibid. Pospielovskii, *Russkaia pravoslavnaia tserkov'*, 294–95. Odintsov, *Gosudarstvo i tserkov'*, 120–21.

173. Odintsov, "Pis'ma," 68.

174. Gordun, "Russkaia pravoslavnaia tserkov'," 124–26.

175. Quoted in Tsypin, *Istoriia Russkoi pravoslavnoi tserkvi*, 159.

176. Odintsov, "Pis'ma," 31.

177. Odintsov, "Pis'ma," 34.

178. Gordun, "Russkaia pravoslavnaia tserkov'," 128–29.

179. Pospielovskii, *Russkaia pravoslavnaia tserkov'*, 304–5. GARF, f. 6991, op. 1, d. 1747, l. 15.

180. N.S. Khrushchev, *Otchet TsK KPSS XXII s"ezdu partii* (Moscow, 1961), 133–34.

181. *Ustav KPSS* (Moscow, 1961), 6.

Sources and Bibliography

I. Sources

Gosudarstvennyi Arkhiv Rossiiskoi Federatsii (GARF), Moscow
  f. 6991   Sovet po religii pri SM SSSR
Rossiiskii Gosudarstvennyi Arkhiv Sotsial'no-Politicheskoi Istorii (RGASPI), Moscow
  f. 17   Tsentral'nyi komitet KPSS
Rossiiskii Gosudarstvennyi Arkhiv Noveishei Istorii (RGANI), Moscow
  f. 5   Otdel propagandy i agitatsii TsK KPSS po soiuznym respublikam
Glavnoe Arkhivnoe Upravlenie FSB RF (various material)

II. Periodicals

Izvestiia (1943–1961)
Pravda (1943–1961)
Zhurnal Moskovskoi Patriarkhii (1943–1961)

III. Collections of Documents

KPSS v rezoliutsiiakh i resheniiakh s"ezdov, konferentsii i plenumov. Moscow: Politizdat, 1985.
O religii i tserkvi. Sbornik vyskazyvanii klassikov marksizma-leninizma, dokumentov KPSS i Sovetskogo gosudarstvo. Moscow: Politizdat, 1981.
Pravda o religii v Rossii. Moscow: Izd-vo Moskovskoi patriarkhii, 1942.
Russkaia pravoslavnaia tserkov' i Velikaia Otechestvennaia voina. Sbornik tserkovnykh dokumentov. Moscow: Izd-vo Moskovskoi patriarkhii, 1943.
Shtrikker, G., ed., *Russkaia pravoslavnaia tserkov' v sovetskoe vremia.* 2 vols. Moscow: Propilei, 1995
Zakonodatel'stvo o religioznykh kul'takh. Moscow: Iuridicheskaia literatura, 1969.

IV. Memoirs

Georgievskii, Evlogii (Metropolitan). *Put' moei zhizni.* Moscow: Moskovskii rabochii, 1994.

Krivoshein, Vasilii (Archbishop). "Metropolit Nikolai (Iarushevich): Vospominaniia Vladyki Vasiliia Krivosheina." *Tserkovno-obshchestvennyi vestnik*, no. 17 (Appendix to *Russkaia mysl'*), June 5, 1997.

———. "Poslednie vstrechi s mitropolitom Nikolaem (Iarushevichem)." *Vestnik russkogo khristianskogo dvizheniia* (Paris), 1976, no. 117: 209–19.

Snychev, Ioann (Metropolitan). *Mitropolit Manuil (Lemeshevskii)*. St. Petersburg, 1993.

Voino-Iasenetskii, Luka (Archbishop). *Ia poliubil stradanie. Avtobiografiia*. Moscow: Izd. im. sviatitelia Ignatiia Stavropol'skogo, 1996.

V. Other Works

Adzhubei, A I. *Te desiat' let*. Moscow: Sovetskaia Rossiia, 1989.

Alekseev, V.A., *Illiuzii i dogmy*. Moscow: Politizdat, 1991.

———. *Shturm nebes otmeniaetsia? Kriticheskie ocherki po istorii bor'by s religii v SSSR*. Moscow: Rossiia molodaia, 1992.

Bogolepov, A.A. *Tserkov' pod vlast'iu kommunizma*. Munich, 1958.

Degtiarev, Iu. M. "Kak Stalin priznal Tserkov'." *Religiia v SSSR. Biulleten' APN* (Moscow), 1991, no. 12: 41–52.

Godienko, N.S. *Sovremennoe russkoe pravoslavie*. Leningrad: Lenizdat, 1987.

Gordun, S. "Russkaia pravoslavnaia tserkov' pri sviateishikh patriarkhakh Sergii i Aleksii." *Vestnik russkogo khristianskogo dvizheniia* (Paris), 1990, no. 158: 82–142.

Khrushchev, S.N. *Pensioner soiuznogo znacheniia*. Moscow: Novosti, 1991.

Konstantinov, D. *Gonimaia Tserkov' (Russkaia Pravoslavnaia Tserkov' v SSSR)*. New York, 1967.

Medvedev, R.A. *N.S. Khrushchev. Politicheskaia biografiia*. Moscow: Kniga, 1990.

Medvedev, R.A., and Ermakov D., *"Seryi kardinal": M.A. Suslov. Politicheskii portret*. Moscow: Respublika, 1992.

Odintsov, M.I. "Drugogo raza ne bylo." *Ateistitcheskie chteniia*, 1989, no. 2: 8–9.

———. "Gosudarstvo i tserkov': Istoriia vzaimootnoshenii, 1917–1938 gg." *Kul'tura i religiia*, 1991, no. 11.

———. "Gosudarstvo i tserkov' v gody voiny." *Otechestvennye arkhivy*, 1995, no. 2, 123–25.

———. *Gosudarstvo i tserkov' v Rossii: XX vek*. Moscow: Luch, 1994.

———. "Khozhdenie po mukam," Parts 1–5. *Nauka i religiia*, 1990, no. 5: 8–10, no. 6: 12–13, no. 7: 56–57, no. 8: 19–21; 1991, no. 7: 1–2.

———. "Krestnyi put' patriarkha Sergiia," *Otechestvennye arkhivy*, 1994, no. 2: 44–80.

———. "Pis'ma i dialogi vremen 'khrushchevskoi ottepeli' (Desiat' let iz zhizni patriarkha Aleksiia)," *Otechestvennye arkhivy*, 1994, no. 5: 25–83.

———. *Religioznye organizatsii v SSSR v gody Velikoi Otechestvennoi voiny 1941–1945 gg*. Moscow: RAGS, 1995.

———. "Russkaia pravoslavnaia tserkov' stala na pravil'nyi put'." *Istoricheskii arkhiv*, 1994, no. 3: 139–40.

———. *Russkie patriarkhi XX veka: Sud'by Otechestva i Tserkvi na stranitsakh arkhivnykh dokumentov*. Moscow: RAGS, 1999.

———. "Uniaty i sovetskaia vlast'." *Otechestvennye arkhivy*, 1994, no. 3: 56–71.

Pikhoia, P.G. "O vnutripartiinoi bor'be v sovetskom rukovodstve. 1945–1958." *Novaia i noveishaia istoriia.* 1995, no. 6: 3–15.

Pospielovskii, Dimitrii. *Russkaia pravoslavnaia tserkov' v XX veke.* Moscow: Respublika, 1995.

Rar Gleb (A. Vetrov). *Plenennaia Tserkov': Ocherk razvitiia vzaimootnoshenii mezhdu Tserkov'iu i vlast'iu v SSSR.* Frankfurt, 1954.

Sakharov, A.N., ed. *Istoriia Rossii. XX vek.* Moscow, AST, 1996.

Shkarovskii, M.V. "Russkaia pravoslavnaia tserkov' v 1943–1957 godakh," *Voprosy istorii,* 1995, no. 8: 36–56.

———. *Peterburgskaia eparkhiia v gody gonenii i utrat 1917–1945.* St. Petersburg: Liki Rossii, 1995.

———. *Russkaia pravoslavnaia tserkov' i sovetskoe gosudarstvo v 1943–1964 gg.: ot peremiriia k novoi voine.* St. Petersburg: DEAN-ADIA-M, 1995.

———. *Russkaia pravoslavnaia tserkov' pri Staline i Khrushcheve (Gosudarstvenno-tserkovnye otnosheniia v SSSR v 1939–1964 gg.).* Moscow: Krutitskoe patriarshee podvor'e, 1999.

Tsypin, Vladimir. *Istoriia Russkoi pravoslavnoi tserkvi, 1917–1990.* Moscow: Khronika, 1994.

Vasil'eva, O. Iu. "Vatikan v gornile voiny," *Nauka i religiia,* 1995, no. 6: 15.

Yakunin, G. "V sluzhenii kul'tu" in *Na puti k svobode sovesti.* Moscow: Progress, 1989, 172–206.

Zubkova, E. Iu. *Obshchestvo i reformy, 1945–1964.* Moscow: Rossiia molodaia, 1993.

———. "O 'detskoi' literature i drugikh problemakh nashei istoricheskoi pamiati." *Istoricheskie issledovaniia v Rossii. Tendentsii poslednikh let (pod red. Bordiugova G. A.).* Moscow: AIRO-XX, 1996, 155–75.

Index

Tatiana A. Chumachenko received her graduate training in Russian history at Moscow State University. Her research on the history of church-state relations in Russia has been supported by the Russian State Social Science Fund and by the "New Perspectives" program of the Moscow Public Science Fund and the Ford Foundation. She teaches in the Department of Modern Russian History at Chelyabinsk State University.

Edward E. Roslof is associate professor of church history at United Theological Seminary in Dayton, Ohio, and the author of *Red Priests: Renovationism, Russian Orthodoxy, and Revolution, 1905–1946*. He completed his doctorate in history at the University of North Carolina, Chapel Hill.